FOLLOWING GOD
CHARACTER SERIES
BIBLE STUDY

An informative **6 WEEK BIBLE STUDY** of life principles for today, to guide the church and the Christian's walk.

David the Shepherd King

THE LIFE AND TIMES OF KING DAVID IN ISRAEL

RICK SHEPHERD

Following God

DAVID THE SHEPHERD KING

ISBN 13: 978-1-61715-534-5

Manuscript editing, text design, and layout by Rick Steele Editorial Services
http://steeleeditorialservices.myportfolio.com

Cover illustration by Daryle Beam/Bright Boy Design

Printed in the United States of America
2022 First Edition

IN HONOR

This Scripture adventure through the times of David, the Shepherd King is presented in honor of several faithful shepherds, pastors who have guided me through the years, beginning with my childhood pastor, Dr. Bob Barker, at First Baptist Church of Chickasaw, Alabama. He was faithful to the Lord, to His Word and to the gospel. Other pastors/shepherds who served alongside him and have had great influence upon my life included Dick Robertson, Frank Marshall, and Jim Moses. I am grateful for and honor other shepherds as well, among whom were James Harris and Bob Riddle in Fort Worth, Texas, Peter Lord and Robbie Goss in Titusville, Florida, Jimmy Draper in Euless, Texas, Jim Hylton in Saginaw, Texas, T. W. Hunt in Fort Worth (a true shepherd of the Word though not as an "official" pastor), and then those I served with on staff—Paul Burleson at Southcliff Baptist Church in Fort Worth, Texas, Wayne Barber at Woodland Park Baptist Church in Chattanooga, Tennessee, and Steve Gaines at Bellevue Baptist Church in Memphis, Tennessee. I am also thankful for and give honor to Pastor Keith Russell at Westside Baptist Church in Jacksonville, Florida, where I was a member for fifteen years during my time of ministry with the Florida Baptist Convention. There, I served under Dr. John Sullivan and David Burton, shepherds of the Lord with a heart for God and the gospel. I also give honor to pastor Sam Shaw at The Orchard Church in Collierville, Tennessee.

Rick Shepherd

Rolesville, North Carolina (2021)

DEDICATION

David, the Shepherd King is dedicated to our four most recent grandchildren, all grandsons—Finn, Asher, James, and Asa. My encouragement to each of you is to be like David, following the Lord from the heart—Love, PapaRick.

Acknowledgments

The *Life of David* and the times surrounding his years reveal a shepherd from boyhood to his dying days. Though David did not serve perfectly, he served well. As someone once pointed out, leaders are those who are proven as to their past, predictable as to their future, though not perfect in the present. That was certainly true of David.

As with any ministry, especially dealing with the Scriptures, I owe special thanks to many. First, to my Lord Himself, for leading me, teaching me, burdening me to dig into this Scripture Adventure. Any good that comes from delving into this study should bring praise and thanks to Him. There is no good in me but Jesus and He is called the Son of David. By His Spirit, He is our Teacher and Leader, our Lord and Savior, our Forgiver, Life, and Leader. He knows what each of us needs and readily guides us in that path.

Second, I am indebted to and grateful for my wife Linda Gail for her encouragement to write these lessons. Her praying for me and encouragement to me means much. Third, many others in the body of Christ have encouraged me to pen these adventures through the Scripture.

Fourth, I am greatly indebted to several resources that have proved very insightful, including:

Barber, Wayne, Eddie Rasnake, Richard Shepherd. *Following God: Kings of the Old Testament* (Chattanooga, TN: AMG Publishers, 1999)

Beitzel, Barry J. *The Moody Atlas of Bible Lands* (Chicago, IL: Moody Press, 1985)

www.thebibleproject.com,

Bridges, Charles. *An Exposition of Psalm 119* (Carlisle, PA: The Banner of Truth Trust, 1827, 1974)

Brown, Francis, et al. *The New Brown-Driver-Briggs-Gesenius Hebrew and English Lexicon* (Peabody, MA: Hendricksen Publishers, 1979)

Dictionary of the Holy Bible, rev. and enlarged ed. (New York, NY: American Tract society, 1886, 1914)

Elliff, Thomas D. *Praying for Others* (Nashville, TN: Broadman Press, 1979)

The ESV Study Bible (Wheaton, IL: Crossway Bibles, 2008)

Grisanti, Michael A. *1 Samuel and 2 Samuel in The Bible Knowledge Word Study, Joshua-2 Chronicles*, ed., Eugene Merrill (Colorado Springs, CO: Cook Communications Ministries, 2004)

MacArthur, John, ed. *The MacArthur Study Bible* (Nashville, TN: Word Publishing, 1997)

Merrill, Eugene H. *Kingdom of Priests: A History of Old Testament Israel* (Grand Rapids, MI: Baker Books, 1987, 1996)

Payne, J. Barton. 1, 2 Chronicles, in *The Expositor's Bible Commentary*, vol. 4. Frank Gaebelein, gen. ed. (Grand Rapids, MI: Zondervan Publishing House, 1988)

www.readscripture.org

Redpath, Alan. *The Making of a Man of God: Lessons from the Life of David* (Grand Rapids, MI: Fleming Revell, 1962)

Ryrie, Charles Caldwell. *The Ryrie Study Bible* (Chicago, IL: Moody Press, 1976, 1978)

Smith, William. *A Dictionary of the Bible* (Philadelphia, PA: The John C. Winston Company, 1884)

Taylor, Richard. *2 Chronicles in The Bible Knowledge Word Study, Joshua-2 Chronicles*, ed., Eugene Merrill (Colorado Springs, CO: Cook Communications Ministries, 2004)

Thomas, Robert L., gen. ed. *New American Standard Exhaustive Concordance of the Bible* (Numbering Classifications from James H. Strong's *Exhaustive*

Concordance of the Bible) (Nashville, TN: Holman Bible Publishers and The Lockman Foundation, 1981)

Unger, Merrill F., ed. *Unger's Bible Dictionary* (Chicago, IL: Moody Press, 1957, revised 1966)

West, Nathaniel. *Studies in Eschatology* (1899). Reprinted as *The Thousand Year Reign of Christ* (Grand Rapids, MI: Kregel Publications, 1993)

Wolf, Herbert. 1 and 2 Samuel, in *The Expositor's Bible Commentary*, vol. 3. Frank Gaebelein, gen. ed. (Grand Rapids, MI: Zondervan Publishing House, 1992)

Zodhiates, Spiros, exec. ed. *The Hebrew-Greek Key Word Study Bible* (NASB), rev. ed. (Chattanooga, TN: AMG Publishers, 1984, 2008) and *The Complete Word Study Dictionary—New Testament* (Chattanooga, TN: AMG Publishers, 1992)

RICK SHEPHERD

Rick Shepherd

RICK SHEPHERD has served in churches in Florida, Texas, and Tennessee, and ministered over fifteen years as Team Strategist for the Prayer and Spiritual Awakening Team of the Florida Baptist Convention. He holds M.Div and Ph.D degrees from Southwestern Baptist Theological Seminary. Rick is one of the founding authors of the Following God® series. He has been married to his wife Linda Gail since 1977. They have four children and seven grandchildren. They are always glad to encourage believers and witness to listening hearts wherever they go. They now make their home in Rolesville, North Carolina.

Preface

What does it mean to be a king? Many monarchs (kings and queens) have marched through history, some filled with pride and wanting all their subjects to follow, even worship, them. A few others have revealed humble hearts as well as humble words and choices, desiring to lead and help others in many ways. Throughout history, both kinds of leaders have influenced others; some in bad ways and others in good ways. How one leads has always made an impact on others for good or evil.

What does it mean to lead as a king? Traditionally, one of the key elements in any kingdom has been protection of people and property. That meant kings have been responsible for protecting their own lives and lands and making sure everything is in place for adequate provision for everyone in the kingdom. Sometimes, that includes making agreements with other kingdoms and peoples, whether for goods or labor or simply for some sort of mutual benefit. Some have sought mutual provision as well as mutual protection. At times that means inevitable battles or skirmishes, even war, to assure provision or protection.

On a personal level, essential to forward progress, a king must have skill in leading, fighting, and managing matters of the kingdom. That makes several qualities necessary. Psalm 78:70–72 gives a summary of David and the Lord's choice of him as king of Israel. David had many of these necessary qualities such as a servant's heart, caring actions, honest character, and skill with people. Those verses state, *"He chose David His servant, and took him from the sheepfolds; from the care of the ewes with suckling lambs He brought him, to shepherd His people, and Israel His inheritance. So he shepherded them according to the integrity of his heart, and guided them with his skillful hands."* David ruled well as a leader and proved a good influence on the people of his land and his generation as well as on thousands throughout history. Though not perfect, his character and skill shine through in many ways.

History has often asked: "What makes a great king?" History has also shown that integrity of heart, honesty, skill with people and provision, and the ability to handle difficulties, all play a significant part. Looking at the lives of people like Saul, the first king of Israel, and David, the second king, reveals that the most important element is always *heart*, specifically, the *heart* of the king. Is it a selfish heart, filled with vanity and glory-seeking, or is it a heart marked by unselfishness, such as a servant's heart for others? One's spirit or heart is crucial; the years of both Saul and David revealed this truth.

This Scripture Adventure is a journey through David's life and his reign as king, a reign with its ups and downs, failures and successes. More than a list of historical facts, David's life and legacy provide us with several life lessons, lessons that can serve to guide us daily, even moment by moment, whether we are serving only as "king" over ourselves or as leader over many. There are many "kingdoms" one can successfully rule or fail to rule. Which kingdoms? The kingdoms of self (with its many areas), as well as kingdoms of home, church, school, a team, a neighborhood or community, a region—even a nation.

Here are some crucial facts when looking at David or any other leader: simply knowing his successes will not make us successful. Nor will knowing his failures keep us from failing, but we can learn. Here are important truth:s

- One can learn from others' failures without failing personally.
- One does not have to succeed in the same way as other "kings" or leaders.

When all is said and done, the crucial questions are these:

- *Have I personally known, worshiped, and walked with the Lord?*
- *Have I pleased Him?*
- *Have I followed Him and His Word?*
- *Have I helped others connect with Him to know and follow Him?*
- *Have I helped others through their life journey?*

David certainly knew the Lord, sought to follow Him, and sought to get others to follow Him and His Word. We can learn from David, from his stands and his stumbles, his successes and failures. After all, it ever remains a matter of the heart—seeking God's heart as well as learning from David's heart for each of our hearts.

Rick Shepherd

CONTENTS

LESSON 1

THE EARLY DAYS OF DAVID

FROM SHEPHERD BOY TO ANOINTING AS KING

David stands out as a king and leader in history, especially in Israel. His story is known almost worldwide. Someone has noted that at one time Psalm 23 was the most-searched item on Google—David wrote that. What was true of him as a shepherd boy proved true as the Shepherd King—he had a heart for God, and he cared about people. What can we learn from him? As with any Scripture adventure, treasures await us. With this particular adventure, the treasures are in abundance, for David speaks to each of us in different ways.

As you walk through this life, consider your own life; not as to whether you are "king" or "queen" of anything, but whether you have a king's heart, a heart for God like David had. That is what God is looking at, and He has never changed. It is what He desired in Adam and Eve and desires in every son or daughter since then, and He knows that kind of heart is impossible to have apart from His working. So, look up to Him, call out to Him, seek Him with a whole heart, and ask Him to change your heart to be like that of Jesus, the ultimate Son of David.

DID YOU KNOW?

Bethlehem

In 1 Samuel 16:1, the LORD told Samuel the next king would be one of the sons of *"Jesse the Bethlehemite."* What does that mean? A man named "Jesse" lived in the small town of *Bethlehem*, a tiny village about five miles south of Jerusalem. In Hebrew, the name "Bethlehem" means "House of Bread," likely a reference to the fields of grain near there. Bethlehem is first mentioned in Scripture in Judges 17:7–8 and was the town of Elimelech, Naomi, Ruth, and Boaz mentioned in Ruth 1:1–2, 19, 22; 4:11. Boaz and Ruth became the great-grandparents of David (Ruth 4:17). Bethlehem became known as *"the city of David"* and it is there that Mary gave birth to the infant *Jesus,* also known as the *"Son of David"* (Matthew 1:1; Luke 1:32; 2:4–20). Micah 5:2 gives a clear Messianic prophecy of a *"ruler in Israel"* coming from Bethlehem. Matthew 2:4–6 reveals the fulfillment of that prophecy along with 2 Samuel 5:2b, noting the birth in Bethlehem of the *"Christ"* or *"Messiah"* who would "SHEPHERD MY PEOPLE ISRAEL" (2 Samuel 5:2b)

Day One

Another Child—The Eighth Son

According to 1 Samuel 16:11 and 17:12, David came along as the eighth son of Jesse. According to 1 Chronicles 2:16, David also had at least two sisters, but we do not know their place in the birth order. Born in Bethlehem to a sheepherding family, David grew up with seven older brothers—no simple feat. What can we learn from Scripture about David and these early days?

Let's review. What do you find about David's position in the family in 1 Samuel 16:10–11?

What was life like for David as the eighth son? What clues do you find in 1 Samuel 17:12–15, 17–18, 20?

David was the eighth son of Jesse, the youngest of the sons and assigned the task of shepherding the family's sheep. Apparently, he was not considered significant, as when the prophet Samuel came to their home, David was not among the brothers presented to Samuel as king candidates. He had the job of taking care of the sheep, though he likely had at least one helper with him so that he *could have* come to the gathering. As the youngest son, David tended the sheep daily. His obedience to his father is seen in his willingness to go to the army camp to check on his three oldest brothers and take them some food along with something for the commander. After his father gave him this task, David left early the next morning, being careful to leave the sheep with *"a keeper."*

What did David do as a shepherd boy? What skill is noted in 1 Samuel 16:23? What further information do you find in the last phrase of 2 Samuel 23:1?

📖 What testimony is given in Psalm 78:70–72? What further insights do you discover about David based on his conversation with King Saul in 1 Samuel 17:34–37?

What does David's conversation with Saul tell you about David as a young boy and young man? Where is David's focus?

David served faithfully and skillfully as a shepherd boy. His many hours in the shepherds' fields around Bethlehem meant not only learning a lot about sheep, but life as well. He had time for reflection and worship. Apparently, David developed skill with a harp, including composing and singing psalms of worship, thanksgiving, and prayer. God saw David as *"a man after His own heart"* and, in his life with sheep and people, David revealed *"the integrity of his heart."* Years later he would be known as *"the sweet psalmist of Israel."*

David also had some adventuresome experiences. History speaks of vast forests near Bethlehem and an abundance of wild animals in David's day. It appears that more than once a lion or bear came looking for a lamb for food. David speaks of fighting and killing the animals, even taking a lamb out of the mouth of the predator, no small feat. This speaks of David's courage, his skill, but most of all his focus on and confidence in the Lord in dealing with dangers, problems, or enemies, whether wild animals or wicked Philistines.

📖 How is David described in 1 Samuel 16:12?

📖 While David is first introduced to us in 1 Samuel 16, God long before saw and knew him. What does God say about this young man in 1 Samuel 13:14?

📖 What further details do you discover in 1 Samuel 15:16, 28?

David came into the house from tending sheep. Here, Jesse, David's seven brothers, and Samuel (and perhaps others) were gathered. Scripture describes David as *"ruddy, with bright eyes, and good-looking"* (NKJV) or *"ruddy, with beautiful eyes and a handsome appearance"* (NASB). Most importantly, God saw David as *"a man after His own heart"* and His choice as the next king. Living in Bethlehem, he would be considered a *"neighbor"* of Saul in Gibeah about 8 or 9 miles from there. In reviewing the chronology of David and his brothers, it is possible that David was around age 10–12, the age when, according to the Lord, he would be considered *"a man,"* certainly capable as a leader.

IN THEIR SHOES

What Does it Take to Be a Man?

Samuel spoke of the LORD desiring *"a man after His own heart"* (1 Samuel 13:14; cf. Acts 13:22). David was that man. Around the age of 10-12, God considered David *"a man,"* capable of following Him and thus able to lead others as king. Jesus revealed His wisdom and understanding of Scripture at age 12 (Luke 2:42, 46–52). What does it take to be a man? Apparently, it is a matter of the heart, knowing God and His Word, willing to listen to others, humble before the Lord and others, always ready to grow and mature, thus able to guide others. These things were true of David and of the Lord Jesus. God always desired leaders to live and act this way. He gave clear direction for selecting a king in Deuteronomy 17:14–20, pointing both to one's heart for God and a humble, growing knowledge of His Word.

Day Two

Another King—Number Two

No doubt David's anointing as the next king surprised Jesse and his sons as well as David. According to 1 Samuel 16:13, *"the Spirit of the LORD came mightily upon David from that day forward."* What would the coming days hold? As with what had gone on already, there were more surprises in store; no fairy-tale script, but rough days and good days, all mixed with perplexities and joys. We can learn from David and how he faced those days.

📖 How did Samuel deal with Saul's actions and attitudes, according to 1 Samuel 15:14, 16–31?

What do you discover about Samuel in 1 Samuel 15:35?

Scripture reveals Saul as a self-focused man rather than a God-focused man. He appears insecure, continually concerning himself with himself, wanting others to honor him. God saw through this pride and sought for *"a man after His own heart."* When Samuel came to Gilgal, he heard *"this bleating of the sheep,"* a sign that not all the livestock had been killed in the Amalekite attack and a sign of Saul's disobedience to the Lord's command. Saul did not understand the depth of Amalekite sin and treachery, nor how their actions had brought the Lord's just sentence of execution upon them; he was only concerned with himself and his rule.

The Lord directed Samuel to go and confront Saul's disobedience; this was a kingship breaker. Samuel dealt with Saul and his sin, revealing his disobedience as rebellion against the Lord and His Word. Samuel obeyed the Lord, made clear to Saul the coming end of his rulership, executed Agag the Amalekite, and went back to his home in Ramah where he *"grieved over Saul"* and his failures. God had a new assignment for Samuel.

📖 How did God deal with Samuel about going to anoint a new king in Bethlehem? What was Samuel's first reaction? Read 1 Samuel 16:1–5.

When Samuel walked into Bethlehem, what did the town leaders do, according to 1 Samuel 16:4–5?

📖 What was Samuel looking for, according to 1 Samuel 16:6–7?

God had some things to teach Samuel. What did God show Samuel when the first-born Eliab walked in, according to 1 Samuel 16:6–7?

📖 How did Samuel respond to the other brothers, according to 1 Samuel 16:8–10?

Samuel assumed that the next king would be strong and tall, looking like a leader. Eliab fit the description in Samuel's mind, but God stopped him, pointing to *His* perspective—*"God sees not as man sees, for man looks at the outward appearance, but the* L*ORD looks at the heart."* While outward appearances may matter to some degree, the most important matter is the heart, the inner man; *character* and *skill* are needed to lead God's way. Having a "heart for God" mattered most. Samuel quickly shifted his focus, rejecting the next six sons. Are there any others?

WORD STUDY
"The Youngest"

In 1 Samuel 16:11, when Jesse spoke of his eighth son David as *"the youngest,"* he used the Hebrew word *qatan* (Strong's # 6996) rooted in *quwt* (Strong's #6962). *Qatan* carries the idea of "diminutive," here apparently referring to David as "the little one" or "the least." It's root word *quwt* can refer to what is cut off or detested, worth nothing. This is not simply a reference to David's age, but to the family's view of him. It appears he was considered below ordinary, certainly no one of any significance. But God thought differently; He saw David as *"a man after His own heart"* and able to be king (1 Samuel 13:14). Always side with what God says, not what family or friends or even enemies say. A seemingly simple shepherd boy may be a king in waiting.

📖 What significance do you find in the family's mention of another son, *"the youngest,"* in the field with the sheep in 1 Samuel 16:11?

📖 Describe David as Samuel saw him in 1 Samuel 16:12.

David did not take the position as king for at least 18 years. What does this tell you about God, His ways, and His Timing?

STOP AND APPLY—*Trusting God's Timing*—David (and others) had to trust God's timing about David being king. Eighteen years...that's a long time, especially for a youth like David, but David had learned some things about God, His ways, how He honors leaders, and how He deals with people. Over the next several years, David had to deal with a vacillating Saul—praising David one moment and ready to kill him the next. Though not easy, David trusted God and His timing. How about you? Any issues with time or timing? Talk to the Lord.

Day Three

David and His Heart—What God Sees

We do not know *when* David wrote Psalm 23, just that he wrote it. It can be assumed that those first years as a shepherd boy, perhaps the first five to eight years, taught him much. Certainly, he learned some skills and understanding of sheep, goats, and wild animals from his father Jesse and from his older brothers. At some point, the care of the sheep was under his leadership, while his brothers took care of other things. We also know that David had helpers with him, servants in the family who worked alongside David. David led them as well as the flocks.

What kind of heart did David reveal in his day-to-day dealings with the sheep? When David was probably no older than age 12, Samuel, though not knowing who or where, already spoke of him as a *"man after His* [God's] *own heart"* (1 Samuel 13:14; Acts 13:22). It is possible David wrote this psalm much later in life after experiencing many trials. Whether that is so or not, Psalm 23 gives us some unique clues about David, about the Lord, and about ourselves. Let's explore Psalm 23 and the heart of David.

DID YOU KNOW?
Who Is the LORD?

In Scripture and often in David's life, we read of *"the LORD,"* a translation of the Hebrew word *Yahweh* (Strong's # 3068) often written with all-capital consonants only—YHWH. Rooted in the Hebrew word *hayah* (Strong's #1961), which means "to exist" or "to be," God is the Eternal, Self-existent God (always being), *"The I AM WHO I AM"* (Exodus 3:14). Most translations use all capitals—LORD—to highlight this unique name. It is found more than 6000 times in addition to being found as *Yah* or in compound words or names such as Azariah ("My Help is the LORD"—for example, in 1 Kings 4:2; Daniel 1:6). The LORD or *Yahweh* is the Creator God, the

Sustainer, the Victorious Warrior and Redeemer, as well as the covenant-making, covenant-keeping God of Israel. This name is included in the title "the Angel of the LORD," referred to by many as the pre-incarnate Christ/Messiah who is noted about thirty-five times in the Old Testament.

📖 David wrote many psalms. Toward the end of his life, he was even called *"the sweet psalmist of Israel"* (2 Samuel 23:1). Read Psalm 23 very carefully. What do you discover about David in this Psalm?

What kind of heart does Psalm 23 reveal?

David readily admitted that the Lord Himself continually shepherded his life, providing for him, protecting him, even considering his weaknesses, like needing *"still waters"* instead of turbulent waters. When David penned this psalm, he expressed his contentment in knowing and following the Lord—perhaps this came after a time of particular trial in David's life. Whatever the case, David expressed his confidence in the Lord as *his* shepherd. He desired to follow Him in the clear tracks He made. Even in places like *"the valley of the shadow of death,"* David knew that the Lord would protect him. (That *"valley"* is a real place near the shepherds' fields near Bethlehem known for thieves, dangers, and potential death). As David used a *"rod"* and a *"staff"* to fight or stave off wolves, bears, or lions, as well as to guide the sheep properly and safely, so the Lord would use His instruments to protect and direct David. He had confidence for the quiet, peaceful days as well as those days of turmoil or trial.

What do you see about shepherding in this psalm? What does it tell you about David's shepherding?

What do you see in Psalm 23 about the Lord's shepherding?

DID YOU KNOW?
Psalms 22, 23, and 24, Together

Psalms 22, 23, and 24 form a "Shepherding Trilogy," a three-part praise hymn, pondering the Lord and salvation in time and eternity. Consider these connections. The Lord Jesus is our *"Good Shepherd,"* our Savior, who *"lays down His life for the sheep"* (Psalm 22 with John 10:11, 14–18), the "Great Shepherd" who, as our Shepherd, guides, equips, and works in us what is *"pleasing in His sight"* (Psalm 23 with Hebrews 13:20–21), and the *"Chief Shepherd,"* our Sovereign Lord and *"King of Glory"* who will return in triumph (Psalm 24 with 1 Peter 5:4). Each Psalm reflects something of the character, ways, and work of the Lord and together picture a beautiful mosaic of prayer and praise to Him. These psalms exhort us to trust and love the Lord, knowing He will care for us now and forever and will be clearly seen as the Victorious Redeemer whatever we may face.

What did David know about the Lord, according to Psalm 23?

While David certainly cared well for his father's sheep, his focus was on far more than sheep. What do you discover about David's view of *God* in Psalm 23?

David saw the Lord as personal and caring for anyone, even for a poor shepherd boy. He saw God as close and comforting, not distant or uncaring, only paying attention to the rich and powerful. In Psalm 23, David testified about how God knew him intimately and personally; this testimony is also seen in several other psalms he penned. David humbly reveals a God-centered attitude, knowing that God worked *"for His Name's sake,"* to reveal Himself and bring glory to Him and His ways. David remained confident in the Lord for his daily needs as well as for the *"forever"* days ahead; *"surely goodness and mercy / lovingkindness shall follow me all the days of my life, and I will dwell in the house of the LORD forever"* (NKJV/NASB—Psalm 23:6).

📖 In Psalm 23, David talks *about* the LORD in verses 1–3 and 6. Then, he talks *to* the LORD in verses 4–5. What do verses 1–3 tell you about David's heart?

📖 What do you discover about David's heart and perspective in Psalm 23:6?

📖 What do you see about David's heart for the Lord in Psalm 23:4–5?

Here in Psalm 23, David reveals his confidence in and comfort from the Lord; how He cared for him day after day. David recognizes God working in his *"soul"* as well as in his external situations. Whatever the circumstance, David knows the Lord will lead him exactly where he needs to be—even through places of darkness or danger. David praises the Lord for His presence and His care, even in those times when enemies are nearby, even perhaps pursuing him or plotting against him. God knew every need David (or any of His children) faced and would provide exactly what was needed when it was needed. David also expresses his confidence in the *"goodness and mercy/lovingkindness"* of the Lord for time and eternity, looking forward to when he would *"dwell in the house of the LORD forever."*

Make it *Personal*: Pray this psalm for *yourself*, inserting your name or yourself in *each* verse where *"my," "me,"* or *"I"* is used. You may want to make a journal entry here or a prayer communicating thanks, praise, confession, personal petition, however the Holy Spirit focuses your heart.

Think of *Others*: Now Pray this psalm for *someone* (or several) God brings to mind. Make this a time of investing in the life and eternity of someone you know.

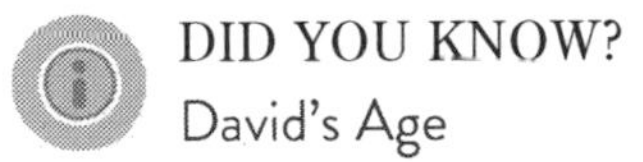

DID YOU KNOW?
David's Age

David was born around 1040 BC, but that does not tell us his age at the various stages of his life. Scripture tells us he was age thirty when he became king and reigned forty years, making him around age 70 when he died (2 Samuel 5:4). Likely, he killed Goliath when he was about age 15. How so? He had three older brothers in the army which required the youngest of the three to be at least 20 (Numbers 1:3; 14:29). That meant brothers 4 through 7 could have been (at most) 19, 18, 17, 16, with David as the eighth son being around age 15. He had been anointed as king before this, possibly at age 10-12. The Bathsheba incident occurred when he was around 48 or 49 and the Absalom debacle occurred when he was around age 64. For further information, see the Chart, "The Life and Times of David" at the end of this Lesson.

STOP AND APPLY—*Needy*—Sheep are very needy. First, they are fidgety, easily agitated or distracted. Second, sheep are frail, susceptible to diseases from many sources, especially insects. Sheep are also easy prey to wild animals or thieves; not cunning, not fighters, easily overcome. Third, sheep easily follow and often stray, even going the wrong way, perhaps after a fellow sheep, though that could lead to a dangerous or even deadly place. Consider your needs and weaknesses. Bring those to the Lord. Ask Him to "shepherd" you, to protect you and provide what you truly need.

Day Four

Shepherd Boy Versus Philistine Giant

Still a young teen or *"man,"* David continued faithfully tending his father's flocks. Three of his older brothers were with King Saul's army dealing with the Philistines. David's dad Jesse called him to go and check on his brothers. That seemed normal enough, but in one of those history-changing events, everything would become anything but normal. What can we learn from this Shepherd Boy?

📖 What do you learn about David in 1 Samuel 17:12–20?

David grew up with seven older brothers (and at least two sisters). It appears that most saw him as the runt of the family, nothing special. He took care of the family flocks and went *"back and forth"* to Saul, apparently to play the harp and soothe Saul's anxieties. Saul and his army had the Philistine menace to deal with. David's dad sent him to check on his three oldest brothers in the Valley of Elah about twelve miles away. David faithfully obeyed, leaving early the next morning after making sure the flock was taken care of by the *"keeper."*

🕮 How did David find out about Goliath, according to 1 Samuel 17:21–25?

🕮 Read 1 Samuel 17:26–27. How did David respond to Goliath's threats and the reactions of the Israeli soldiers?

🕮 Describe Eliab's reaction to David's words in 1 Samuel 17:28? How did David respond, according to 1 Samuel 17:29–30?

When David came to the Israeli army camp, he went to where his brothers were, and, about that time, Goliath showed up with his threats, another day in his forty-day challenge (1 Samuel 17:16). David saw the great fear of the soldiers and questioned what was going on. Whoever could kill this giant would be given Saul's daughter, and his family would pay no taxes.

In anger, David's oldest brother Eliab questioned David's presence with the army, maligning his role as shepherd over *"those few sheep"* and accusing him of only coming to see *"the battle."* David responded with his own questions, revealing his simple request for knowing what was occurring.

🕮 What occurred next? Note the events from 1 Samuel 17:31–33.

🕮 What did David have to deal with in his meeting with Saul, according to 1 Samuel 17:33–39? Where was David focused?

📖 What did David do as he left Saul, according to 1 Samuel 17:40?

Saul heard about David's inquiry. David told Saul he was ready to fight Goliath. When Saul objected, David rehearsed how he had dealt with an attacking *"lion or a bear."* David compared Goliath to one of the attacking animals, though Goliath's wrong was even worse. He was taunting *"the armies of the living God."* David would deal with him in the same way. While Saul sought to 'help' David by loaning him his armor, David chose to fight his way without Saul's armor; he picked up *"five smooth* [brook] *stones"* as he prepared to face the giant.

📖 How did David respond to the site and words of Goliath, according to 1 Samuel 17:41–47?

📖 Read 1 Samuel 17:48–49. What did David do as the giant approached?

📖 Summarize the summary given in 1 Samuel 17:50–54.

Goliath taunted David when he saw him, but David did not focus on his words or actions, but on the Lord and his relationship with Him: *"I come to you in the name of the LORD of hosts, the God of the armies of Israel, whom you have taunted."* David was confident in God, focused on honoring Him. He would prevail, *"that all the earth may know that there is a God in Israel."* Then, David *"prevailed over the Philistine with a sling and a stone"*—simple words about a simple action but also a life-changing and nation-changing action in their affect.

David went to the battlefield and there cut off the head of Goliath with Goliath's sword, then took his weapons to his own tent. The Philistines fled, and the Israelite soldiers chased them, insuring an Israeli victory. On their return, the Israelites *"plundered"* the abandoned Philistine camp. Saul, perhaps more concerned with his own appearance, did not readily recognize David. Perhaps David was "just another servant" in his court. Whatever the situation, David's victory over Goliath changed that.

📖 What would happen next? What do you discover in 1 Samuel 18:1–6?

📖 Read 1 Samuel 18:7–9. How did these events begin shaping life for David?

IN THEIR SHOES

Jonathan, the Friend

Though a very capable warrior, Jonathan did not rise up to confront Goliath. Instead, he had a front-row seat to the events of David's victory over Goliath; he was doubtless impressed with this young man, about 25 years younger than him. First Samuel 18:1 clearly states, *"The soul of Jonathan was knit to the soul of David, and Jonathan loved him as himself."* Though technically in line as the next king after his father Saul, Jonathan gladly entered into a covenant friendship with David that included his readiness to follow David as the next king (1 Samuel 18:3–4; 20:13–17, 42; 23:16–18). Jonathan revealed his love and loyalty to David over and over, always seeking to protect him and at the same time remained loyal to his father and his duties (1 Samuel 19:1–7; 20:1–42; 2 Samuel 1:17, 22–27).

Soon after David's meeting with Saul, Saul's son Jonathan, though more than twenty-five years older than David, made a covenant agreement with him. The covenant 'ceremony' included trading robes and armor (including his sword, bow, and belt), and as found in historical records, meant unswerving loyalty to one another; each would defend the other to the death and seek to help and bless in any way possible (the person and any family members).

Alongside the strategic occurrence of a covenant between Jonathan and David, Saul sent David on several raids against the Philistines. David proved victorious time after time. As a result, the people saw David in a new light, a light Saul did not appreciate; in fact, Saul became *"very angry."* Many ascribed to David victory over *"his ten thousands,"* while the songs or statements about Saul only spoke of *"his thousands."* In 1 Samuel 18:9, these momentous words pointed to a brewing storm: *"and Saul looked at David with suspicion from that day on."*

STOP AND APPLY—Where Is Your Focus?—It is easy to focus on surrounding circumstances, the words of others (spoken or written), or one's own inadequacies. David faced all those but chose to focus on the Lord and His abilities. When he faced Goliath, he kept his focus on the Lord, not on the giant. What 'giant' are you facing? What are people saying or writing? Look at the Lord and His Word; focus on Him.

DAY FIVE

FOLLOWING MY SHEPHERD

What can we learn from David, the *Shepherd Boy—Shepherd King*? God is no respecter of persons and, as He was faithful to David as his *"Shepherd,"* so He is available to the willing heart today. He can be *your* Shepherd, in the mundane days 'keeping sheep' as well as the momentous days of honor or challenge or danger. David faced all of that. We can learn from him.

IN THEIR SHOES

Priests Reigning

While most did not see David as a future king, many believers throughout history have failed to remember that God destined each believer to *"reign in life"* daily through Jesus Christ (Romans 5:17). One day each believer will reign with Him as a *"priest,"* even sitting on the Throne with Him. Consider those promises in 2 Timothy 2:12; 4:8 (*"crown of righteousness"*); 1 Peter 2:9 (a *"royal priesthood"*); Revelation 3:21 (as overcomers on His Throne); 5:10—believers from *"every tribe and tongue and people and nation"* will be a *"kingdom and priests to our God; and they will reign upon the earth."* Revelation 20:4, 6 reveals that the resurrected saints will reign with Christ as *"priests of God"* during the Millennium and Revelation 22:5 speaks of the redeemed reigning forever.

Most people think of themselves in their family as one of the "also born" rather than as future kings or queens. David certainly faced that. What was David's primary connection, according to Psalm 23:1?

How does David's connection speak to you about *your* connection? This would be a good time to write a "Letter to God" or a "Letter to Your Heavenly Father." He is your best friend, even a covenant friend. He knows what you are going through and what you are thinking; putting it on paper or on screen may help you think through just how awesome it is to have the "LORD" as your *"Shepherd."*

As you close your "Letter," include some faith statements of trust in the Lord (whether you *feel* them or not). Use Scripture, perhaps verses, sentences, or phrases from some of David's psalms or other Scriptures.

Confess the truth. Pick one or two of the psalms of David, read each through, and make each a personal prayer for yourself and/or for someone you know. Here are some of David's psalms: Psalms 2–5, 22–24, 34–38, 51–52, and 54. For a fuller list see the last page of the Chart, "The Life and Times of David" at the end of this lesson. You may want to write your prayer or a portion of a prayer in the space here or in your personal journal.

What challenges are you facing now, at this season of life? Any "Goliaths," "Sauls," or even family or friends like David's brothers challenging you in some way? Make some personal applications. Here are four principles to follow whatever your challenge(s). In the space given after these four principles, write your personal applications.

First, keep the Lord as your focus. Look at Him, His character and power. He will never betray you, misuse you, or change on you.

Second, recall His Word. His promises are good. David penned Psalm 12 in which he states, *"the words of the* LORD *are pure words; as silver tried in a furnace on the earth, refined seven times"* (12:6). No one refines precious metals seven times—it's a Scripture picture, a Hebrew way of showing complete refinement with absolutely no impurities—that's God's Word. Recall what God has said and stick to it. Say His Word to yourself. Pray His Word to Him. Obey His Word.

Third, trust God and His plans. He never wrings His hands wondering what to do or paces back and forth in front of His throne. He knows what He is planning and what He is doing.

Fourth, trust God's timing. He is sometimes "two minutes 'til too late," but He is never late...or early. He is always on time.

My Applications:

Make the call. Call on the Lord for "what next?" Several times, David faced a "what next?" season in his life. He took the next step. Bring before the Lord your current season and as much of the *next* season you see. Talk to Him about it. Ask Him for wisdom about your next step, just *one* step. James 3:17–18 describes the *"wisdom from above."* Bring your life and decision(s) into the light of those verses. You may want to write your *one* step in the space below. It may be simple or hard, big or small. Whatever the case, write it out, pray it over, and obey, trusting God in how He is leading you.

TAKEAWAYS
The Early Days of David

There are *eight* takeaways from *The Early Days of David*: 1) Never presume on God or God's will. 2) God can change leaders and followers based on what He knows and sees, including one's disobedience or obedience to Him from the heart. 3) Never underestimate God's ability to put in place who or what He wants in place. 4) God looks at the heart, the inner person more than the outer person. 5) What many, or perhaps most, despise, God may prize. 6) God works based on His perfect Timing, not human timing or the current circumstances. 7) God will always be true to His character and His Word. 8) God wants us to trust Him, no matter how bleak the circumstance may appear or how wrongly others act.

Lord, thank You for the walk and testimony of David. He was not perfect, but he looked to You most of the time. May I too have a *heart* for You, seeking You and Your will whatever my age or season of life. Like David, I pray Psalm 139:23–24—*"Search me, O God, and know my heart; try me and know my anxious thoughts; and see if there be any hurtful way in me, and lead me in the everlasting way."* I also pray, *"Let the words of my mouth and the meditation of my heart be acceptable in Your sight, O LORD, my rock and my Redeemer"* (Psalm 19:14). Thank You for Your compassion, concern, and care for me and Your willingness to teach me and lead me. In Jesus' Name, Amen.

The Life and Times of David			
DATE BC	AGE David (Approx)	EVENT (Locations are Highlighted with Bold Text)	SCRIPTURE Psalms of David are in Bold Text
1040-970 BC	Birth-Age 70	David was born ca. 1040 BC in Bethlehem, Judah and died in 970 BC in Jerusalem, Judah. It is thought David penned 75 Psalms. Where possible, each is printed in Bold Print at the time it was penned (if known).	1 Samuel 9–31 and 2 Samuel 1–24, 1 Kings 1; 2:1–12, 1 Chronicles 3:1–9; 10–29
1040	Birth	David was born in Bethlehem, the son of Jesse, the grandson of Obed, and the great-grandson of Boaz and Ruth.	Ruth 4:12, 17, 21–22 1 Chronicles 2:12–13
		David was born the eighth son to Jesse (Ephrathite of Bethlehem) his father and his unnamed mother in Bethlehem. Seven older brothers: Eliab, Abinadab, Shammah (or Shimea), Nethanel, Raddai, Ozem, unnamed son (possibly died early). David had two sisters (possibly half-sisters), Zeruiah and Abigail.	1 Samuel 16:6–11; 17:12, 58; 1 Chronicles 2:13–16; Matthew 1:6 Psalm 51:5
		David was born in Bethlehem, in the territory of Judah and was a member of the tribe of Judah.	Genesis 49:8–12 1 Samuel 16:1; Micah 5:2; Matthew 2:2–6
	Ages 5-15?	David tended the flocks of his father Jesse in the shepherds' fields around Bethlehem.	1 Samuel 16:11, 19; Psalm 78:70–71 (Asaph)
1040-1010	Birth-Age 30	David lived under the reign of King Saul in Israel (approximately 1050-1010 BC). Saul, born around 1082 BC, began to reign around the age of 31 (1 Samuel 13:1), about 42 years older than David.	1 Samuel 9–31 Acts 13:21

ca. 1030-1028	David was about age 10-12.	1 Samuel 13:14—After Saul's disobedience, the prophet Samuel spoke about *"the LORD"* seeking *"a man after His own heart"* to be the next king in place of Saul.	1 Samuel 13:7b–13, 14; Acts 7:46; 13:22
	Ages 8-15	David skillfully played the harp in his childhood and early teens.	1 Samuel 16:16, 18
	Ages 8-15?	In his childhood or youth, tending his father's sheep near Bethlehem, David sometimes encountered a bear or a lion, perhaps several times. He slew each one.	1 Samuel 17:34–37
1030-1028	About age 10-12	God sent Samuel to Bethlehem. He observed the seven oldest sons of Jesse, each of whom the Lord rejected as king. Samuel asked if there was another son. Then, they brought in David, the eighth and *"the youngest,"* from tending the sheep. He appeared *"ruddy, with bright eyes, and good-looking"* (16:12).	1 Samuel 16:1–10, 12
	Age 10-12	At the house of Jesse in Bethlehem, Samuel anointed David as the next king of Israel. [Samuel around age 74-76]	1 Samuel 16:11–13
	Age 10-12	*"The Spirit of the LORD came upon David from that day forward"* (1 Samuel 16:13b). *"I have given help to one who is mighty; I have exalted one chosen from the people. I have found My servant David; with My holy anointing oil I have anointed him."* (Psalm 89:19b–20) [NKJV] Psalm 89:21–29 gives God's prophecy of the Messiah to come, the Greater Son of David.	1 Samuel 16:13b; 18:12 Psalm 89:19b–20 and 89:21–29 (written by Ethan).
1010-970	Ages 30-70	David *"shepherded"* the people of Israel *"according to the integrity of his heart, and guided them by the skillfulness of his hands"* [NKJV] (Psalm 78:72).	Psalm 78:72 (written by Asaph)
1030-1025?	David, Ages 10-15	The Spirit of the LORD departed from Saul after his disobedience. Saul, troubled in spirit, had David come to play his harp and Saul became *"refreshed and well"* in spirit.	1 Samuel 16:14–23
	Ages 10-15	David served as Saul's armor bearer and occasionally returned to Bethlehem to keep his father's sheep.	1 Samuel 16:21 and 17:15
1026/ 1025	Age 14 / 15	David carried food to the Valley of Elah where his three older brothers were serving in Saul's army. As soldiers, they would be age 20 or older; the other four brothers possibly ages 16-19, not yet 20 (not old enough to be in the army). David was the eighth son and youngest (or one of the youngest), possibly age 14 or 15.	1 Samuel 17:17–22 [Army soldiers' aged 20, see Numbers 1:3, 20; 26:2, et al]
1026/ 1025	Age 14/15	David questioned why no one answered Goliath's challenge. David offered to face him in battle.	1 Samuel 17:23–30

1026/ 1025	Age 14/15	David (around age 14-15) spoke with Saul (around age 56-57) about facing the Philistine giant Goliath. Saul gave David his armor which did not fit. David chose to fight using his sling and smooth stones from the brook in the Valley of Elah.	1 Samuel 17:31–39
		David faced Goliath the giant using his sling and *"five smooth stones from the brook"* in the Valley of Elah.	1 Samuel 17:40–47
		Using his sling, David threw one smooth stone, hit Goliath in the forehead, and slew him. Then, David cut off Goliath's head.	1 Samuel 17:48–51
1026/ 1025	Age 14 / 15	Saul questioned who David was. David identified himself as *"the son of your servant Jesse the Bethlehemite"* (1 Samuel 17:58).	1 Samuel 17:55–58
1026/ 1025	David, around age 14 /15. Jonathan, around age 41 (26/27 years older)	Jonathan, firstborn son of Saul, entered into a covenant with David, giving him his robe, armor, sword, bow, and belt. In giving his royal robe of future kingship, he acknowledged something of David's future role as king in Saul's and Jonathan's place. Jonathan was born around 1067 BC, 26/27 years older than David.	1 Samuel 18:1–4
	Age 14 /15	Saul ordered David to stay at court with him in Gibeah.	1 Samuel 18:2
1025- 1018?	Ages 15-22	At Saul's orders, David went out to fight the Philistines and became a leader over *"the men of war."* He proved very wise and victorious in the battles.	1 Samuel 18:5–6, 13–16
	Ages 15-22	After many victories over the Philistines, David's fame spread throughout the land. Saul became jealous, angry, and vengeful.	1 Samuel 18:6–11
1024?	Age 16?	Saul promised to give his daughter Merab to David as a wife, but she married Adriel instead.	1 Samuel 18:17–19
1023- 1018	Ages 17-22	Saul sought to give David his daughter Michal, hoping she would be a snare to him or that the Philistines would kill him in battle.	1 Samuel 18:20–30
		Saul sought to kill David, but Jonathan intervened on David's behalf.	1 Samuel 19:1–8
		Saul again sought to kill David at his home in Gibeah, but Michal helped him escape safely.	1 Samuel 19:9–17 **Psalm 59**
		David fled to Samuel at Ramah and told him all Saul had done. Saul sent three teams of servants to Ramah, then went himself to capture David. Each group encountered the Spirit of God and prophesied.	1 Samuel 19:18–24
		David fled back to Gibeah to Jonathan who promised to protect David as part of his covenant relationship. David and Jonathan strengthened their covenant, with David promising to protect Jonathan's descendants.	1 Samuel 20:1–23

		Jonathan fulfilled his promise, giving David warning of Saul's intent to kill David. Jonathan and David agreed to stand for one another as covenant partners. David fled to Nob.	1 Samuel 20:24–42
1018	Age 22?	In Nob, David received from the priest Ahimelech the Tabernacle *"showbread"* for him and his men and *"the sword of Goliath."*	1 Samuel 21:1–9; Matthew 12:3–4
1018	Age 22?	Dealing with Saul became so difficult that David fled into Gath (enemy Philistine lands) to live under Philistine king Achish.	1 Samuel 21:10
		Because of the reaction of David's Philistine captors serving under king Achish in Gath, David pretended to be insane and thus escaped. David probably penned Psalm 34 at this time (note the kingly title "Abimelech" in the Title of Psalm 34). Psalm 56 deals with David's trust in God while captive by the Philistines in Gath.	1 Samuel 21:11–15 **Psalms 34 and 56**
		David fled from Gath to *"the cave of Adullam,"* where his brothers and his father's house joined him.	1 Samuel 22:1 **Psalm 57?** (Title)
		About 400 men noted as *"in distress… in debt, and … discontented"* joined David in his wilderness hideaway at the cave of Adullam. David *"became captain over them."*	1 Samuel 22:2 David possibly penned **Psalm 142** at this time.
1018	Age 22?	David and his men next went to Mizpah and sought safety for his father and mother with the king of Moab. David remained *"in the stronghold"* in the wilderness (perhaps in Moab or at Masada).	1 Samuel 22:3–4
1017	Age 23?	The prophet Gad directed David to leave the stronghold and go into the land of Judah. David *"went into the forest of Hereth"* in Judah.	1 Samuel 22:5
1017	Age 23?	Doeg the Edomite told Saul of David's encounter with the priest Ahimelech in Nob. Saul called Ahimelech and his family to his headquarters at Gibeah of Ramah. Saul falsely accused the priest and had Doeg the Edominte slay him and his family (85 men) as well as the people of the town of Nob.	1 Samuel 22:6–18, 19; **Psalm 52** (Title)
1017	Age 23?	Abiathar, a son of Ahimelech, *"escaped and fled after David."* He told him of the slaughter. Abiathar joined with David and his men.	1 Samuel 22:20–23
		Informed of the Philistine raid on the Judean town of Keilah, David *"inquired* [Hebrew—*shaal,* to ask, request] *of the LORD"* about whether to attack the Philistines. God said *"Go."*	1 Samuel 23:1–2

		When David's men proved hesitant to fight the Philistines, David *"inquired of the LORD once again"* and the LORD again said *"Go."* He gave David and his men victory at Keilah.	1 Samuel 23:3–5
		Saul sought to capture David at Keilah. Through the priestly *"ephod"* Abiathar had brought, David inquired of the LORD about whether he would be safe or captured in Keilah. Then, David and his 600 men fled.	1 Samuel 23:6–13. David possibly penned **Psalms 27** and **31** at this time.
		David's ranks had grown to 600 men at this time.	1 Samuel 23:13
		David and his men hid in the strongholds of the hills and forests in the Wilderness of Ziph as Saul sought to capture and kill him.	1 Samuel 23:14–15
		Saul's son Jonathan, David's covenant friend *"before the LORD,"* sought to encourage and strengthen David in the forests of Ziph. He assured David about being the future king with Jonathan at his side.	1 Samuel 23:16–18
		Men from Ziph came to Saul at Gibeah ready to deliver David to him out of *"the hill of Hachilah"* in the forests of Ziph.	1 Samuel 23:19–24a **Psalm 54** (Title)
Spring of 1016	Age 24?	David went from Ziph to the Wilderness of Maon. Saul sought him but left to deal with a new Philistine threat. David fled to En Gedi.	1 Samuel 23:24b–29 **Psalm 35; 63** (Title)
1016		With 3000 men, Saul sought David in the Wilderness of En Gedi, particularly in the remote area of *"the Rocks of the Wild Goats."*	1 Samuel 24:1–2
		David, hiding in a cave, cut the corner of Saul's robe (perhaps one of the *tzitzit* (cf., Numbers 15:37–41)). He had the opportunity to kill him but did not. David honored God and God's *"anointed"* king Saul. Afterward, David came out and spoke to Saul showing his innocence. Saul asked David to spare his descendants, then left. *"David and his men went up to the stronghold"* (Masada?).	1 Samuel 24:3–22 Numbers 15:37–41 David possibly wrote **Psalm 57** at this time.
1014	Age 26?	Samuel died around age 88-90 and was buried at Ramah. Samuel lived from around 1104/02 BC to 1014 BC	1 Samuel 25:1a
1014	Age 26?	David and his men moved to the Wilderness of Paran in the NE section of the Sinai Peninsula.	1 Samuel 25:1b

Spring of 1013	Age 27	In Maon and Carmel, David sought help and food for his men from the wealthy Nabal who refused and maligned David. Abigail, Nabal's wife, averted David's attack of them and their property. Nabal died soon after and David asked the widow Abigail to be his wife.	1 Samuel 25:2–42
Fall of 1013	Age 27	David also took Ahinoam of Jezreel as his wife. Saul gave his daughter Michal, also David's wife, to Palti as his wife.	1 Samuel 25:43–44
Spring of 1012	Age 28	David and his men hid again in the hill of Hachilah in Ziph. With 3000 men, Saul again sought to capture David. With opportunity to kill Saul, David refused to strike *"the LORD'S anointed."* Saul and David parted.	1 Samuel 26:1–25
1012	Age 28	Amazingly, because of Saul's relentless opposition, David escaped to the land of the Philistines to serve Achish, king of Gath.	1 Samuel 27:1–4
1012-1011	Ages 28-29	The Philistines gave David and his 600 men the village of Ziklag where their wives, children, and livestock lived (about 3000 people in that village). They lived there 16 months (27:7).	1 Samuel 27:5–7. David possibly penned **Psalms 10, 13**, and **22** during this time.
1012	Age 28	More men joined David at Ziklag to fight on his side.	1 Chronicles 12:1–7
1011	Age 29	David and his men raided the towns of the Geshurites, the Girzites, and the Amalekites, perpetual enemies of Israel. David feigned loyalty to the Philistine king Achish.	1 Samuel 27:8–12
	Age 29	King Achish made David one of the *"chief guardians"* in his army.	1 Samuel 28:1–2
	David, age 29/30. Saul, 72.	Saul sought guidance from a forbidden medium at Endor, refusing to inquire of the LORD.	1 Samuel 28:3–25 1 Chronicles 10:13–14
	Age 29/30	More men joined David at the stronghold and at Ziklag.	1 Chronicles 12:8–22
	Age 29/30	David and his 600 plus men sought to join with the Philistine army at Aphek as they prepared to fight Saul and his forces near Jezreel.	1 Samuel 29:1–2
1010	Age 30	The Philistine leaders rejected David and his men and ordered them to leave their ranks. David and his men left the next morning traveling from Aphek back to Ziklag.	1 Samuel 29:3–11
		On the third day, David and his men arrived at Ziklag and saw it burned. All their families and livestock had been kidnapped by the marauding Amalekites.	1 Samuel 30:1–3

		All the men wept and then David's men spoke of stoning him. David, *"greatly distressed,"* turned to the LORD and *"strengthened himself in the LORD his God."*	1 Samuel 30:4–6
1010		David sought the LORD using the ephod of Abiathar the priest. *"Shall I pursue this troop"* of Amalekites? The LORD directed David to pursue and assured him of victory.	1 Samuel 30:7–8
		David and his 600 plus men began their march. At the Brook Besor, 200 *"weary"* men stayed behind. David and 400 continued.	1 Samuel 30:9–10
		As they marched, they found an Egyptian slave near death, abandoned by an Amalekite master three days before. They gave him food and water. He provided needed information on the Amalekite camp location.	1 Samuel 30:11–15
		David and his men came to the Amalekite camp as they were celebrating their victories and their great plunder. David and his men attacked and fought all night and the next day, conquering and rescuing all their families and all the plunder.	1 Samuel 30:16–20
		Back at the Brook Besor camp David distributed the spoil among his men, including the 200 *"weary"* men, despite the protest of the 400 plus, some of whom were *"wicked and worthless* [literally translated, *"sons of Belial"*]." David initiated a statute—*"As his part is who goes down to the battle, so shall his part be who stays by the supplies; they shall share alike"* (1 Samuel 30:24).	1 Samuel 30:21–25
		From Ziklag, David sent portions of the spoil to the elders/leaders in several towns of Judah.	1 Samuel 30:26–31
		Saul, Jonathan, and the Israeli army faced defeat and death at the hands of the Philistine army. The Philistines took the bodies of Saul and his three sons from Mount Gilboa and hung them on the wall of the city of Beth Shan. The men of Jabesh Gilead traveled all night to rescue the bodies of Saul and his sons and bury them at Jabesh.	1 Samuel 31:1–13
1010	Age 30	On his third day back at Ziklag, David received from an Amalekite runner the report of the deaths of Saul and Jonathan on Mount Gilboa. He mourned the deaths of Saul and Jonathan and executed the Amalekite who claimed to have killed Saul. David's *"Song of the Bow"* lamented their deaths.	2 Samuel 1:1–27
1010	Age 30	When the nurse of Jonathan's 5-year old son Mephibosheth heard about Jonathan's death, she fled from Jerusalem, but in running fell injuring the child so that he became lame in his feet.	2 Samuel 4:4

	Age 30	David *"inquired of the LORD"* about moving from Ziklag. God instructed him to go to Hebron in Judah. He moved there with his family and his men.	2 Samuel 2:1–3
1010	Age 30	David became king of Judah with his capital in Hebron for 7 ½ years.	2 Samuel 2:4–7, 11
1010-1008	Ages 30-32	Abner, commander of Saul's army, made Ishbosheth (age 40), the son of Saul, rival king over Israel at Mahanaim. Ishbosheth reigned two years. Joab led David's army.	2 Samuel 2:8–10, 13
		The rival kingship of Ishbosheth led to a civil war. Abner killed Joab's brother Asahel. Many men of both armies fell, but the *"house of David"* ... *"grew stronger and stronger."*	2 Samuel 2:12–32; 3:1
1010-1003	Ages 30-37	During the 7 ½ years at Hebron, David fathered six sons by six wives: Amnon, Chileab (Daniel), Absalom, Adonijah, Shephatiah, and Ithream.	2 Samuel 3:2–5; 1 Chronicles 3:1–4a
1008	Age 32	Abner, initially loyal to Ishbosheth, came over to David's side. Abner also brought Saul's daughter Michal to David as his wife. At Hebron, David made a covenant of peace with Abner and several men from Israel.	2 Samuel 3:6–21
	Age 32	David's commander Joab, not trusting Abner and wanting to avenge the death of his brother Asahel, killed Abner in Hebron.	2 Samuel 3:22–27
	Age 32	In Hebron, David mourned the death of Abner and spoke against Joab and his brother Abishai for their evil ways in killing Abner.	2 Samuel 3:28–39
1008	David, age 32	Baanah and Rechab, captains of Israel's army, assassinated Ishbosheth in his bed in Mahanaim and brought his head to David in Hebron. David executed them for their wicked deeds.	2 Samuel 4:1–3, 5–12
Around 1008/ 1007 Perhaps as late as 1003	Around Age 32/33? (after the civil war) Perhaps up to age 37	The elders of Israel came to David in Hebron yielding to David as the king over all Israel. With great joy, David and these leaders celebrated a covenant feast as King David made a covenant with them. This occurred during the time period after the Israeli civil war and before the move to Jerusalem (most likely in the months immediately after Ishbosheth's assassination).	2 Samuel 5:1–3 1 Chronicles 11:1–3; 12:23-40
1010–970	Age 30-70	David ruled in Hebron a total of 7 ½ years (ages 30-37) and in Jerusalem 33 years (ages 37-70), reigning 40 years (ages 30-70).	2 Samuel 5:4–5 1 Chronicles 3:4

1003-970	Ages 37-70	David and his men captured Jerusalem and moved there, making it his capital, *"the stronghold of Zion," "the City of David." "So David went on and became great, and the LORD God of hosts was with him"* (2 Samuel 5:10).	2 Samuel 5:6–10 1 Chronicles 11:4–9
1003-990	Ages 37-50?	David added more concubines and wives in Jerusalem. David had more sons (likely 13) as well as daughters, including Tamar, sister of Absalom.	2 Samuel 5:13–16 1 Chronicles 3:5–9; 14:3–7
1002	Age 38	The Philistines came to the Valley of Rephaim southwest of Jerusalem to fight against King David. He escaped to *"the stronghold"* (likely the Cave of Adullam).	2 Samuel 5:17–18
	Age 38	While at the Cave of Adullam with the Philistines encamped in the Valley of Rephaim, David longingly spoke of drinking from the well of Bethlehem, then garrisoned by Philistines. Three of his thirty *"mighty men" "broke through the camp"* there and retrieved a container of water from the well. They brought it back to David, but in honor of them and their risk and *"to the LORD"* he poured it out.	1 Chronicles 11:15–19
	Age 38	David *"inquired of the LORD"* about whether to fight the Philistines. The LORD gave him victory at Baal Perazim.	2 Samuel 5:19–21 1 Chronicles 14:8–12
	Age 38?	The Philistines came to fight David in the Valley of Rephaim again. David *"inquired of the LORD"* again and the LORD gave him a specific battlefield strategy and another victory.	2 Samuel 5:22–25 1 Chronicles 14:13–16
1002	Age 38?	David won many victories. *"Then the fame of David went out into all lands, and the LORD brought the fear of him upon all the nations."*	1 Chronicles 14:17
1000-991	Age 40-49	David began to subdue various nations surrounding Israel. First, he conquered the Philistines on the western side of Israel.	2 Samuel 8:1
1000-996	Age 40-44	David defeated Moab to the east of Israel and east of the Dead Sea. They began to pay tribute.	2 Samuel 8:2
1000-996	Age 40-44	To the north, David defeated Hadadezer, son of the king Rehob of Zobah, north of Damascus, Syria. He also conquered territory at the Euphrates River.	2 Samuel 8:3–4, 7–8 1 Chronicles 18:4 Psalm 60

1000-996	Age 40-44	Possibly in more than one instance, David defeated the Syrians and placed garrisons in Damascus. Syria paid tribute to David.	2 Samuel 8:5–6; 10:1–19; 1 Chron 19:1–19
997-996	Age 43-44	Toi king of Hamath (north of Damascus) sent his son Joram / Hadoram to bless David and give gifts of silver, gold, and bronze.	2 Samuel 8:9–10 1 Chronicles 18:9–10
997-996	Age 43-44	David dedicated to the LORD all the plunder, tribute, and gifts he received from conquering Syria, Moab, the Ammonites, the Philistines, the Amalekites, and Zobah.	2 Samuel 8:11–12
996?	Age 44?	To the south, David defeated Edom and placed garrisons there. Second Samuel 8:13 refers to *"the Valley of Salt,"* a region south of the Dead Sea, near Edom. Varying versions of this verse show David defeating either *"Syrians"* or *"Edomites."* It likely refers to Edomites, since it speaks of *"the Valley of Salt."* Psalm 60 points to this as well.	2 Samuel 8:13–14 1 Chronicles 18:12–13 **Psalm 60**
1001 & after	Age 39 and following	Through his reign and through his 'cabinet,' *"David administered judgment and justice to all his people"* (2 Samuel 8:15).	2 Samuel 8:15–18 1 Chronicles 18:14–17
995?	Age 45?	David gave thanks to the LORD for His deliverance from Saul and for the many victories He had given to David and his men.	2 Samuel 22:1–51 **Psalm 18:1–50**
995?	Age 45? Mephibosheth, possibly around age 20, had a son, Micah.	Sometime after consolidating the kingdom of Israel and Judah, David sought to show *"kindness"* to any of the family of Jonathan, his covenant friend. Ziba, the servant of the house of Saul informed David about Jonathan's son Mephibosheth living in LoDebar, lame in his feet. David restored to Mephibosheth all the lands of Saul and brought him to Jerusalem to live and eat at the king's table.	2 Samuel 9:1–13 [1 Chronicles 9:40, Mephibosheth (also known as Merib-Baal) had a son Micah]
995-993?	Age 45-47?	A famine occurred in Israel for three years. Then, David sought the LORD who revealed that the famine was because of Saul's slaughter of several Gibeonites who should have been protected as covenant partners of Israel. David gave the Gibeonites seven men of Saul's house and the Gibeonites executed them in Gibeah of Saul.	2 Samuel 21:1–9 [cf., Joshua 9:3–27; 10:1–11]

993?	Age 47?	David retrieved the bones of Saul, Jonathan, and the seven men and buried them. The famine stopped in answer to prayer.	2 Samuel 21:10–14 1 Samuel 31:11–13
993?	Age 47?	While fighting in Philistine territory against the giants there, David *"grew faint"* and almost lost his life at the hand of Ishbi-Benob, one of the giants. Joab's brother Abishai came to David's aid and killed the giant. This led to a new level of caution concerning David.	2 Samuel 21:15–17
993?	Age 47?	David's men urged, even demanded, that David not go out to battle since he was considered *"the lamp of Israel"* who needed to remain alive.	2 Samuel 21:17
993?	Age 47?	The Israelites had at least three other battle encounters and victories against Philistine giants—at Gob against the giant Saph / Sippai, at Gob against Lahmi a brother of Goliath, and at Gath against a 12-finger, 12-toe giant.	2 Samuel 21:18–22 1 Chronicles 20:4–8
Spring, 993?	Age 47?	General Joab and his army fought the Ammonites and besieged Rabbah. David stayed in Jerusalem (likely at the urging of his men, but not inquiring of the LORD about this).	2 Samuel 11:1; 21:17 1 Chronicles 20:1
Spring, 993?	Age 47?	At the urging of his men, David stayed home from battle at Rabbah. At his palace in Zion / Jerusalem, he awoke from a daytime nap and from his rooftop saw Bathsheba bathing. He called for her, committed adultery with her, and she conceived a child.	2 Samuel 21:17; 11:2–5
	Age 47	David plotted to bring Uriah the Hittite, Bathsheba's husband home from Rabbah to be with his wife. As one of David's mighty men and a faithful soldier, Uriah remained loyal to his task as an active-duty soldier. He did not go home to Bathsheba.	2 Samuel 11:6–13
	Age 47	David deceptively plotted to have Uriah killed in battle. Uriah died in battle at Rabbah, and Bathsheba mourned his death.	2 Samuel 11:14–26
	Age 47	David brought Bathsheba to the palace to become his wife and she gave birth to their son. *"But the thing that David had done displeased the LORD"* (2 Samuel 11:27).	2 Samuel 11:27
	Age 47, 48	David's sin and guilt tormented him like *"the fever heat of summer"* (Psalm 32:4)	Psalm 32:3–4 (**Psalm 32**)

	Age 48	*"The LORD sent Nathan"* the prophet to David to confront him about his sin toward the LORD, Bathsheba, and Uriah. David confessed his sin and Nathan told him of God's forgiveness and that he would not die. He also told him of the consequences that would befall his house—David would pay fourfold. It would begin with the death of Bathsheba's newborn son.	2 Samuel 12:1–15 Psalm 32:1–11; 51:1–19 (**Psalm 51**-Title)
	Age 48	The newborn son became ill, *"struck"* by the LORD. David fasted and prayed. The child died on the seventh day. David worshiped the LORD and returned to his regular schedule. David professed his faith in one day seeing that child again.	2 Samuel 12:15b–23
991	Age 49	David and Bathsheba married after Uriah's death. After being married to David, Bathsheba gave birth to a son whom they named *Solomon*. The Lord called him *Jedidiah*, *"Beloved of the LORD."*	2 Samuel 12:24–25 Matthew 1:6
	Age 50 and afterward	2 Samuel 5:14 and 1 Chronicles 3:5 reveal that David and Bathsheba (Bath-shua) had four sons: Shammua/Shimea, Shobab, Nathan, and Solomon. Solomon is listed fourth which may indicate his birth order, though that is unlikely. In the genealogies of Jesus, Joseph is a descendant of David and Bathsheba through Solomon, and Mary is a descendant of David and Bathsheba through Nathan.	2 Samuel 5:14 1 Chronicles 3:5 Matthew 1:1, 6, 16 Luke 3:23, 31
990	Age 50	David and his men captured the city of Rabbah of the Ammonites. He captured several other Ammonite cities as well.	2 Samuel 12:26–31 1 Chronicles 20:1–3
990-980	David, Age 50 to 60? Solomon, a young child, ages 4-10?	David taught and trained his young son Solomon in the wisdom and ways of God. Solomon wrote of this time speaking of when he was *"tender and the only son in the sight of my mother"* (Proverbs 4:3). Later, Solomon taught his son(s) as David had taught him (Proverbs 1:8–33; 2–3; 4:10–27; 5–7, et al).	Proverbs 4:3–9
985	David, age 55 Absalom, age 22	In Jerusalem, David's son Amnon plotted and then raped Absalom's sister (Amnon's half-sister) Tamar. Afterward, he hated Tamar. She left in shame and went to her brother Absalom's house. When informed, David became very angry, but did nothing.	2 Samuel 13:1–21
983	David, age 57 Absalom, age 24	Absalom hated his half-brother Amnon because he had raped his sister Tamar. Two years later, he carried out his plot to kill Amnon. Absalom (age 24) invited his brothers to a sheep shearing feast time at Baal Hazor, near Ephraim, where Absalom ordered his servants to kill Amnon.	2 Samuel 13:23–29

983	David, age 57 Absalom, age 24	David received false news that all of his sons had been slain by Absalom. David's nephew Jonadab informed him that only Amnon had been slain. David's other sons returned to Jerusalem.	2 Samuel 13:30–33, 34b–36
	David, age 57 Absalom, age 24	Absalom (age 24) fled from David and Jerusalem to Geshur to his grandfather Talmai, king of Geshur, where he stayed three years. David was comforted after Amnon's death but continued to grieve over the absence of his son Absalom, longing to see him.	2 Samuel 13:34a, 37–39
980	David, age 60	Joab convinced a woman of Tekoa to approach David to encourage him to bring Absalom (age 27) back to Jerusalem. David agreed and sent Joab to bring him back, but David would not see him.	2 Samuel 14:1–24
980-978	David—60-62 Absalom-27-29	During these days, Absalom's fame as the king's son continued to grow. All considered him handsome. His family increased—a total of three sons and a daughter (Tamar, likely named after her aunt).	2 Samuel 14:25–27
980-978	David—60-62 Absalom-27-29	Absalom (age 27-29) waited two years to see David but could not.	2 Samuel 14:25–28
980	David, age 60	Hiram became king of Tyre in 980 BC.	2 Samuel 5:11–12 1 Chronicles 14:1–2
980-978?	Age 60 and afterward	Shortly after becoming king of Tyre, Hiram provided timber from cedar trees and skilled craftsman to build David's palace in Jerusalem.	2 Samuel 5:11 1 Chronicles 14:1
980-970	Age 60 and afterward	By all that the LORD had done, *"David realized that the LORD had established him as king over Israel, and that his kingdom was highly exalted, for the sake of His people Israel"* (1 Chronicles 14:2).	2 Samuel 5:12 1 Chronicles 14:2
978	David, age 62 Absalom, age 29	Absalom, after waiting two years to see his father David, set Joab's barley field on fire to get his attention so he could finally see his father. Joab made arrangements and Absalom met with David.	2 Samuel 14:28–33
Around 977	Age 63?	David sought to bring the Ark of the Covenant from the house of Abinadab in Kirjath- Jearim to Jerusalem.	1 Samuel 7:1–2a 2 Samuel 6:1–2

Around 977	Age 63?	In his *first* attempt, with great rejoicing, David sought to bring the Ark of the Covenant to Jerusalem on a Philistine-style cart instead of on the shoulders of Levites, failing to follow the Lord's Word in carrying the Ark (see Numbers 3:30–31; 4:15; 7:9; 10:21; Deuteronomy 10:8). The cart tilted at the threshing floor of Nacon. When Uzzah (likely a grandson of Abinadab) touched the Ark to keep it from falling, the LORD, angered, struck him dead. In fear of God, they placed the Ark in the house of Obed-Edom for *three* months. *"The LORD blessed Obed-Edom and all his household."*	2 Samuel 6:1–11 1 Chronicles 13:1–14; Numbers 3:30–31; 4:15; 7:9; 10:21; Deuteronomy 10:8
Around 977	Age 63	David prepared a Tent to house the Ark of the Covenant in Jerusalem and organized the various priests and Levites to carry and receive the Ark of the Covenant into the Tent in Jerusalem.	1 Chronicles 15:1–28
Around 977	Age 63	*Three months later*, in the *second* attempt after the *first* failed, David moved the Ark using God's appointed means of the Ark being carried on the shoulders of the Levites. David, along with many elders and priests, brought the Ark of the Covenant into the Tent in Jerusalem with great worship and celebration. .	2 Samuel 6:12–19 1 Chronicles 15:2, 11-15, 26; 16:1–36; Psalm 96:1–13; 105:1–15; 106:1, 47, 48
Around 977	Age 63	When David arrived in Jerusalem, his wife Michal despised David *"in her heart"* and rebuked him for his public display. David, in turn, exalted the LORD and affirmed God's choice of him as king.	2 Samuel 6:16, 20–23 1 Chronicles 15:29
Around 977	Age 63	David placed Asaph and his brothers in Jerusalem to minister before the Ark of the Covenant in the Tent there, while Obed-Edom and his relatives plus Zadok and his relatives ministered at the Tabernacle remaining in Gibeon.	1 Chronicles 16:37–42
976	David, age 64, Absalom, 31	Absalom (age 31) rebelled against his father David and committed treason, seeking to become king of Israel.	2 Samuel 15:1–12
	Age 64	David fled from Jerusalem along with several loyal followers. They escaped from the coup Absalom had organized.	2 Samuel 15:13–37 **Psalm 3** (and **63**?)
	Age 64	Fleeing with David, Zadok and several Levites carried the Ark of the Covenant from Jerusalem. David ordered them to return to Jerusalem with the Ark and they did so.	2 Samuel 15:24–29
	Age 64	Absalom (age 31) came into Jerusalem.	2 Samuel 15:37b

	Age 64	As David fled, he met Mephibosheth's servant Ziba who spoke deceptively to David accusing Mephibosheth of deserting the house of David. David gave to Ziba all that belonged to Mephibosheth.	2 Samuel 16:1–4
	Age 64	As David journeyed, Shimei of the family of Saul cursed David and those with him. David's men desired to slay Shimei, but David would not. He listened and entrusted himself to the LORD in facing this defamation.	2 Samuel 16:5–14 **Psalm 7**
	David, age 64 Absalom, age 31	Absalom came into Jerusalem to establish himself as king. Hushai feigned loyalty to Absalom to help David's cause. Ahithophel sided with Absalom, giving advice to promote Absalom against David. Hushai helped thwart Ahithophel's counsel, sent warning to David, thus saving his life. Thwarted, Ahithophel killed himself. David and those with him made it safely to Mahanaim.	2 Samuel 16:15–23; 17:1–29
	Age 64	David stayed in Mahanaim while his army went out in three bands. David urged them to *"deal gently for my sake"* with Absalom. David's army defeated Absalom's army, slaying 20,000 men, but *"the forest* (wild beasts) *devoured more people that day than the sword devoured"* (18:6–8). Joab killed Absalom trapped in tree limbs. David mourned the death of his son Absalom.	2 Samuel 18:1–33
	Age 64	Joab rebuked David for honoring Absalom above those who had fought for David. David then began honoring them in the gate of the city of Mahanaim. David came back to the Jordan River area and Gilgal. Shimei asked his pardon which David gave. Mephibosheth came and told of Ziba's deception. Barzillai (age 80), a very wealthy man, honored David at the Jordan, giving him his servant Chimham. Barzillai then returned home.	2 Samuel 19:1–39
	Age 64	At Gilgal, the men of Judah and the men of Israel quarreled over the king's return.	2 Samuel 19:40–43
	Age 64	Sheba, labeled *"a worthless"* man (Hebrew, *Belial*, "empty, worthless") incited a rebellion against David. The men of Israel *"withdrew from following David"* and followed Sheba. The men of Judah remained loyal to David and brought him from the Jordan River area to Jerusalem.	2 Samuel 20:1–2
976	Age 64	David came to Jerusalem and ordered his men to stop Sheba's revolt. As the new army commander, Amasa and the men pursued Sheba. Joab killed Amasa. Joab then led the army to the town of Abel Beth-maacah and set up a siege. The people of the town executed Sheba, ending the revolt. Joab and his army returned to Jerusalem. David continued to reign.	2 Samuel 20:3–26

	Age—Mid 60s	After beginning to dwell *"in his house"* and experiencing what the LORD had done in giving David *"rest on every side from all his enemies,"* David told Nathan the prophet that he wanted to build a Temple dwelling for *"the ark of God"* which was *"inside tent curtains."* Nathan told him, *"Go, do all that is in your mind, for the LORD is with you"* (2 Samuel 7:3).	2 Samuel 7:1–3 1 Chronicles 17:1–2
	Age—Mid 60s	The *"same night"* after Nathan had spoken to David about building a dwelling for the Ark of the Covenant, God came to Nathan and told him to tell David not to build *"a house"* for Him, but that David's descendant would build that house.	2 Samuel 7:4–7, 13 1 Chronicles 17:3–6, 12
	Age—Mid 60s	The LORD of Hosts spoke to Nathan the prophet about His promises for David, including an eternal kingdom. In this revelation to Nathan, which he then told to David, God made a non-revocable, unconditional covenant with David to sit one of his descendants enthroned as King Forever. These covenant promises were partially given to David's son Solomon, but are ultimately fulfilled in the life, ministry, death, resurrection, ascension, and eternal reign of the Lord Jesus Christ, the Son of David.	2 Samuel 7:8–16, 17 1 Chronicles 17:7–14 Luke 1:31–33 Revelation 11:15–17; 19:6
	Age—Mid 60s	Nathan went to David and told him all the promises God had spoken about him, his descendants, his *"house"* or family, the people of Israel, and the building of a *"house for My name."*	2 Samuel 7:17 1 Chronicles 17:15
	Age—Mid 60s	David *"sat before the LORD,"* praising Him and thanking Him for the promises of the Davidic covenant for him and for Israel. He prayed for the fulfillment of those promises based on God's Word to him.	2 Samuel 7:18–29 1 Chronicles 17:16–27
	In later years	Many prophets spoke of the coming Messiah. For example, Isaiah prophesied about the *"child"* and *"son"* to come who would reign *"on the throne of David and over his kingdom."*	Isaiah 9:6–7
	Hundreds of years later…	The Angel Gabriel came to Mary in Nazareth and spoke to her of the coming Messiah to Whom she would give birth. Gabriel said, *"the Lord God will give Him the throne of His father David"* (Luke 1:32).	Luke 1:26–38
975	Age 65	Satan tempted David to number Israel, possibly an expression of David's pride in his military might or concern over his present condition. David instituted a census of the population and the army. Joab questioned his motives and his actions, but David proceeded. The census covered most of Israel and took over nine months.	2 Samuel 24:1–9 1 Chronicles 21:1–8

974	Age 66	*"David's heart condemned him"* for the census. God sent the prophet Gad with a choice of one of three judgments. He chose the judgment of three days chastening from the Angel of the LORD. 70,000 men died in a plague.	2 Samuel 24:10–15 1 Chronicles 21:9–15
	Age 66	David saw the Angel of the LORD ready to bring judgment on Jerusalem. He humbled himself before the LORD, confessing his sin.	2 Samuel 24:16–17 1 Chronicles 21:16–17
	Age 66	David went to Araunah/Ornan the Jebusite, bought his threshing floor on Mount Moriah, and offered burnt offerings and peace offerings to the LORD on the altar David placed there. God answered David's prayer with fire at the altar and stopped the plague.	2 Samuel 24:18–25 1 Chronicles 21:18–30
	Age 66	David recognized the threshing floor of Araunah/Ornan as the place for *"the house of the LORD God"* and began preparations for the building of the Temple there which King Solomon later built.	1 Chronicles 22:1–5 2 Chronicles 3:1
971?	Around Age 69?	David told Solomon how years earlier God had revealed that David would have a son to be named *"Solomon"* and that he would reign as king and build the Temple (1 Chronicles 22:9–10).	2 Samuel 7:12–13 (see also verses 1–2, 5–11) 1 Chronicles 22:6–16
971	David, age 69, Adonijah, age 35?	David's fourth-born son Adonijah (and likely the oldest living son at that time) sought to exalt himself as the next king, enlisting Joab as his army commander and Abiathar as high priest.	1 Kings 1:5–7
971	David, age 69	Adonijah held a coronation feast at En Rogel, near Jerusalem, but did not invite Nathan the prophet nor Adonijah's brother Solomon.	1 Kings 1:8–10
971	Age 69	Nathan the prophet conferred with Bathsheba about Solomon's rightful place as the new king. She went into the palace to David confirming his desire that Solomon was to reign and informing him of Adonijah's actions. Nathan entered confirming her account.	1 Kings 1:11–27
971	Age 69	David confirmed Solomon as the *LORD'S* choice and *his* choice as the next king. He instructed them in what to do to install Solomon as king, anointing him at the Gihon Springs at the foot of Zion (Jerusalem) in somewhat of a private ceremony. Several people responded with rejoicing in a thunderous uproar.	1 Kings 1:28–40

971	Age 69	Adonijah and his group heard the uproar. Abiathar's son Jonathan reported the news of Solomon's anointing as the new king with David's affirmation. All dispersed; Adonijah fled to the Altar in fear. As the new co-regent, Solomon consigned him to his house.	1 Kings 1:41–53
971?	Likely around Age 69	David confirmed Solomon as the next king (1 Chronicles 23:1–2). Solomon served in a role as co-regent with his father David.	1 Chronicles 22:6–19; 23:1–2
971?	Age 69?	David commanded the leaders in Israel to help Solomon. Since the land had rest from all their enemies, they could devote time and energy to building the Temple in Jerusalem. David urged them, *"now set your heart and your soul to seek the LORD your God"* to build the Temple *"for the name of the LORD."*	1 Chronicles 22:17–19
971 or 970	Age 69-70	David organized the Levites and priests into 24 courses to serve at scheduled times throughout the year in service for the coming Temple (Included gatekeepers, singers, instrumentalists, and worship leaders who would prophesy and lead in praise and thanks). David later conveyed this to Solomon.	1 Chronicles 23:2–32; 24:1–31; 25:1–31; 26:1–32; 28:13, 21
971 or 970	Age 69-70	David (likely with Solomon) organized his army into various divisions, each one assigned to a specific month for duty. He assigned various men to oversee the king's storehouses throughout the land, as well as overseers for the king's farms, crops, and livestock. David also had various counselors to consult.	1 Chronicles 27:1–34
	Age 69?	David instructed Solomon about following the LORD, acting wisely toward those who acted wickedly or righteously.	1 Kings 2:1-9
	Age 69?	In Jerusalem, David gathered the various tribal leaders, as well as worship leaders, David's select *"mighty men"* of war, and the army to affirm Solomon as the next king.	1 Chronicles 28:1–8
	Age 69?	David charged his son Solomon to *"know"* the LORD and to *"serve Him with a whole heart and a willing mind"* (28:9).	1 Chronicles 28:9–10, 20
	Age 69?	David revealed the detailed Temple plans given him by the LORD and gave them to Solomon. That included the plans for the priestly divisions, the various furnishings and instruments to be used in the Temple, and the ministry of the Temple.	1 Chronicles 28:11–19, 21
	Age 69?	David addressed *"the entire assembly"* gathered in Jerusalem and commanded them to honor Solomon as king and called them to make an offering to help build the Temple. The people gave abundantly and *"willingly ... with a whole heart."*	1 Chronicles 29:1–9
	Age 69?	David *"blessed the LORD,"* praising and thanking Him for all He had done. He prayed for the people's hearts to be fixed on the LORD and for Solomon's heart to remain loyal to the LORD and His Word.	1 Chronicles 29:10–19

	Around Age 69	David called the people to worship the LORD. They offered many sacrifices, held a great feast, and for a second time crowned Solomon as the new king in a public ceremony. Solomon reigned with great majesty and authority.	1 Chronicles 29:20–25
971 and 970	Age 69, 70	In David's old age, he became frail and had difficulty staying warm. Abishag came to attend to David and help keep him warm. His attendants sought to honor him.	1 Kings 1:1–4
970	Age 70	After reigning 40 years, David died in Jerusalem. People honored him and his memory, faithfully recording his deeds as king.	1 Chronicles 29:26–30 1 Kings 2:10–12
1030-970, Ages 10-70	Most of David's Life	Via pre-psalm headings or Scripture references, approximately 75 *Psalms* are considered written by David. *Psalm* 2 (Acts 4:25); 3–9; 11–32; 34–41; 51–65; 68–70; 86; 95 (Hebrews 4:7); 101; 103; 106–110; 122; 124; 131; 133; 138–145 (see Willem A. VanGemeren, *Psalms*, Introduction in *The Expositor's Bible Commentary*, vol. 5 (Grand Rapids: Zondervan Publishing House, 1991), p. 33, n. 74).	
1040–970	David's Life	In Acts 13:22–23, 34–36, the Apostle Paul spoke of David's reign, of God's statement of him as "A MAN AFTER MY HEART," and of Jesus being born in his lineage as the Son of David. Paul gave a Summary Statement of David's life and reign: *"David, after he served the purpose of God in his own generation, fell asleep, and was laid among his fathers"* (Acts 13:36).	Acts 13:22–23, 34–36
AD 26-30 through Today	Messiah Jesus, Ages 30-33, His Ministry and in the Early Church	Jesus the Messiah was called or referred to as the *"Son of David"* or similar 25 times in the New Testament: Matthew 1:1; 9:27; 12:3, 23; 15:22; 20:30, 31; 21:9, 15; 22:42, 43, 45; Mark 10:47, 48; 12:35; Luke 1:32; 3:31; 18:38, 39; 20:41; John 7:42; Romans 1:3; 2 Timothy 2:8; Revelation 5:5; 22:16	*Genealogical* Notes: Matthew 1:1, 6; Luke 3:31; Romans 1:3; 2 Timothy 2:8; Revelation 22:16

This data has come from comparing Scripture with Scripture. Some of the comparative chronological data has also_come from http://www.bible.ca/archeology/bible-archeology-maps-timeline-chronology-1samuel-16-20-saul-jonathan-david-1019-1012bc.htm [Accessed November 4, 2016]. In *Kingdom of Priests*, Eugene H. Merrill gives some helpful chronological data.

Notes

Lesson 2

On the Run

DAVID'S DAYS RUNNING FROM SAUL AND SEEKING THE LORD

David did not have the picture-perfect childhood. He faced many challenges even as a young boy. When "fame" seemed to be in his grasp or at least near at hand, Saul became jealous to such an extent that he wanted to kill David. As David entered his late teens, his circumstances and many of his relationships were filled with challenges.

What would David do? He was now "on the run," seeking to dodge another spear or arrest or attack from the hand of Saul. Have you ever wanted to do the will of God only to have detractors show up in your life, each with "clear" suggestions? David dealt with that. So did the "Son of David," our Lord Jesus. He had several seeking to show Him what He needed to do to be the ideal Messiah. The only problem: most of what others said did not match what His Father said.

Whatever we face, we must continually look to the Lord. We find David doing that in the psalms he penned. Likely, he penned far more than we have in our Bibles. First Kings 4:32 states that Solomon penned a little over one thousand songs and three thousand proverbs, many of which are not in the Bible and have been lost for millennia. It is quite possible David wrote as many psalms with many disappearing over time, especially in light of his many years "on the run," probably from ages 18 or 19 to 30. How do we know David looked to the Lord? Every time one of his poems, prayers, or songs surfaces, he is calling on the Lord, sometimes complaining to the Lord, but often praising and thanking the Lord. In any case, the Lord was at the center of his focus. David's focus is a good example to follow.

You may not be "on the run," but there are certainly some challenges facing you, some you did not expect. God is no respecter of persons. As He allowed challenges in David's life and even in Jesus' life, so He will in your life, in my life, in all His children's lives. What is God doing? What is He saying? Let's listen carefully so we hear clearly, learn and love more fully, and obey more precisely.

IN THEIR SHOES
Run Where?

David was on the run from Saul. *Where* did he go? *Several* places are mentioned, including his home in Bethlehem, his new home with Michal in Gibeah, and Ramah where Samuel lived. David and his men also went to Nob, to Gath over which the Philistine Achish ruled as king, and the cave of Adullam. He took his family to Mizpah of Moab, and he went to the *"stronghold"* (perhaps Masada) in the Judean Wilderness. In addition, David and his men went to the city of Keilah in Judah, the wilderness of Ziph at Horesh, the Hill of Hachilah at Horesh, *"in the wilderness of Maon, in the Arabah to the south of Jeshimon,"* the strongholds (and caves) of the wilderness of Engedi, the wilderness of Paran, and the village of Ziklag in Philistine territory, where they stayed for 16 months.

Day One

Saul Is Upset

As David proved himself a capable warrior against the Philistines, the people of the land began to take notice. They spoke and even sang about David slaying *"his ten thousands,"* while they stated that Saul had slain *"his thousands."* This did not sit well with Saul; he became jealous of David. First Samuel 18:9 reports, *"and Saul looked at David with suspicion from that day on."* What would this mean? What can we learn from David and from this relationship?

What do you find David doing in 1 Samuel 18:10?

Saul allowed his jealousy and anger to control him so much that he began agreeing with evil thoughts from an evil spirit. What does Saul try to do in 1 Samuel 18:10?

How often did this happen, according to 1 Samuel 18:11?

What did Saul try next? Read 1 Samuel 18:12–16 and note what occurs in these verses. What were some of Saul's thoughts toward David?

📖 What scheme did Saul plan, according to 1 Samuel 18:17? Note David's response in verse 18.

In these verses, we see Saul having thoughts of killing David, even while he was playing his harp for Saul's benefit. Saul threw his spear at David, but he escaped—not just once, but at least twice. The Lord had departed from Saul and appears to be with David in some way. Saul sensed that and became afraid of David. Instead of going to the Lord about this, Saul tried to rid himself of David, and perhaps was seeking to rid himself of God's influence. Saul sent David on more military missions against the ferocious Philistines. It appears Saul was seeking to let the Philistines kill him, but David experienced victory after victory, becoming quite a noteworthy young leader. To gain David's confidence and further endanger David in more battles, Saul sought to give him his oldest daughter, Merab, but David refused.

📖 What would Saul do next? Read 1 Samuel 18:20–29?

📖 After this, what occurred in David's life and military career, according to 1 Samuel 18:30?

When Saul saw that his daughter Michal loved David, he sought to use that. He got his servants involved, even telling them what to say to convince David to come into the "family." At every turn, Saul sought ways to get David killed. None of this worked. When he saw David's success and the love his daughter Michal had for David, Saul feared David even more and saw him as his *"enemy."* The more David faced the Philistines, the more skill and cunning he showed. David's name became *"highly esteemed."*

📖 Saul next sought to enlist his oldest son Jonathan to deal with David. Read 1 Samuel 19:1–8. What occurred at this juncture?

IN THEIR SHOES
How Much Is Enough?

How many times did Saul seek to kill David? In 1 Samuel, we read about sixteen attempts—1) Saul threw a spear at David, the first spear attack (18:10–11), 2) Saul's second spear attack (18:11), 3) Saul appointed David commander to fight Philistines (wanting his death in battle) (18:13), 4) Saul sought to give David his daughter Merab as a wife, hoping he would be killed in battle (18:17), 5) Saul gave his daughter Michal as his wife, still hoping for his death at the hands of Philistines (18:20–30), 6) Saul ordered Jonathan and his servants to kill David (19:1–6), 7) Third spear attack (19:9–10), 8) Saul sent messengers to ambush David at his and Michal's house (19:11–17 with Psalm 59), 9) David escaped to Samuel's house in Ramah. Saul sent men to Ramah to capture David (19:18–20), 10) Saul sent a second team to Ramah (19:21a), 11) Saul sent a third team to Ramah (19:21b), 12) Saul himself went to Ramah (19:22). Saul continued to desire David's death (20:3–42). Saul had the priests of Nob slain because of their contact with David (22:6–23), 13) David escaped from the town of Keilah before Saul arrived with his forces (23:7–13), 14) Saul pursued David in the wilderness of Maon, but stopped after hearing of Philistine aggression (23:24–29), 15) Saul sought David in the wilderness of Engedi (24:1–22), 16) Saul sought to kill David in the wilderness of Ziph (26:1–25). After this, David fled into Philistine territory.

Saul admitted that he wanted to put David to death, but Jonathan was not a willing accomplice. He spoke to his father with wisdom and reason, defending David. He pointed out that David had brought great victories for Israel against the Philistines and had not sinned against Saul in any way. For a season, Saul listened to his son Jonathan, agreeing not to put David to death. Instead, Saul welcomed him into his presence and counsel, and David continued to prosper as a military leader against the Philistines.

📖 What occurred soon after, according to 1 Samuel 19:9–10?

📖 What did Saul seek to do, according to 1 Samuel 19:11?

📖 Read 1 Samuel 19:12–17. How did David's wife Michal respond to the situation?

IN THEIR SHOES
Psalm 59

David prayed and later composed the words of Psalm 59 when Saul sent men to David's and Michal's house to ambush and kill him. The *Title* to Psalm 59 states, "A Mikhtam of David, when Saul sent men, and they watched the house in order to kill him." In this tense situation, David looked to God to *"deliver me from my enemies"* and to *"set me securely on high away from those who rise up against me"* (59:1). In his innocence and dependence, David focused his attention on the LORD and His deliverance.

Saul once again sought to kill David as David played the harp. David escaped and went home to his wife Michal in Gibeah. Saul ordered some of his servants to lie in wait at David and Michal's house in order to kill him the next morning. That night Michal warned him and helped him escape through a window. Then, she placed a statue with goat's hair in a bed so that it looked like David asleep in the bed. The servants came and found the ruse of Michal, but she defended herself, telling her father that David had threatened her and escaped.

STOP AND APPLY—What Are You Running From?—Each of us faces certain situations or people from which we want to run. There were times when David wanted to have *"wings like a dove"* to fly away and *"be at rest,"* but he placed his trust in the Lord (Psalm 55:6–8). During another time of danger, David's friends urged him to run away. He penned the words *"how can you say to my soul, flee as a bird to your mountain"* while expressing his personal trust in the Lord (Psalm 11:1–7). We must do the same, whatever or whoever is tempting us to be "on the run"—*"in the LORD I take refuge"* (Psalm 11:1a).

Day Two

Time with Samuel and On the Move

David knew his life was in danger. Saul's jealousy had risen to fever pitch, and he wanted to be rid of David. What could David do? He knew Samuel could be trusted. How would Samuel help him, and what would he learn from Samuel?

To where did David escape, according to 1 Samuel 19:18?

DID YOU KNOW?
Where Is Ramah?

Ramah, also known as *Ramathaim-zophim*, lay in the Tribal Territory of Ephraim in the central part of Israel, about three miles north of *Gibeah* where Saul lived. Ramah was situated about eighteen miles north-northwest of *Jerusalem.* Samuel was born to Elkanah and Hannah in Ramah and lived there most of his life, except during his time in Shiloh (1 Samuel 1:1–2, 19–20; 2:11; 3:21; 7:17; 19:18). He also had a School of the Prophets there, apparently housed in *"Naioth"* which simply means "dwellings" referring to the dwellings of the prophets. At his death, Samuel was buried in Ramah (1 Samuel 25:1).

What did David do when he arrived at Samuel's house in Ramah? Why do you think David went there?

📖 Read 1 Samuel 19:19–20. What did Saul do in response to David's escape?

📖 What occurred with each group sent to capture David? Read 1 Samuel 19:21–24 and note your answers.

How do you see God protecting David in these incidents in Ramah?

DID YOU KNOW?

What and Where Is Naioth?

The term *"Naioth"* (Strong's #5121 and #5116a) means "dwelling" or "habitation." *Naioth in Ramah* may simply refer to the "dwellings" of the school of the prophets located in Ramah; those prophets are who Saul and his men (four groups) encountered when they sought to capture David there (1 Samuel 19:18–24; 20:1).

With Saul's servants seeking to kill him, David fled to Samuel's house at Ramah and told him all that had occurred. They went to *"Naioth,"* probably the location or dwellings of Samuel's school of prophets in Ramah. David's brief reprieve with Samuel gave him some breathing room, but likely it did more than that. Samuel would have spoken to David clear wisdom from God about God's ways and about what it meant to follow Him. He would have also prayed for David then and in the coming days. Certainly, David knew these things. Samuel's intercession for David over the next months and years would certainly make a difference.

Saul sent three teams of men, one after the other, to capture David, but each encountered the prophets in Ramah and those men *"prophesied"* there. Saul then came, and he too *"prophesied."* The Lord used these encounters to protect David, who escaped from Ramah back to Gibeah where he met with Jonathan.

📖 What could David do? What do you discover in 1 Samuel 20:1–24?

📖 How did Saul react to these events, and how did Jonathan respond, according to 1 Samuel 20:25–42?

Doubtless very concerned, David fled back to Jonathan, and they talked over the matter. Considering Saul's actions and the covenant relationship David and Jonathan shared, Jonathan proposed a plan to warn David if anything was amiss. On the second day of the New Moon meals, Saul erupted in anger against Jonathan over David's absence. Saul clearly wanted David dead. On the third day, as a faithful covenant friend, Jonathan confirmed Saul's intentions, giving David clear warning. David fled to Nob.

📖 What do you find David doing in 1 Samuel 21:1–9?

📖 David left Israeli territory and fled to Gath, to Achish the king there. What occurred there, according to 1 Samuel 21:10–15?

📖 Many note this incident in Gath as the setting for *Psalm 34*. Read that psalm in light of David's situation. What insights do you discover? Write those here.

David came to Nob where Ahimelech the priest resided with his family. David came in stealth mode, not telling Ahimelech about Saul's anger and vengeance toward him. Perhaps David was not sure if he could trust Ahimelech, or he could have said what he did trying to protect Ahimelech from Saul's anger. In any case, David received bread, even the show bread from the Tabernacle, and Goliath's sword. He left Israeli territory and fled to Philistine Gath, where he sought asylum with King Achish. The king's servants spoke against David's presence; they knew him to be a valiant warrior and no friend of the Philistines. David sensed the tension and feigned being a madman. Later, David penned Psalm 34 about his trust in the Lord and how he called on Him in the midst of his fears. He knew the Lord had protected him; it is always right to walk in the fear of the Lord more than in the fear of any man or many men.

STOP AND APPLY—*The Fear of the Lord*—Proverbs 9:10 states, *"the fear of the LORD is the beginning of wisdom and the knowledge of the Holy One is understanding."* In Genesis 22:12, the Angel of the LORD revealed to Abraham that fearing the Lord was at the heart of *"worship"* (Genesis 22:5, 12). Fearing the Lord is not a terror of Him, though certainly appropriate, considering how holy and awesome He is. He deserves and calls for a reverence for Him, a fear of insulting or diminishing Him in some way or failing to acknowledge how great He really is. To see Him more and more as He is, is to be ready to hear Him more clearly, follow Him more closely, and love Him more fully. We see that in David. Do we see that in each of our hearts?

DAY THREE

LEADING NEEDED

David needed to be led by the Lord. As he continued to live life on the run, he discovered others who needed to be led by a capable leader and certainly needed to be led by the Lord. So, David became leader of a rag-tag group of men. What can we learn from David and his needy men? What kind of leading do each of us need day by day? What influence can each of us bring into others' lives to help them follow the Lord?

DID YOU KNOW?
Where Is the Cave of Adullam?

The *"Cave of Adullum"* is located near the town of Adullum, in the foothills of the Tribal Territory of Judah, about ten miles east of Gath and about thirteen miles west of Bethlehem. Many consider the context of Psalm 142, penned by David as he prayed for deliverance from his persecutors, to be this cave. According to some, the Hebrew word *"adullum"* speaks of "a hiding place" or "refuge."

Read 1 Samuel 22:1–2. Where did David go? Who gathered around him there?

📖 What did David do about his family, according to 1 Samuel 22:3–4?

📖 What further leadership did David receive, according to 1 Samuel 22:5?

David escaped from Gath and fled to the cave of Adullam where his brothers and his family joined him. Others heard of David and where he was. About four hundred men joined David, and he became *"captain over them,"* leading men much in need. Scripture describes them as *"in distress"* (pressures of some sort), *"in debt"* (money or labor problems), and *"discontented"* (literally, "bitter of soul," unhappy about Saul's slipshod reign, possibly hurting in some way, perhaps offended or wronged and, for many, angry about it). These willingly followed young David, who was running from Saul.

For safety, David took his family and the four hundred men to Mizpah of Moab, a small town in southern Moab east of the Dead Sea. David continually focused on the Lord, telling the king there, *"let my father and mother come and stay with you until I know what God will do for me."* David left there and went to *"the stronghold"* (possibly a location in the mountains of Moab or the location of Masada). The prophet Gad gave him further direction to leave there and go into Judah. David traveled to the *"forest of Hereth,"* south-south-west of Bethlehem.

DID YOU KNOW?
The Prophet Gad

The Prophet *Gad* first appears when David is in Moab securing his parents in a safe place. Gad gave David a word from the LORD: *"Do not stay in the stronghold; depart, and go into the land of Judah"* (1 Samuel 22:5). David obeyed and traveled to the forest of Hereth. In later years, the LORD assigned to Gad the task of giving David the choice of one of three chastisements for his sin of numbering Israel's troops, perhaps a matter of pride in numbers and military might. Gad obeyed; David chose three days of pestilence (2 Samuel 24:1–14). In the midst of the calamity, God sent Gad instructing David to make an offering *"on the threshing floor of Araunah the Jebusite,"* the location of Abraham's sacrifice years before (2 Samuel 24:15–25; 1 Chronicles 21:9–30; 2 Chronicles 3:1). Gad served as David's *"seer"* or prophet, writing of David's *"reign, his power, and the circumstances which came on him in Israel"* (1 Chronicles 29:29–30).

In 1 Samuel 22:6–23, we read the sad story of Saul's madness. He continued in his jealous vengeance against David and anyone who came near him. Wanting to know about David's ways and travels, he summoned and questioned the high priest Ahimelech about his involvement in David's life. As a result, through Doeg the Edomite, he executed Ahimelech and his family, all priests from Nob. Only Abiathar, one of the sons of

Ahimelech, escaped and fled to David, telling him the details of what happened. David grieved over the events and the deaths of the priests, but assured Abiathar that he would be safe with David.

📖 While in the *"forest of Hereth,"* David received word that Philistine marauders were fighting against and stealing grain from the Israeli town of Keilah, a few miles away. The people of Keilah needed help. What did David do, according to 1 Samuel 23:2?

IN THEIR SHOES
"Inquire"

David prayed often; he *"inquired of the LORD,"* seeking His guidance. The word *"inquire,"* a translation of the Hebrew word *sha'al* (Strong's # 7592), means "to ask, to make a request." The record reveals this word often in David's life; seeking whether or not to go a certain direction, what to do, where to go, when, or how (1 Samuel 23:2, 4; 30:8; 2 Samuel 2:1; 5:19, 23).

📖 According to 1 Samuel 23:3, how did David's men respond to him? What does 1 Samuel 23:4 say about how David responded to their fears?

When David heard about the Philistines seeking to steal grain from Keilah, he first inquired of the Lord if he should go and help them. The Lord instructed him to go, but his men were resistant. David prayed *again*, and again the Lord led them to go, promising victory. They traveled there and delivered the town from the oppressive Philistines.

📖 What would happen next? What did Saul plot to do, according to 1 Samuel 23:7–8?

📖 Read 1 Samuel 23:9–13. How did David respond to the news that Saul was coming against him?

📖 What did David do in these days, according to 1 Samuel 23:13–15?

Saul received the news about David and his exploits in Keilah. He planned to attack David there, but David sought the Lord and escaped before Saul arrived. He and his men traveled from place to place, going into several *"strongholds"* in the *"wilderness of Ziph."* There God protected him from Saul's pursuit.

📖 What occurred in David's and Jonathan's lives at this juncture, according to 1 Samuel 23:16–18?

📖 How did the Ziphites respond to David's presence in their territory, according to 1 Samuel 23:19–26? What did Saul do during this time? What stopped Saul from pursuing David, according to 1 Samuel 23:27–28?

📖 What occurred next? Read the events of 1 Samuel 23:29; 24:1–22. What happened in the encounter between Saul and David?

What do you discover about David? What insights do you glean about Saul from these events, especially in his words to David?

As David traveled about, Jonathan found him at Horesh and encouraged him, especially in dealing with Saul's intentions against him. He assured David that he would indeed be the next king and Jonathan would support him fully. The two made another covenant and Jonathan returned to his house. At this time, the Ziphites informed Saul of David being near them, and Saul went seeking David, but David escaped to Engedi. Saul once again sought him but failed. David had opportunity to kill Saul. Instead, he cut off the edge of Saul's robe (perhaps a corner *tzitzit*). When Saul was some distance away, David pleaded with Saul to stop and assured him he had no intentions of harming him. Saul admitted David would one day be king: the two parted ways.

Day Four

We Keep on Learning How to Lead

During David's years "on the run," he had many things to learn. He had been a capable shepherd, capable military leader against the Philistines, and began proving himself a skilled captain over the six hundred men who joined him during these years. What did David have to learn? What can we learn from him as he experienced this process, this "training school on the run"?

IN THEIR SHOES
David's Retreat

In 1 Samuel 25:1, we read that David went south to the *"wilderness of Paran"* after the death and burial of Samuel. Scripture does not tell us why he did this, but the fact that he traveled far south into the wilderness of Paran may indicate his need to "get away" after Samuel's death. Samuel had a significant influence in David's life over the last ten-plus years. From David's anointing in Bethlehem at the hand of Samuel to David's brief sojourn in Ramah running from Saul, Samuel had treated David with respect and prayed for him. David knew this. Perhaps David needed to pause for a time and make sure he was on track for the days ahead, for all God wanted to do.

After Samuel's death and burial in Ramah, David went south to the *"wilderness of Paran."* Read the account presented in 1 Samuel 25:2–42. What occurred, and what significance do you see in these events?

DID YOU KNOW?
Where Is Carmel?

"Carmel" which means "God's vineyard" or "fresh vineyard" is sometimes translated "fruitful field" or "fertile field" (see Strong's # 3759). *"Carmel"* referred to an area of rich pastureland about 8 miles south of Hebron and about one mile north of the wilderness of Maon where David and his men lodged at one time (1 Samuel 23:24–25). David sought some 'neighborly' supplies from Nabal who lived in Maon and whose sheep grazed in the nearby Carmel area (see 1 Samuel 25:2, 4–8, 15–16,

40). This area and city of *"Carmel"* does not refer to Mount Carmel to the north which borders the Jezreel Valley and is just south of modern-day Haifa.

Sometime after his sojourn in the wilderness of Paran, David and his men encountered the shepherds and flocks of Nabal, whose name means "fool." David's men did not interfere with Nabal's shepherds, but rather proved to be a protection. Later, David sent his men to ask for a few supplies, certainly not a strange request or an overwhelming amount. Nabal responded in anger and greed. David prepared to attack. Nabal's wife Abigail received word of her husband's untoward response and prepared provisions for David and his men, hoping to quell any negative consequences. When she met David and his men on the march, she spoke with wisdom and graciousness. David, sensitive to what was occurring, recognized the error of his mission, received the provisions, and retreated from attacking Nabal and his estate. When Nabal found out what had occurred, he was angered, possibly had a stroke, and, ten days later, died. First Samuel 25:38 attributes Nabal's death to the Lord striking him, what some consider as God's judgment. After this, David married Abigail.

David and his men sought protection in the wilderness of Ziph, particularly on *"the hill of Hachilah,"* a prominent location from which to see the surrounding countryside and watch for any of Saul's troops. What occurred? Read 1 Samuel 26:1–25 and summarize the encounter.

IN THEIR SHOES

"A Partridge in the Mountains"

David compared Saul's pursuit of him to searching for *"a single flea"* or as a man hunting *"a partridge in the mountains,"* both considered impossible tasks. David continually sought to make clear that what Saul was doing was useless and senseless. There was no reason for Saul to chase David who had nothing against Saul and who twice chose not to kill Saul when he could have (see 1 Samuel 24:2–15; 26:1–20).

What occurred next? Read 1 Samuel 27:1–4. What rationale did David use in his next move?

While David and his men sought refuge on *"the hill of Hachilah"* in *"Ziph,"* the Ziphites traveled to Gibeah to inform Saul of David's presence there. After confirming this, Saul and his men began seeking David. David escaped, refused to harm Saul, and sought to convince Saul to stop chasing him. Both men departed from there. David and his six hundred men chose to travel to and live in Philistine territory rather than face possible death from Saul and his men. Since David was in Gath with King Achish, Saul stopped chasing him.

IN THEIR SHOES
David as Captain

The 400 men who joined David are described as *"in distress, ... in debt, and... discontented;"* David became *"captain over them,"* exerting influence and skill in warfare and in character (1 Samuel 22:2; 30:23–25). The Hebrew word translated *"captain"* is *sar* (Strong's # 8269), meaning "chief" or "commander." Several times Scripture describes David's men as *"mighty men,"* valiant, trained for war (e.g., 2 Samuel 23:8, 9; 1 Chronicles 11:10; 12:1, 8).

📖 What did David ask for, according to 1 Samuel 27:5–7? What came as a result of this request?

📖 What did David and his men do in the coming months, according to 1 Samuel 27:8–12? How did Achish respond to David's reports, according to 1 Samuel 27:1–2?

David wisely asked King Achish for a place to live. Achish gave David, his men, and their families the village of Ziklag, where they lived for the next sixteen months. The total population of these men and their families could have been around three thousand or more. From there David and his men raided several Canaanite villages but reported to Achish that they had raided villages of Judah. Achish believed the ruse, and David continued in his favor.

📖 How did Saul respond to his situation, according to 1 Samuel 28:1–25?

Saul failed to receive any kind of response from his prayers. In frustration, he went to Endor and sought the services of a medium or witch. In a very strange encounter Saul saw "Samuel" or some manifestation like him and heard the judgment against him for his disobedience. Much debate has arisen around this incident. Whatever occurred, Saul showed his heart, even disobeying the Word of the LORD in this (Deuteronomy 18:10–14). The next day, he died in battle with the Philistines (about 72 years of age).

📖 What do you discover about David and his men in 1 Samuel 29:1–2?

📖 How did the Philistine leaders react to the presence of David and his men? Read 1 Samuel 29:3–5 and record your insights.

📖 Record your observations from the events of 1 Samuel 29:6–11.

Traveling at the rear with King Achish, David and his men journeyed with the Philistine troops to Aphek. Amazingly, they planned to fight with the Philistines against Saul and the Israelite troops. The leaders of the Philistines saw David and his men and protested their presence, demanding they leave. Achish sought to convince the Philistines that David and his men would be useful; they did not agree. David and his men left camp the next morning, traveling back to Ziklag.

📖 What did David and his men find when they arrived at Ziklag, according to 1 Samuel 30:1–5?

📖 How did David's men respond to this calamity? How did David respond, according to 1 Samuel 30:6–8?

What occurred next? Read 1 Samuel 30:9–20 and note what happened.

DID YOU KNOW?

Who Were the Amalekites?

In Genesis 36:12, Amalek is noted as a son of the concubine Timna and Eliphaz, a son of Esau, who became a chief among his people. The Amalekites developed significant military might. They *"did not fear God"* and proved to be underhanded thugs, first mentioned attacking the rear of Israel's exodus from Egypt to Mount Sinai, aiming at *"the stragglers"* who were *"faint and weary"* (Deuteronomy 25:17–19). Joshua led a battle against them and Exodus 17:16 notes, *"the LORD will have war against Amalek from generation to generation"* (Exodus 17:8–16). They proved a menacing force during the period of the judges (Judges 3:13; 6:3, 33; 7:12; 10:12; 12:15). Having passed the limits of rebellion, the LORD ordered Saul to execute the Amalekites, but he did not, for which Samuel rebuked him and pronounced Saul's kingship coming to an end (1 Samuel 15:2–3, 8, 13–29, 32–33). David and his men dealt with them (1 Samuel 30:1–18). Over 500 years later, the influence of Amalek continued through Haman, a descendant who ruled in the kingdom of Persia. Through Mordecai and Esther, he faced defeat and execution (Esther 3–7).

When David and his men reached Ziklag, they saw smoke rising; Amalekite raiders had kidnapped their families and livestock and burned the village. The men began to weep and sob at this calamity. In their *"embittered"* condition they spoke of stoning David, though he was obviously not to blame. David too wept, *"greatly distressed,"* and quickly *"strengthened himself in the LORD his God."* Then, David *"inquired of the LORD,"* seeking whether to pursue the raiders.

The Lord directed David and his men to pursue the Amalekites. When they came to the Brook Besor, two hundred of the men stayed, too weary to go any further. They established a camp to keep their supplies there. David and four hundred men soon found a lone Egyptian slave in a field, having been abandoned by his Amalekite master. Near death, David and his men revived him, and he gave them much-needed intel about the location of the Amalekite camp. David and his men attacked the camp, defeating the Amalekites and recovering their families and all the plunder the Amalekites had stolen from various villages.

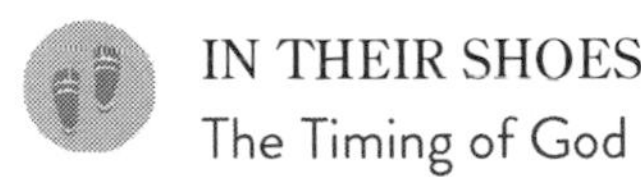

IN THEIR SHOES
The Timing of God

David and his men arrived at Ziklag just in time... not just in time to stop the Amalekites, but to prepare for the chase. Then, they found an abandoned Egyptian slave almost dead without food and water for three days... just in time...He led them to the Amalekite camp... just in time... The Amalekites were feasting, probably drunk, and likely unready for battle. David and his men conquered them, recovered their families, and traveled back to Ziklag with all the plunder. From there, David sent gifts to several Judean towns, just after Saul had been slain. This, too, was just in time for David to be seen and acknowledged as the new king. Over and over, God's timing worked His plan for David and Israel.

STOP AND APPLY—*Training for Reigning*—It is obvious that during his "on the run" years, God was training David for reigning over Israel. What does God do today to train His children for reigning? Romans 5:17 reminds us that those who *"receive the abundance of grace and of the gift of righteousness"* are those who will *"reign in life through the One, Jesus Christ."* Believers are meant to reign now...and then, forever. God is working in our lives, teaching us how to rule...over self by His power, over circumstance by trusting Him, over temptation and sin by following Him and His Word. Pause and consider how God might be working in *your* life in this season.

DAY FIVE

FOLLOWING MY SHEPHERD

David "on the run" has some things to show us, not only about David, but also about the ways of God and how He works in our lives. There is always something (or someone) we are dealing with in one way or another. Sometimes it's a "Saul." At other times it may be those like Doeg the Edomite or the people of Keilah who would give up on us, even though we had been a help in some way. At other times, we may find them on our "team" yet wanting to be selfish and ungiving like some of David's men. Cultures and times change, but people do not. For the most part, people are people in whatever country or city we find ourselves. We can learn from David and what he faced during his "on the run" season.

📖 David revealed his leadership in the events after their victory over the Amalekite raiders. What do you discover in 1 Samuel 30:21–31? Note the reactions of some of David's men, David's responses, and David's actions toward his men and toward others in Judah.

When David and the four hundred men returned to camp at the Brook Besor, some of the men wanted to keep all the plunder for themselves. David wisely intervened, assuring that all shared equally in the *"spoil,"* a decision that later became an *"ordinance"* in Israel. David also sent several gifts to various villages and towns in Judah where he and his men had been. Doubtless, with the death of Saul and knowing David's character, care, and skill, these village leaders would regard David as a capable future king.

IN THEIR SHOES
Everyone Matters

When some of David's men wanted to keep all and not give any of the plunder to the 200 who stayed at the Brook Besor camp, David stated, *"As his share is who goes down to the battle, so shall his share be who stays by the baggage; they shall share alike"* (1 Samuel 30:24). That later became a law in Israel. The principle holds true throughout Scripture. In the New Testament, those who pray, give, or serve share in the answers, the victories. As 1 Corinthians 3:8 states, *"Now he who plants and he who waters are one; but each will receive his own reward according to his own labor."* *Everyone* matters.

During David's march and victory over the Amalekites, Saul and the men in his army were facing humiliation, judgment, and defeat at the hands of the Philistines. In 1 Samuel 31, we read the horrific account of the defeat and deaths of Saul and his sons Jonathan, Abinadab, and Malchi-shua. In their celebration, the Philistines beheaded them and hung the bodies of Saul and his sons on the walls of Beth-shan. The men of Jabesh-gilead heard of this and retrieved those bodies, giving them proper honor and burial.

📖 What do you discover in 2 Samuel 1:1–16? How did David respond to the words of the Amalekite young man?

📖 Read 2 Samuel 1:17–27. Record your insights into David's words, *"the song of the bow."*

David returned with his men to Ziklag and on the third day back there, an Amalekite young man came with news of the deaths of Saul and his sons. He falsely portrayed himself as the one who killed Saul and David ordered his execution. Then, David, in grief sang *"the song of the bow"* over the deaths of Saul and Jonathan, stating twice in his lamentation *"how the mighty have fallen!"*

It becomes obvious in reviewing David's life that *relationships* matter. How we relate to

God and to others matters to God and to each of us. God has some clear guidance for daily life. David discovered this over the years. Hundreds of years after David, the apostle Paul wrote to believers in Rome, pointing them to what matters for now and eternity.

📖 Read Romans 12:1–2. What is essential for any believer, according to those verses?

📖 How important is it to have a right attitude? Consider Romans 12:3, write your insights, and make any personal applications the Holy Spirit brings to mind.

📖 Every believer is gifted in some way. Read Romans 12:4–8 and 1 Peter 4:10–11. What do you learn about God's work of equipping each believer?

📖 What is true of each believer? How should each regard what God has given? What is vitally essential, according to 1 Peter 4:11?

IN THEIR SHOES

Don't Give in to Evil

Jesus told His disciples *"a parable"* so that *"at all times they ought to pray and not to lose heart."* (Luke 18:1–8). The phrase *"to lose heart"* is a translation of the Greek word *egkakeo* and literally means to give in to evil (Strong's # 1457b). What evil?

Scripture shows us that the *"flesh"* is evil, *"hostile toward God,"* never wanting to follow Him (Romans 8:5–8). This world or *"age"* is described as *"this present evil age"* (Galatians 1:4) and the devil is called *"the evil one"* (Matthew 6:13; 2 Thessalonians 3:3). Each of those opposes God, prayer, believers, and the will of God. How do we *not* give in to evil? Give time to prayer, especially reading, thinking, and praying in the Scriptures. David knew much of the Word, thought much on God's Word, and prayed often (see Psalm 1:1–6). We should do the same.

Paul thought through the seven gifts in Romans 12. Consider Romans 12:9–15 and compare them with the seven gifts in verses 6–8. Some see verses 9–15 as applying in parallel fashion to the gifts in verses 6–8, so that, for example, one with the gift of prophecy should show love without hypocrisy, abhor what is evil and cling to what is good—good words for anyone, especially one who speaks God's Word. Note your insights about the spiritual realities found in these verses.

What did Paul command in Romans 12:16–21? Consider why this would be so important. Think of this considering what you have learned from David and what he faced in his twenties, leading six hundred men and their families. Do you see any parallels or common threads? Write your insights and any applications to your life.

How vital is it to know how to deal with evil in daily life? How important is this in leading others—self, home, school, church, job, community, and so forth?

TAKEAWAYS

David's Time on the Run

There are *three* takeaways from David's time *"On the Run."* 1) *Remember* God—His Word, His promises, His ways. 2) Be *Realistic* about people. Not one person is

God—there's only One—nor will any be Christlike all the time. Most changes take time; sometimes those changes come quickly. 3) Be *Real* by loving God and loving people. Lead them to Him and His Word, ever looking to Him to grow them up from childish ways to mature ways.

What stands out to you in these verses about dealing with people or leading people?

Lord, thank You that You do not leave me alone in the daily grind of life. Thank You for the training You are doing in my life, day by day, week by week, year by year. May the skills You are giving me and working in me be useful for my life and in the lives of those around me. May my attitudes reflect trust in You like David showed in dealing with Saul, even when he could have taken advantage of his enemy. Show me how to be grateful for the rough days as well as the more pleasant times. And I pray for grace to love and lead others (whether one person or many) Your way, toward You and Your Word. May they, in turn, love and lead others. You endured and loved and led, following Your Father. Work that in my life as You work in my life. In the name of Jesus, our Lord and Leader, Amen.

Notes

Lesson 3

King David

THE FIRST HALF OF DAVID'S REIGN AS KING

Israel was a divided nation when David became king of Judah (one of the twelve tribes) at the age of 30. Abner, commander of Saul's army, made Ishbosheth, one of Saul's sons, the new king over Israel (the other eleven tribes). The anointing as future king that Samuel had poured on David many years before, became current reality for the tribe of Judah. David did not force it to happen; he could have killed Saul more than once, but he followed his conscience and his principles, looking to the Lord to put him on the throne at the right time, in the right way, in the right place.

What would happen next? How would David establish order and begin to govern? He had been through a decade of training in reigning and that occurred with a questionable "kingdom" of men who were in "debt," in "distress," and "discontent"—what a challenge! Not only that, David had been on the run from Saul and his men in place after place; David had hidden in at least fifteen places starting with his home in Bethlehem. Now came the challenges of leading some who had not been overly pleased with the last king, Saul, and others who invested their lives in the line of Saul against David.

Each of us faces some kind of challenge or perhaps many challenges on many fronts. What should we do when we face such challenges? David provides a good example. He was not perfect, not like the Lord in everything he did, but he stayed focused on the Lord for the most part. We too must stay focused, not on our problems or challenges, but on the Lord. Pastor and author, Peter Lord, once wisely stated, "Gaze on God; glance on the problems." That is good counsel, because we human beings are fickle and fragile. God is neither.

As we walk through the early days of David's reign as king, it is vital to look carefully at David and those around him, listen to the Lord attentively, read His Word expectantly, and pray, seeking the wisdom of God for the challenges, perplexities, or problems each faces.

DID YOU KNOW?
Hebron

David prayed, asking the LORD about going up to *"one of the cities of Judah."* The LORD directed him to go from Ziklag to *Hebron*, located about 18 miles south of Jerusalem. It was the home of Abraham for several years and the location of the burial cave of Abraham, Sarah, Isaac, Rebekah, Jacob, and Leah (Genesis 23:1–20; 25:7–10; 49:29–33; 50:12–13). David moved there and the men of Judah anointed him king over Judah. Two years later David became king over all Israel and stayed in Hebron five and a half more years (total of seven and a half years in Hebron). David lived in Hebron from age 30 to almost 38 and fathered six sons there.

Day One

Where Do We Go from Here?

David and his six hundred men had just won a decisive victory over the Amalekite raiders. They returned to Ziklag with great plunder. Now what? Within a matter of three days, David received news of the deaths of Saul and Jonathan as well as many others of Saul's army. He lamented their deaths, especially that of Jonathan and Saul. David probably wandered what he should do next? How should he live now? He would no longer need to run from Saul. Knowing what David did can help us as we face major (and minor) decisions day by day.

📖 According to 2 Samuel 2:1a, what was the first thing David did after his lament over Saul and Jonathan?

📖 Based on 2 Samuel 2:1b, what was the second thing he did?

📖 Who moved to Hebron with David, according to 2 Samuel 2:2–3?

DID YOU KNOW?
The Men of Jabesh-Gilead

The men of Jabesh-gilead showed great valor in their all-night march to retrieve the bodies of Saul and his sons from the wall of Beth-shan. They took them back to Jabesh and gave them an honorable burial. This is very significant in light of the city's history. Over 300 years before, the people of Jabesh-gilead refused to fight in the battle against the errant tribe of Benjamin. As a result, the men of that city were slain, and 400 virgin women from there were given to the almost-extinguished tribe of Benjamin (Judges 21:1–23). Years later, at the beginning of Saul's reign, Nahash and his Ammonite army threatened Jabesh-gilead but Saul and his army soundly defeated them, saving the city (1 Samuel 11:1–11). Saul was like a national hero to the people there; the men who risked their lives to retrieve his body would have grown up hearing the stories of Saul and his army. David spoke of God's blessings on these men for their valiant deed and told of his being the new king of Judah (2 Samuel 2:4–7).

📖 What happened next, according to 2 Samuel 2:4? What did they do, and what significant news did they bring to David?

📖 How did David respond, according to 2 Samuel 2:5–7?

The first thing David did was pray; he *"inquired of the LORD"* about moving back into Judah. But where? The second thing David did was pray *again*; the Lord carefully directed him to move to Hebron. He took his two wives and his men with their families and settled into life in Hebron. The men of Judah came to him and *"anointed David king over the house of Judah,"* a fitting move on their part and part of the plan of God for David. It was also important for David to know about the valor of the men of Jabesh-gilead in recovering the bodies of Saul and his sons and giving them an honorable burial. David sent word to them, desiring the blessing of the Lord for them. He also spoke of himself being the newly anointed king of Judah.

DID YOU KNOW?
David's Sons Born in Hebron

During his seven and a half years in Hebron, David had six sons born, each by a different wife—1) Amnon by Ahimoam the Jezreelitess, 2) Chileab by Abigail, 3) Absalom by Maacah, 4) Adonijah by Haggith, 5) Shephatiah by Abital, 6) Ithream by Eglah (2 Samuel 3:2–5).

📖 What do you discover about Israel during these days? What occurred between Judah and Israel, according to 2 Samuel 2:8–11 and 3:1?

📖 What did Abner, the commander of Saul's army (2 Samuel 2:8a), do to strengthen David's reign, according to 2 Samuel 3:6–11?

Saul's army commander Abner pulled together the details to make Saul's son Ish-bosheth king over Israel (the tribes other than Judah). Civil war erupted with Joab leading David's army and Abner leading Saul's army. The rivalry between those two men intensified, and the war between the two groups escalated. The *"House of David"* continually grew stronger while the *"House of Saul"* grew steadily weaker. Ish-bosheth and Abner could see what was going on. Tensions increased, especially between those two men.

Ish-bosheth accused Abner of sexual relations with Saul's concubine Rizpah. Abner erupted in anger at Ish-bosheth and began talking about transferring the rule over Israel to David so that he would rule the entire land, *"from Dan even to Beersheba"* (northernmost to southernmost). Ish-bosheth became fearful of Abner, apparently knowing that Abner could follow through with this threat. He would reign only two years.

📖 Read 2 Samuel 3:12–21. What did Abner do? How did David respond?

📖 When Joab learned of Abner's meeting with David, he revealed his suspicions about him. Read 2 Samuel 3:22–30. What did Joab say and do, according to these verses?

📖 How did David respond to the death of Abner, according to 2 Samuel 3:31–39?

Abner began seeking ways to hand over the reins of Israel to David. He sent messengers to David, and David received them and the offer with the condition that his wife Michal be given back to him. Though awkward, this was accomplished. Abner spoke to the leaders of Israel about David being the king of the whole nation of Israel, pointing to what God had said and the ways God had worked to bring this about. Abner also spoke to the men of the tribe of Benjamin, part of the "House of Saul." In addition, he traveled to Hebron to speak to David. All agreed that David should be king over the whole nation. David sent Abner in peace to make the arrangements.

Joab and his soldiers came in from a raid and heard that Abner, Saul's army commander, had met with David and that David sent him away in peace. Joab was suspicious *and* still feeling vengeful toward Abner who had killed Joab's brother Asahel earlier. With great animation, he told David of his concern and caution but said nothing of his thoughts of vengeance. Joab sent men to bring Abner back. Soon after Abner arrived, Joab murdered him, most likely more for Abner's role in Asahel's death than his link to Saul. David mourned Abner's death and spoke of the innocence of him and the kingdom over this travesty. David saw this act of Joab and his men as *"evil"* and spoke of the Lord dealing with the difficult *"sons of Zeruiah"* (Joab and Abishai, Asahel had died).

📖 What occurred next? Read 2 Samuel 4:1–3, 5–12 and summarize the events of those days.

How did David show his character in these events?

DID YOU KNOW?

What about Mephibosheth?

At the time of David's initial kingship in Hebron, Jonathan's son and Saul's grandson Mephibosheth would have been about five or six years of age. In 2 Samuel 4:4, we read of how Mephibosheth became crippled and unable to walk. Normally, all the descendants of a former king were executed by the new king. What would happen to him? About fifteen years later, because of his covenant relationship with Jonathan, David brought Jonathan's son Mephibosheth to live in his palace and provided for him everything needed (see 2 Samuel 9:1–13).

News of Abner's death in Hebron affected Ish-bosheth and those around him. Soon after, two of Saul's commanders assassinated Ish-bosheth and carried his severed head to David in Hebron. They thought they would receive David's praise and favor. Instead, David, focused his attention on how the Lord *"redeemed my life from all distress"* and spoke of the news of Saul's death as deserving judgment. Now more so, David saw these two *"wicked men"* who stealthily killed *"a righteous man"* as deserving execution for their deed. David ordered them executed. Then, David's men honorably buried Ish-bosheth's head in Abner's grave.

🕮 What do you discover in 2 Samuel 5:1–5?

What do you see as significant in the phrase *"before the LORD"*?

The men of Israel regarded David as one of them, and themselves as *"your bone and your flesh."* He had been a leader for them under King Saul, and now they acknowledged the Lord calling David to *"shepherd My people"* as ruler over all Israel. At Hebron they entered into a covenant relationship with David *"before the LORD,"* pointing to their sense of accountability to the Lord and trusting His watch-care over them. David ruled for seven and a half years from Hebron, then thirty-three more years from Jerusalem.

DID YOU KNOW?
Covenant King

The leaders of Israel came to David, noting themselves as *"your bone and your flesh,"* words used of a covenant relationship (2 Samuel 5:1). Adam stated similar words to his wife (Genesis 2:23). Abner spoke of David making *"a covenant"* with Israel (2 Samuel 3:21). David agreed and soon after entered this covenant as the *"shepherd"* and *"ruler"* over Israel (2 Samuel 5:1–3). Knowing of His coming crucifixion, noting the New Covenant, Jesus spoke to His disciples of giving *"My body"* and *"My blood of the covenant"* (Matthew 26:26, 28). Jesus, the greater *"Son of David,"* is *the* Covenant King of believers (Micah 5:2, 4–5a; 2 Samuel 5:2b; Matthew 2:6).

STOP AND APPLY—Covenant Loyalty—David and the leaders of Israel entered a covenant relationship in which David agreed to *"shepherd"* and be *"ruler"* over Israel. This meant showing love and loyalty to the people. They had already seen this is his commanding of Israel's troops against aggressive Philistines. He could be trusted. That is the covenant loyalty we see in our King Jesus. Believers need to show that loyalty and love to Him and to one another, with *"love"* being the "mark" of a disciple (John 13:35).

Day Two

The Early Days in Jerusalem

From his headquarters in Hebron, David reigned as king over all of Israel, all twelve tribes. Those first years were foundational for what his reign would look like, and he did what he thought best day after day. He dealt with injustices, sought to honor his word, and govern in a way pleasing to the Lord. What would his reign look like? What marks would he make and leave?

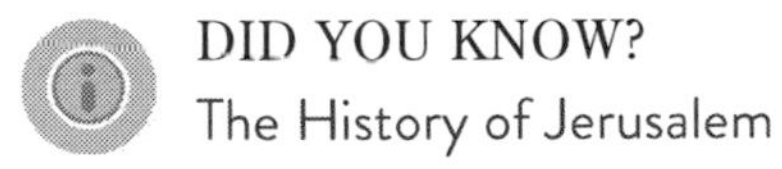

DID YOU KNOW?
The History of Jerusalem

Jerusalem is first mentioned in Genesis 14:18 as *"Salem,"* meaning "peace." At that time, Melchizedek ruled as *"king of Salem"* and *"priest of God Most High"* (*El Elyon*). He met Abram in *"the valley of Shaveh"* or *"the King's Valley"* on the north side of Jerusalem coming from his decisive defeat of the four-king confederation. The Jebusites (part of the Amorites) ruled the city in the days of Joshua (Judges 1:8, 21). The Jebusites thought they were impervious and taunted David saying *"the blind and lame"* could stop him. David and his men entered through a water tunnel and captured the city. It became *"the city of David,"* his capital.

📖 What do you discover in 2 Samuel 5:6–10?

📖 What significant truth do you read in 2 Samuel 5:10?

At the end of the time in Hebron, David led an assault team to Jerusalem and captured the city from the Jebusites. Thinking their city invincible, the Jebusites mocked David, but, in spite of their mockery toward him, he indeed conquered the city by invading through a water tunnel. He called Jerusalem *"the city of David,"* making it his capital. Certainly, David's skill as a commander made a difference, but his success ultimately came because *"the LORD God of hosts was with him."*

STOP AND APPLY—Who Is *With* You?—David ruled well as king. His success came because *"the LORD God of hosts was with him."* In His call to make disciples, Jesus told His followers *"I am with you always, even to the end of the age"* (Matthew 28:20). What a promise! The reality is not so much *who* we are or *what* we know or can do, but who is with us, especially the Lord Himself. He makes the eternal difference!

The writer of 2 Samuel gives information about the building of David's palace in Jerusalem in 2 Samuel 5:11–12, though the actual building of his palace probably did not occur until around 980 BC, over twenty years later, when King Hiram of Tyre sent cedar logs of Lebanon as well as Tyrian stone masons and carpenters. These details are given revealing David's kingship, not the chronological order of his reign (cf. 1 Chronicles 14:1–2).

📖 Early in his days in Jerusalem, David had to deal with Philistines again. What do you discover in 2 Samuel 5:17–21?

Record any additional insights from 1 Chronicles 14:8–12, especially verse 12.

When the Philistines heard about David reigning in Jerusalem, once again they gathered for battle, this time in the *"valley of Rephaim"* west-southwest of Jerusalem. David escaped to *"the stronghold,"* possibly the Cave of Adullam. Likely while there, David *"inquired of the LORD,"* seeking His guidance and victory. The Lord answered, directing David to go into battle and assuring him of victory. That victory occurred at a location known as *"Baal-Perazim,"* meaning "the break-through of Baal." There, after their victory, the Israelites gathered the abandoned Philistine idols and carried them away. First Chronicles 14:12 notes that under David's order, his men also *"burned"* those idols.

Summarize the significant event which occurred during this time at the Cave of Adullam, according to 1 Chronicles 11:15–19.

What do you discover about David from this incident?

While at the Cave of Adullam, David longingly mentioned drinking from the well of Bethlehem. Though not ordered to get water from that well, the "three" revealed their hearts of loyalty to David and their skill in military matters. They brought the water back to David, and he refused to drink it, regarding it as like their own lifeblood. He valued them and their sacrificial effort and revealed his heart as a leader and a man of God as he poured it out like an offering before the Lord.

DID YOU KNOW?
The Valley of Rephaim

The *Valley of Rephaim* is about 3 or 4 miles west-southwest of Jerusalem, between Philistine territory and Israel. It is likely named after the giants called *Rephaim* over the centuries (see Genesis 14:5; Numbers 13:32–33; Deuteronomy 2:10–11, 20–21). David defeated the Philistine army twice in this area.

📖 What further data do you find in 2 Samuel 5:22–25?

📖 What common element do you find in 2 Samuel 5:19 and 23?

Soon after, the Philistines came back to the same valley, seeking to battle David and the Israelites. Once again, David *"inquired of the LORD"* and the Lord gave the go-ahead along with a different strategy for the battle. This time, he was to go a different route and wait on *"the sound of marching in the tops of the balsam* [Hebrew-*baka* shrubs/trees or *mulberry*] *trees,"* apparently God's signal to attack. David and his men *"struck down the Philistines from Geba* (or *Gibeon) as far as Gezer"* further west.

In each challenge, David sought the direction of the Lord in prayer rather than charging ahead in his own steam or in some man-made strategy. David revealed his heart for the Lord; specifically, for seeking, worshiping, and following Him. He desired to obey Him in all of life, not only in the 'religious' areas as some did, but in all areas.

In David's first years in Jerusalem, he continued to stabilize the kingdom of Israel. He faced problems and challenges from time to time, but God was working in him and through him. We can learn from David, what he did right and what he did wrong.

📖 Read 2 Samuel 8:1–2. What two people groups did David defeat?

📖 What further conquests are recorded in 2 Samuel 8:3–8?

📖 What response did David have from Toi king of Hamath, according to 2 Samuel 8:9–10?

📖 What do you discover about David in his actions as described in 2 Samuel 8:11–12?

David defeated the Philistines, including conquering the capital city of Gath. He also defeated Moab, who began giving him tribute. In addition, David and his army overcame the leaders of Zobah, a kingdom north of Damascus along with several Arameans (Syrians) seeking to help king Hadadezer of Zobah. Along with capturing much gold and bronze from Zobah, David also received ongoing tribute from the Arameans. After these victories, king Toi of Hamath (also north of Damascus) sought to placate David with silver, gold, and bronze. David continually focused on the Lord and his relationship with Him; he took all of the plunder and gifts from these tribute nations as well as from other conquests and dedicated them to the Lord. Likely, later he gave these treasures and metals as material to be used in building the Temple in Jerusalem.

STOP AND APPLY—Where Is Your Focus?—Sometimes one's attitude comes more from focus than circumstances. Someone who has just gone through a cataclysmic storm is much more grateful for a sunny day, even if it means blistering heat. Someone recovering from surgery is often much more grateful for a good meal. It's about perspective. David's focus was on the Lord. That should be true of each of us, no matter what our circumstances. Pause and Pray. Perhaps there is a need to *refocus* and find the Lord's refreshing.

Day Three

Stabilizing the Kingdom and the Heart

David continued stabilizing the Kingdom of Israel by dealing with surrounding nations. His focus on the Lord did not waver in these days or in these encounters. David did not seek to bring people to focus on him or his skills, but on the Lord, His greatness, and power.

📖 Battles continued. What further conquest do you read about in 2 Samuel 8:13–14? The Scriptures are clear about who gives victory. What do you see in 2 Samuel 8:14b?

📖 What do you discover about David and his heart attitude in 2 Samuel 22:1–51 (a parallel to Psalm 18:1–50)?

David and his army delivered a decisive defeat over the Edomites in the *"Valley of Salt"* near the Dead Sea, and David placed garrisons in Edom. The writer is careful to note *"the LORD helped David wherever he went,"* giving him wisdom for battle in victory after victory. David subdued all the kingdoms bordering Israel, bringing a greater measure of peace and safety to the nation. In a song of praise to the Lord, David penned Psalm 18, summing up the many ways the Lord had given victory over Saul and many surrounding nations.

WORD STUDY
Kindness

David spoke of showing *"kindness"* to any descendant of the house of Saul *"for Jonathan's sake."* The word *"kindness"* is a translation of the Hebrew word *chesed* (Strong's #2617), meaning "covenant mercy" or "covenant kindness." It refers to a covenant action of love which shows forgiveness and helpfulness. It is often translated *"mercy"* or *"lovingkindness."* David's actions of kindness and grace toward Mephibosheth reveal his faithfulness to the covenant relationship between him and Jonathan.

How did David reveal his heart in his covenant actions toward Jonathan's son Mephibosheth? Read 2 Samuel 9:1–8?

What further details do you discover in 2 Samuel 9:9–13?

David took seriously his covenant relationship with Jonathan. Sometime in his 40s, David intentionally sought to show *"kindness for Jonathan's sake."* A house-manager named Ziba informed David about Jonathan's son Mephibosheth living in the home of Machir, son of Ammiel, in Lo-debar, an out-of-the-way area east of the Jordan River and just south of the Sea of Galilee. Even though he was lame in both feet, David restored to him the lands of his grandfather Saul (considerable wealth), ordered Ziba to care for the lands, and brought Mephibosheth to Jerusalem where he daily ate at the king's table.

DID YOU KNOW?
Lo-debar

The area known as *Lo-debar* (which means "no pasture" or "nothingness") contained the home of a wealthy man, Machir, son of Ammiel which served as Mephibosheth's temporary home. *Lo-debar* (also known as *Debir*) lies about five miles east of the Jordan River and about nine or ten miles south of the Sea of Galilee. Mephibosheth moved from this place of relative obscurity into David's palace..

📖 According to 2 Samuel 10:1–5, what incident occurred that affected further relations with surrounding nations? Further details are found in the account in 1 Chronicles 19:1–5.

📖 David continued to stabilize the nation of Israel by dealing with the opposition of surrounding nations. At this time, he had to deal with the Ammonites and certain mercenary Arameans (Syrians). What actions do you discover in 2 Samuel 10:6–14? Summarize what you find.

📖 What occurred after this, according to 2 Samuel 10:15–19?

News came to David about the death of King Nahash of the Ammonites. He sent a delegation to express *"kindness"* to Nahash's son Hanun, since Nahash had shown *"kindness"* to him (Hebrew—*chesed*—*"kindness"*). Certain young *"princes"* of the Ammonites suspected David of sending a spying delegation, so they treated the delegation with great disrespect. Because of this the Ammonites became *"odious"* to David. When the Ammonites realized their situation, they hired several Arameans (Syrians) to battle Israel. To deal with the issue, David sent his commander Joab along with the army and his *"mighty men."*

Using excellent strategy, skill, and prayerful dependence on the Lord, Joab and his men experienced victory over the Ammonites, who retreated into the city of Rabbah to fight another day. Joab returned to Jerusalem. The Arameans called for more Arameans from Zobah and other lands north of Damascus. David gathered his army, crossed the Jordan River, and attacked the Arameans, soundly defeating them, including Hadadezer's commander Shophach. The servants of Hadadezer then made peace with David and began serving him. Dealing with the Ammonites and Arameans was thus settled for a while.

IN THEIR SHOES
Covenants Matter

The faithfulness of the LORD to Israel is based on who He is and what He has promised, including the covenants He has made with the children of Abraham through Isaac and Jacob. When the Israelites made a covenant with the deceptive

Gibeonites, God took their actions seriously. He chastened Israel for Saul's failure to honor the Gibeonite covenant found in Joshua 9. David honored his covenant with Jonathan and others. He honored the Gibeonite covenant as well (see 2 Samuel 21:1–14).

📖 David continued stabilizing the nation. During this time a famine occurred in Israel. After three years, David sought the Lord and discovered that the famine was judgment from the Lord for Saul's offenses against the Gibeonites, ignoring Israel's covenant with them. Read 2 Samuel 21:1–14 and summarize what occurred.

In his zeal for Judah and Israel, Saul sought to exterminate the Gibeonites, in violation of the covenant agreement Joshua and the leaders had made with them hundreds of years before. Saul ignored the covenant agreement, but God did not. He chastened Israel for Saul's wrongs, and Israel faced three years of famine. David desired to make things right with the Gibeonites. Dealing with this in some manner as a covenant violation, the Gibeonites executed seven men from the lineage of Saul. At this time, David also honored the lives of Saul, Jonathan, and the seven men by giving them an honorable burial in Gibeah.

📖 Review the covenant agreement Israel made with the Gibeonites in Joshua 9:3–27, especially verses 18–21. What did Joshua and the leaders decide to do in this situation?

📖 According to Joshua 9:19–20, what consequences did the Israelites realize they would face if they broke this covenant agreement with the Gibeonites?

📖 In looking over what occurred in Joshua 9 and 10, what continued protection should Israel have given the Gibeonites?

In Joshua's day, Joshua and the leaders decided to honor the covenant agreement and give the Gibeonites a measure of protection rather than having them executed as Canaanites. They let them live, making them servants to the Israelites. The Israelite leaders recognized that God would bring His wrath upon them if they broke the covenant agreement, so they followed the course of making them *"hewers of wood and drawers of water"* for the people of Israel.

Joshua 10 records the planned attack of five Canaanite kings and their armies against the city of Gibeon and the Gibeonites. Joshua and the Israelite army defended the city of Gibeon and the Gibeonites. God gave Israel a decisive victory over those five Canaanite city-states and their people. God even brought miraculous results in His bigger plan to give the Israelites victories and the land of Canaan. This is not a license to presume upon God, but an example of God's merciful actions toward His people and His covenant promises. He honors covenants and reveals that in Joshua 10 as well as in 2 Samuel 21.

These historical events should have signaled to Saul and the Israelites that God honors covenant agreements, even with Gibeonites. With that in mind, they should have protected them instead of trying to exterminate them or rid the land of them. Because of His covenant agreement with Israel and Israel's covenant agreement with the Gibeonites, God dealt with the nation of Israel in the matter of the Gibeonite slaughter.

STOP AND APPLY—Dealing with Others' Offenses—There are times when we must deal with the offense(s) of others. In Matthew 18:15–35, Jesus directed His disciples about restoring relationships. He said that if a *"brother sins,"* go to him/her and seek to bring reconciliation. If he or she does not listen, then go with one or two others, always seeking to restore the relationship. Jesus emphasized always having a forgiving attitude, even when one refuses to listen. Paul wrote about dealing with a sinning believer and *"so-called"* believers in Corinth (see 1 Corinthians 5:1–13). In Romans 12:16–21; 14:1–23; Galatians 6:1–10 and 1 Thessalonians 5:14–15, he also gives clear direction and wise counsel about dealing with others' offenses, sins, and weaknesses.

Day Four

Wrong, Wrong, Wrong

David had a *"heart"* for God, but he was not perfect. As the saying goes, he had "feet of clay;" he always had to be on guard since he, like any other, was susceptible to temptation and wicked thoughts, motives, and actions. Perhaps unaware at first, David focused too long on the young woman bathing on a rooftop. He then turned tempting, lustful thoughts into immoral intentions and committed adultery with Bathsheba. What he did was wrong, wrong, wrong—wrong toward God, wrong toward Bathsheba and her family, wrong toward Uriah and the other soldiers, wrong toward the nation of Israel. How could this happen?

DID YOU KNOW?
Wartime in the Springtime

In David's day, kings, commanders, and armies set their war strategies and battle plans according to the season. Winter was never a good time to fight because of the cold and the winter rains, but it proved a wonderful time to prepare for future fighting. When Springtime came, nations, kingdoms, city-states, or alliances were ready for war (for example, see 2 Samuel 11:1a; 1 Chronicles 20:1a). That proved true year after year, in war after war, battle after battle.

Historical records reveal that David continued dealing with troubles near Israel; in his late forties, he almost lost his life dealing with Philistine giants (see 2 Samuel 21:15–17). His men demanded that he not go into battle; seemingly good advice, but not settled in prayer. That is the setting for what occurred next in David's life, matters from which we can hopefully learn to be better on guard ... and deal with sin God's way.

📖 What military matters occurred during this time, according to 2 Samuel 11:1? How might this connect to the advice of his military men as found in 2 Samuel 21:17?

📖 Note that Rabbah was the capital city of the Ammonites. What do you discover about the Ammonites in 2 Samuel 10:14?

📖 According to 2 Samuel 11:1, what was David doing in Jerusalem? Consider this strategic time.

📖 When David should have been battling Ammonites, he faced a different kind of battle. Read 2 Samuel 11:2–5. Record your observations.

Joab defeated the Arameans (Syrians) and Ammonites; the Ammonites ran to their capital city Rabbah, where they hid from the Israelites behind the walls of that city. Joab returned to Jerusalem. When Spring came, Joab took Israel's army to Ammon to besiege Rabbah (about 24 miles east of the Jordan River). David did not go with him but stayed in Jerusalem, likely on the advice of his military. He did not inquire of the Lord about this.

In Jerusalem, instead of being leader in a battle, David took an afternoon nap, and then, walking on his roof, saw young Bathsheba taking a rooftop bath. Around age 47, David faced a battle of lust and adultery; he sinned in thought, then action. In his position of power, he caved in to the evil of his flesh; after looking and pondering, he had her brought to his palace where he lay with her. She became pregnant.

IN THEIR SHOES
Roadblocks

David is an example of ignoring and crashing through *roadblocks;* he did not have to commit adultery and murder. 1) He did not pray. Instead, he unwisely did what his men demanded and stayed in Jerusalem. 2) He did not fulfill his responsibility. He listened to unwise advice about not going to battle instead of taking responsibility for being king, including battles (2 Samuel 21:15–17). 3) He did not listen, though informed that Bathsheba was the daughter of Eliam, one of David's loyal *"mighty men"* (2 Samuel 23:34). 4) He did not think of others, even Uriah, another of his loyal *"mighty men"* (2 Samuel 23:39). 5) He tried to cover his sin. He devised many plans, but faced several setbacks—Uriah ignored the extras *"from the king,"* remaining loyal to his men and his task (2 Samuel 11:8–13). 6) He became desperate and deceitful, not thinking of God or His Word; David sent Uriah's "death sentence" letter with him back to commander Joab at the siege of Rabbah (2 Samuel 11:14–24). 7) David ignored his conscience, rationalizing about war and death (2 Samuel 11:25). 8) For months, David ignored the conviction of God; his guilt drained him as *"the fever heat of summer"* (Psalm 32:3–4). Finally, when Nathan confronted him, David admitted his sin and received God's forgiveness as well as His chastening (2 Samuel 12:1–23; Psalm 32; 51).

After finding out that Bathsheba was pregnant, David sought to cover up his sin by evil scheming, bringing Uriah, a trusted and skilled soldier and one of David's *"mighty men,"* from the frontlines of battle. David's plans failed, not once, but twice. Desperate and becoming more deceitful, David resorted to an underhanded "death sentence" letter sent to Joab at the hand of Uriah himself. This betrayal was inexcusable, and Uriah died in battle.

📖 Read Psalm 32:3–4. What did David experience over the next few months?

📖 What occurred next? Read 2 Samuel 12:1–6 and record David's response to Nathan's story.

David experienced intense guilt over his adultery and scheming murder. He describes his experience like one being drained by *"the fever heat of summer"* (Psalm 32:4), like a summer temperature of 103 degrees that drains one's energies. David's guilt and God's heavy hand of conviction pressed and drained him. How long? Apparently, for several months. Then, the Lord sent the prophet Nathan with a story. David became incensed and angry over the cruel and uncompassionate actions that Nathan described of an unnamed Israelite man.

📖 What changed? According to 2 Samuel 12:7–8, what four things did the Lord remind David of through Nathan's words?

📖 The Lord focused David's attention on the heart of the matter. What do you discover in 2 Samuel 12:9a? The Lord noted David's *"evil"* and then delineated it. What further details do you discover in 2 Samuel 12:9b?

IN THEIR SHOES
Dealing with Philistine Giants

In 2 Samuel 21:15–17, David came close to losing his life in a battle with the Philistine giant Ishbi-benob. Abishai, Joab's brother and *"chief of the thirty,"* an obvious leader among David's *"mighty men,"* killed Ishbi-benob (2 Samuel 23:18–19). David's men (perhaps overly cautious) then demanded that he not go out and battle any more. David's men proved victorious over several other Philistine giants in at least three other battles (2 Samuel 21:18–22; 1 Chronicles 20:4–8).

📖 What would be the consequences of David's actions, according to 2 Samuel 12:10–12?

Nathan made clear to David *"you are the man!"* and then spoke the Lord's words to him. The Lord had 1) anointed David as king, 2) delivered him from the hand of Saul, 3) gave David *"his master's house,"* and 4) gave him the riches and position of king over Judah and Israel. He could have given David even more. David acted in self-will and evil, despising *"the word of the LORD,"* sinning against Him as well as against Bathsheba, Uriah, and many others. Consequences would come. *"The sword"* (troubles and death) would be perpetual in David's *"house"* for all to see.

📖 Read 2 Samuel 12:13–15. How did David respond? What further insights do you discover in Psalm 32:1–2, 5?

📖 What further words of wisdom did David give in Psalm 32:6–11?

David confessed his sin—*"I have sinned against the LORD."* Nathan assured David that the Lord forgave him and that he would not die, but consequences would come, the first being the death of the child to be born. When David penned Psalm 32, he rejoiced in the blessing of forgiveness, recalling the months of heavy guilt and inner sorrow. He spoke of God's forgiveness for his wrongs—his *"sin," "iniquity,"* and *"transgressions"*—and he called others to draw near to the Lord, rejoicing in how He would give *"deliverance"* as well as clear guidance. He also warned about not being like *"the horse or as the mule,"* stubborn or reluctant to come to the Lord, experiencing sorrows rather than joy in the mercies and forgiveness of the Lord.

📖 What occurred next? Read 2 Samuel 12:16? What did David do in response to the child's illness? Based on 2 Samuel 12:17–21, how did this affect those in the palace?

📖 After the child died, how did David view this matter, according to 2 Samuel 12:22–23?

David revealed his heart in several ways. He knew he had done wrong and had confessed his sins. The first thing he did after the child became ill: David *"inquired of God for the child,"* he prayed. He fasted that first day and night, seeking God and His graciousness. Those in the palace sought to comfort and help in any way they could, but he continued fasting. When the child died, they were afraid to tell David, but he sensed something had changed. When he discovered the child had died, he arose and *"worshiped"* the Lord, then resumed his normal routine. His servants perplexed, David assured them with his trust statement that he had been praying that perhaps the Lord would be *"gracious to me"* and allow the child to live. David also believed he would see this son again—*"I shall go to him,"* a statement many view as affirming eternal life.

📖 What do you discover in 2 Samuel 12:24–25? How do these verses highlight the care and love of God?

📖 What did David do next, according to 2 Samuel 12:26–31? Do you see any significance in these actions? If so, note your insights.

The LORD showed grace and mercy to David. Throughout Scripture, God's grace and mercy are evident. "Grace" refers to what God kindly and lovingly gives which we have not earned and do not deserve. "Mercy" refers to how God lovingly withholds what we have earned and deserve for our sins, our wrongs, our injustices toward others—we have earned and deserve justice, penalties, or payments for our wrongs, but God withholds that, treating us with forgiveness, revealing His covenant kindness and love.

Probably about a year after being married, David and Bathsheba gave birth to another son, whom they named Solomon. *"The LORD loved him"*—Nathan the prophet brought a message from the Lord that the child's name was Jedidiah, meaning "beloved of the LORD." After this, Joab captured Rabbah, the place where Uriah had died, but he called for David to come and camp and fight against it so that the victory would be his. David did that, conquering the city as well as other Ammonite cities. Once again David was protecting Israel, fulfilling his role as king and military leader.

STOP AND APPLY—*Dealing with Wrongs*—How did David deal with his wrongs? First, he failed to deal with them and his guilt. That produced more intense inner turmoil. Finally, after hearing the clear words of Nathan the prophet, David admitted his sins and cried out to God for forgiveness. The Lord forgave him and, in His love, began chastening him for his wrongs. David did not become perfect, but did begin doing what was right as king, providing for his family and protecting Israel. What do you need to do at this point in your life? Are there any wrongs needing correction? What right words do you need to hear or speak, and what right direction should you follow?

Day Five

Following My Shepherd

Following the Lord as Shepherd does not mean walking in perfection, but it does mean going in the right direction. David discovered that in many ways with many relationships. David discovered new depths of the grace and mercy of God as well as new insights into his own sin and God's holiness. We can learn from David. We, too, have much to learn and apply as we follow day by day.

"Grace" and *"Mercy"*—Read the verses given below and note your insights about *"grace"* and *"mercy,"* how they reveal the Lord and how they speak to you and your situation.

1 Timothy 1:2

2 Timothy 1:2

Hebrews 4:16

2 John 1:3

The word *"holy"* appears more than 500 times in the Old and New Testaments (Strong's #6918, #6944 [Old Testament], and #40 [New Testament]). It means "set apart," especially "set apart for a unique purpose." In the Old Testament, God dwelt in the *"Holy of Holies,"* the inner room set apart for His dwelling in the Tabernacle and later the Temple in Jerusalem, *"the holy city."* The priests wore *"holy"* garments representing their duty to be *"holy"* to Him, set apart to serve and worship Him and lead others to worship and obey Him. How holy is God? How does He see sin?

📖 Read the verses below and note your insights.

Isaiah 6:3–7

Isaiah 57:15–19

Psalm 16:10–11 with Acts 2:24–28, 29–40

Real love cares about every area of life. God's love is holy love. That means in His love, God corrects. It is called His chastening love. Look at the following verses and note your insights.

Proverbs 3:11–12

Hebrews 12:5–11

📖 How forgiving is God? What does the Scripture say about His forgiveness? Read the verses below and note your insights and any applications the Holy Spirit brings to mind.

Luke 24:44–49

Acts 13:32–39

Ephesians 1:7–8

WORD STUDY
"Served"

The word *"served"* used of David in Acts 13:26 is a translation of the Greek word *hupereteo* (Strong's #5256, "to serve" [as an under-rower—*huperetes*]). It refers to servants (often slaves as a result of war conquests) who rowed the ancient Roman and Greek ships. There was no one lower than these "under rowers." While the contrast between king and servant is clear, David had a servant's heart and faithfully served the Lord and His purposes above those of himself.

📖 What further insights do you glean from the testimony of David's life in Paul's words in Acts 13:36?

God is indeed holy, and sin is very serious! He does not wink at sin or give a grandfatherly chuckle about the "cute" ways of wayward children. From the start, He said death would come for disobedience (Genesis 2:17; 5:5). Adam disobeyed and ate of the forbidden fruit; the "Fall" occurred, and everything in the universe began groaning in the agony of evil brought by Adam's self-will (Romans 5:12; 8:18–25).

The Good News: God is love. He never abandoned His people or His purposes. He came into the Garden of Eden with a promise of the *"seed"* of the woman crushing the head of the evil serpent, one day ridding the world of all evil, every vestige of sin (Genesis 3:15; Romans 5:17). Jesus came as that *"Seed"* of the woman, lived sinless, went to the cross where He paid for every sin, and now offers His eternal forgiveness to any who will come to Him, repent of sin, believe Him, and receive Him into one's life as Lord and Savior (Galatians 4:4–7; John 3:16–18; 6:35–40, 44–47).

God's unabandoning love also means He keeps working on His children; He never abandons His purpose to have a family of sons and daughters made in the image of Christ (see Romans 8:29; Colossians 3:10). That means He corrects and chastens (or *"disciplines"*), continuing to teach and train in many ways through every season of life. He is the Master Designer who continues working, sculpting, building, and growing us according to His perfect design based on the Person of Jesus Christ, the *"Image"* He delights in and desires to see in each of us (Genesis 1:26–27; Romans 8:29; Ephesians 2:10; 4:13).

DID YOU KNOW?
The Son of David

The title *"Son of David"* is used of Jesus 25 times in the New Testament. In Revelation 22:16, Jesus Himself stated, *"I am the root and the offspring of David,"* pointing to His eternality as the Creator of all and to His humanity as a Man coming as *"the son of David"* through the womb of Mary. Jesus the Messiah was called or referred to as the *"Son of David"* or similar 25 times in the New Testament: Matthew 1:1; 9:27;

12:3, 23; 15:22; 20:30, 31; 21:9, 15; 22:42, 43, 45; Mark 10:47, 48; 12:35; Luke 1:32; 3:31; 18:38, 39; 20:41; John 7:42; Romans 1:3; 2 Timothy 2:8; Revelation 5:5; 22:16.

Forgiveness is real. Scripture makes it clear that God is holy, and sin must be dealt with through a righteous penalty and payment, a death approved of by Him. That occurred in Jesus, God's *"only begotten Son"* (John 3:16). Jesus told His disciples to spread the message of His *"forgiveness of sins"* through His death and resurrection. Peter delivered this message to the eager crowd on Pentecost Sunday, and thousands responded in repentance and faith in Jesus as their Lord, Messiah, and Savior. That message spread across the land, from Jerusalem into Judea, Samaria, and then began traveling to *"the end of the earth"* (Acts 1:8, ESV).

God used many people through the ages. David served as one link in God's chain of redemption. Through David's greater Son, Jesus Christ, *"the Son of David,"* salvation came. Acts 13:36 states, *"David...served the purpose of God in his generation"* and then died. The word *"served"* in this verse is a translation of the Greek word *huperetes* (Strong's #5256), literally translated "served as an under rower" referring to the servants who rowed the ancient Roman and Greek ships. There was no one lower than these "under rowers." Though the contrast between king and servant is clear, David had a servant's heart and faithfully served the Lord and His purposes above those of himself.

TAKEAWAYS—
The First Half of David's Reign as King

There are *seven* takeaways from *The First Half of David's Reign as King.*

1) Never stop trusting God and never stop praying.
2) Follow God's leading through His Word and His Spirit.
3) Trust God's Timing.
4) Remember with gratitude those who have walked with you on the journey.
5) Keep on looking to the Lord for Wisdom and Strength—through prayer, through God's Word, through wise people.
6) Always stay on guard against temptation, sin, and evil from any direction.
7) Stay grateful for God's mercy, grace, love, and forgiveness and stay humble, living as His servant throughout life.

Lord, thank You for the true picture You give of David in Your Word. He was not perfect, erring in many ways, but most of the time he sought You and served faithfully as king. Thank You for forgiving Him, though his sins brought much hurt and harm to many, like mine and every other person's sins have done over the years. Thank You for not giving up on Your purposes, Your people, on David, or on me. May I be a faithful "under rower" as he was, serving Your purposes in my generation. In the name of Jesus, our faithful *"Son of David"* and Savior, Amen.

LESSON 4

THE SHEPHERD KING IN NEW PASTURES

CHALLENGES OF REIGNING IN THE PRESENT AND PREPARING FOR THE FUTURE

Around the time David turned 50 years of age, he had added Bathsheba to his list of wives, and they soon had a son named Solomon. David was walking in some new pastures, living in the aftermath of both his victorious conquests and his deceptive days. Solomon was a young child; many of David's other children were now young adults. Israel had become well-established as a stable nation, and the day-to-day tasks of reigning were being carried out. These things being true did not mean there were no ongoing challenges.

David faced the challenges of his various children, some of which we will explore in greater detail. David was still learning what it meant to know the Lord as his shepherd, and then, in turn, to shepherd his family and the nation. David knew successes and failures, and these became apparent in this season of his life over the next two decades. The Lord had more to teach him, more to reveal, more for him to do. How would David respond?

How are we to respond to the challenges each of us faces... in knowing how to follow the Lord, in dealing with our personal lives, in interacting with and leading our families, in fulfilling our responsibilities in our employment, or in handling various situations, including financial challenges, health issues, and relationship matters? David faced all these things and more. What can we learn from him? What does God have to teach us through His Word?

Walking through these years of David's life will help us get a better perspective on our lives whatever the season or situation. David did some things wrong, some things right, and some things differently than you or I would have done them. God still worked in and through him. He will do the same in your life, in my life, in various lives of those around us. Ask the Lord to make you sensitive to His still, small voice as we walk together through these days of David.

IN THEIR SHOES
David's Family

David had at least seven wives and nineteen sons; Amnon was David's first-born son (2 Samuel 3:2–5; 5:13–16; 1 Chronicles 3:1–9; 14:3–7). He also had several daughters, but we only know the name of one, Tamar (2 Samuel 13:1; 1 Chronicles 3:9). Though God had specifically stated that no king of Israel should *"multiply wives,"* David disobeyed, following the prevailing custom of other kings (Deuteronomy 17:17; 2 Samuel 12:11). David had several concubines as well (2 Samuel 16:21–22; 1 Chronicles 3:9).

Day One

Family Matters

David had several wives and several children born by those wives. How did he handle family matters? How did he deal with discipline issues, teaching right and wrong, helping his children see what God had said or done?

📖 David would have been well aware of the words of Moses, especially about daily living and home life. Read Deuteronomy 6:4–9. What counsel did Moses give to God's people in verses 4–5?

📖 Where were these words from God to be, according to Deuteronomy 6:6?

📖 What further application did Moses give as recorded in Deuteronomy 6:7–9?

Just before their entry into Canaan, Moses gave the people *"the commandments, the statutes and the judgments"* God had given him to teach them so that they would obey and prosper in their new home. Their relationship to the Lord their God stood as the foundation for everything. Added to that were the words of God given by Moses. Moses carefully and clearly instructed them that God's words were to be *"on your heart,"* ready at hand and in heart to know and obey.

With the command to love God came the command to teach His words *"diligently"* to their children in all of life— in the house, walking on the road, wherever they might be.

This was for their benefit and blessing. God did not necessarily require a formal teaching time. Rather, He pointed to their daily lifestyle, speaking and teaching from the time one woke up to bedtime at night, rising up, sitting, walking, and lying down; in other words, anytime, all the time.

In addition, these words were to be so close and real that they would be as though written on their hands (touching everything they did) and on their forehead (making a difference in everything they thought about and every direction they looked). The word of God should affect every entry or exit from house or property, every discussion or decision (*"doorposts"* and *"gates"*).

IN THEIR SHOES

Did Solomon Write the *Book of Proverbs?*

The *Book of Proverbs* notes the writing as *"the proverbs of Solomon"* (Proverbs 1:1; 10:1; 25:1). Much discussion and debate has occurred over some of the verses because of different writing styles. It is possible that Solomon included proverbs he heard or read from other sources. What we have in the *Book of Proverbs* presents the wisdom of Solomon and others and how it applies to various situations and relationships. Ultimately, the Spirit of God superintended these words, and they apply to us today—the *"wisdom from above"* versus mere earthly wisdom (James 3:17a; 2 Peter 1:21).

Likely in his mid-50s, David had a large family. What do you discover about his relationship with his young son Solomon, according to Proverbs 4:3?

Based on Proverbs 4:1–2, how did Solomon view the father-son relationship and responsibility?

This could be a record of Solomon quoting his father David. First, what did David teach his son, according to Proverbs 4:4–5?

Solomon remembered some of the things his father David taught him, even in his *"tender"* years. Apparently, he was also very special to his mother Bathsheba, who, although she had other sons, regarded Solomon as unique. Perhaps David had told her of what God had revealed in years past (perhaps when David was in his 40s): God revealed that David would have a son to be named *"Solomon,"* meaning "peaceful" who would be king and build *"a house for My name"* (1 Chronicles 22:8–10). That kind of revelation from the Lord would certainly affect how David and Bathsheba saw this son.

Remembering the times when his father taught him, Solomon revered what David had said as *"sound teaching"* important for gaining *"understanding;"* never *"abandon"* that *"instruction."* When David taught Solomon, he emphasized the *"heart"* firmly holding the truth in order to truly *"live."* This mirrored the word of the Lord from Deuteronomy 6:6—*"these words...shall be on your heart."* It would be vital to get *"wisdom"* and *"understanding,"* and to never *"forget"* the father's instructions or *"turn away"* from them.

📖 What benefits would come to the obedient person, according to Proverbs 4:6, 8, and 9?

📖 What David said affected Solomon. How did Solomon direct his son—what to do, according to Proverbs 4:10–13?

📖 Read Proverbs 4:14–27. What further teaching did Solomon give about what not to do and why?

The person who acquires *"wisdom"* and *"understanding,"* will find those to be like trustworthy guards in life who will *"watch over you."* Not only that, but wisdom and understanding would *"exalt"* one, filling that life with *"honor"* as well as *"grace"* and *"beauty."* To value this teaching would mean a meaningful life, victorious and honored in many ways.

Solomon took to heart the words of his father David. He held fast the words David taught him, and then, in turn, he taught his son about how to live day by day. It would mean a right walk avoiding *"the path of the wicked."* Solomon spoke of staying away from *"evil men."* He is known for his words, *"watch over your heart with all diligence, for from it flow the springs of life,"* echoing both Moses' words in Deuteronomy 6 and David's words in Proverbs 4 (Proverbs 4:23).

📖 What further insights about family do you glean from Psalm 127, which Solomon wrote? Who builds a good house and gives it proper protection, according to verse 1?

📖 Psalm 127 seems to echo some of the thoughts of David about his family and the families of many he knew. Who is the clear focus in verses 1 and 3?

📖 What are some of the potential benefits of one's children, according to Psalm 127:4–5?

A house that will stand must come from God's activity among those in that house, or it will eventually prove empty or vain (not eternally valuable). The Lord is the Builder of lives and homes as well as the protector, giving wisdom for guarding one's life, one's relationships, and one's home. God is the giver of life and the giver of children in a home. Children can be a defense and protection for parents and others as well as for fellow siblings. As one properly guides the children in the home, so those children give wise guidance within the community. David and Solomon knew the reality of these truths, both the successes and failures.

STOP AND APPLY—Proverbs Are Not Promises—The various *"proverbs"* and *"sayings"* given in the *Book of Proverbs* are clear instructions for relationships, for how to view a host of matters, including money, fame, morality, the ways of men and women, even business matters. They are proverbs for living well, not promises that all will go well for the obedient person; there are devious people in this world. Galatians 1:4 speaks of *"this present evil age,"* noting the tenor of the times in any period. We should always follow God and His Word, trusting Him to lead us in His will His way. He promises rewards for faithful obedience and an eternity with Him that is beyond description.

Day Two

Troubles at Home

The Bible does not deal with people based on any measure of their perfection, but on their real-life choices. God made clear from the beginning His will for marriage to be one man and one woman in a covenant relationship for life (Genesis 2:18–25). Jesus Himself affirmed that (Matthew 19:4–6). Many ignored God's direction, including

David. Problems arose. As you walk through these Scriptures, note any warning signs or possible detours needed in your life. Look for ways to walk with God and to help others know Him and walk *with* Him, not against Him or ignoring His Word.

Based on 2 Samuel 13:1–2, what struggle do you see going on in Amnon's mind?

IN THEIR SHOES
David's Relatives

David dealt with many different family dynamics. It is possible that some of David's relatives lived in or near David's residence in Jerusalem. Certain relatives had a negative impact. David's third-born brother Shimeah (or Shammah) had a son Jonadab, who was a *"friend"* with and a cousin of Amnon, David's first-born son (1 Samuel 16:9; 2 Samuel 13:3; 1 Chronicles 2:13). Jonadab gave wicked counsel to Amnon about acting with trickery toward Amnon's half-sister Tamar (2 Samuel 13:4–6). About two years later, Jonadab gave further information about Amnon's death via Absalom's plan (2 Samuel 13:30–33).

Scripture introduces us to David's nephew Jonadab, noted as *"a very shrewd man."* What kind of wicked counsel did he give his cousin Amnon, according to 2 Samuel 13:3–5?

What happened next? Read 2 Samuel 13:6–14 and summarize what occurred.

Amnon changed. What do you discover in 2 Samuel 13:15–18?

📖 Read 2 Samuel 13:19–22. What did Tamar do? How did Absalom respond? How did David respond?

Amnon faced lustful thoughts and wrong intentions toward his beautiful half-sister Tamar. David's nephew Jonadab (son of David's brother Shimeah) was a *"friend"* of Amnon but labeled as *"a very shrewd man."* He gave Amnon wicked counsel to trick Tamar into being alone with him. Amnon followed the plan and raped his half-sister, Tamar. In shame, she went to her brother Absalom's house. David heard what occurred, became angry, but did nothing. Absalom became silent toward Amnon, hating him for what he had done.

📖 What did Tamar's brother Absalom do about Amnon's wickedness and Tamar's grief, according to 2 Samuel 13:23–29?

📖 How did David and his sons respond to the murder of Amnon, according to 2 Samuel 13:30–36?

DID YOU KNOW?
Absalom's Grandfather in Geshur

After the ambush and murder of his half-brother Amnon, Absalom escaped to *Geshur* where his grandfather Talmai ruled as king. Geshur is located just over 100 miles north of Jerusalem, east of the Sea of Galilee. Absalom was the son of David and his wife Maacah, the daughter of Talmai (2 Samuel 3:3). Absalom stayed in Geshur three years.

📖 According to 2 Samuel 13:37–39, what did Absalom do? What was going on in David's mind and heart?

📖 What occurred next, according to 2 Samuel 13:30–39?

Absalom became angry about how Amnon had treated his sister Tamar but said nothing. He waited two years, his anger apparently fuming under the surface. Then, he hatched a plot of revenge. He invited *"all the king's sons"* and his father David to a sheep-shearing event, a time of work and festivity. David would not go lest too many people be *"burdensome,"* but he agreed to Amnon going with all his other sons (Amnon's half-brothers). There, Absalom commanded his servants to murder Amnon when he was *"merry with wine."* After the servants killed Amnon, the king's sons fled the gathering.

David received a report that all his sons had been slain and began to grieve. Jonadab reported that only Amnon had been killed; it was all part of Absalom's revenge over Tamar. When David's sons came into Jerusalem, they, the king, and his servants *"wept very bitterly"* over Amnon's death. Absalom fled to his grandfather's home in Geshur, east of the Sea of Galilee, and stayed three years. While David eventually came to terms with Amnon's death, he continued to long for Absalom.

📖 Joab recognized David's longing for Absalom's return. He convinced a woman of Tekoa to come and talk with the king with the words he gave her. What do you discover in 2 Samuel 14:1–20?

📖 How did David respond, according to 2 Samuel 14:21–22?

📖 Read 2 Samuel 14:23–24. What did Joab do, and how did David respond to these events?

Joab convinced a woman of Tekoa to come to King David with a ruse; she came and told her story. David responded with concern, but soon discovered the issues at hand. He spoke to this woman about her story and suspected Joab's involvement. David agreed to send for Absalom; Joab went north to Geshur and brought Absalom back to Jerusalem, but David refused to see him.

📖 According to 2 Samuel 14:25–33, what did Absalom do in this Jerusalem "exile" of sorts?

DID YOU KNOW?
Fire in the Grain Field

God made it clear that the Israelites were to be careful about fires in any field of crops—barley, wheat, or any other crop (Exodus 22:6). If a fire broke out and consumed any grain, the person responsible for the fire should make restitution for the lost grain. Absalom's order to his servants to burn Joab's barley field was in direct violation of the Word of God given through Moses; there is no mention of him making restitution for the barley that had burned.

Absalom wanted to see his father David, but David never called for him. Absalom waited. After two years, he called for Joab twice and still had no response; then he took matters into his own hands. Absalom ordered his servants to set fire to Joab's barley field. That got Joab's attention, and soon Absalom saw his father David, but all was not well.

STOP AND APPLY—Barley Field Fires?—When Absalom could not get the attention of his father or Joab, he had his servants set fire to Joab's barley field. Scripture was clear; this was illegal and unnecessary, but Absalom did it anyway (see Exodus 22:6). While David and Joab may have been negligent, Absalom's self-centered plan was not the answer. We do not need to take matters into our own hands; Scripture is clear about how to make an appeal or clear up offenses. Don't set fire to any "barley fields," but call on the Lord for His grace and wisdom; follow His lead.

Day Three

David's House and God's House

Around 980 BC, Hiram became king of Tyre. David turned 60 years of age, and Hiram offered to bring cedar trees to build David a new palace. It was a momentous time in David's life, the beginning of his final full decade, age 60-70. God also spoke to him about not building a *"house"* for the Ark and about His promises for David, his descendants, an eternal kingdom, and His care for Israel. David had clear revelation about God's will for him and for Israel. We need to pay attention to the words and faithfulness of God.

📖 What did King Hiram of Tyre do for David, according to 2 Samuel 5:11 (also found in 1 Chronicles 14:1)?

📖 How did David respond to the actions and gifts of King Hiram? Read 2 Samuel 5:11–12 and note your insights.

When Hiram became king of Tyre, he sent cedar trees and many craftsmen in stone and wood to build *"a house for David,"* a new palace. David had lived in Jerusalem for over twenty years and this new *"house"* appears to have been a nicer dwelling than he had for those first years. This new palace helped cement in David's mind his reign as well as God's work in establishing the kingdom of Israel.

One of the great events in David's reign was the placement of the Ark of the Covenant in Jerusalem. First, what do you discover about the days of Saul in 1 Chronicles 13:3b?

When David spoke of bringing the Ark of the Covenant into Jerusalem, he mentioned the situation in the days of Saul, apparently the entire forty years—*"for we did not seek it in the days of Saul."* An overview of Saul's reign shows little to no prayer or seeking God and His will. David's statement appears to confirm this sad reality. David had a different view, praying often and wanting what God could do.

📖 Read 1 Chronicles 13:1–14 along with 2 Samuel 6:1–11. What did David desire to do? What occurred at this time?

📖 What did David do after the death of Uzzah, according to 2 Samuel 6:10?

David and thirty thousand *"chosen men"* went to Kiriath-jearim to the house of Abinadab to bring the Ark of the Covenant to Jerusalem. This seemed *"right in the eyes of all the people."* They placed the Ark on a cart like that of the Philistines many years before. Driving the Ark at the threshing floor of Nacon, the cart became unstable; Uzzah reached out to keep the Ark from falling to the ground. When he did, God struck him dead *"for his irreverence."* What could they do now? God's action frightened David, and he ordered the Ark to be left at the house of Obed-edom. For three months, the Ark stayed at his house and *"the LORD blessed Obed-edom and all his household."* What would David do next?

📖 Read 1 Chronicles 15:1–2. What changed?

📖 What occurred, according to 1 Chronicles 15:3–24?

📖 Summarize the events that occurred next, according to 1 Chronicles 15:25–28 and 2 Samuel 6:12–19.

IN THEIR SHOES
God's Way to Carry the Ark

When David tried to move the Ark of the Covenant on a cart like the Philistines had used over sixty years before, the Lord's anger began to burn. *"For his irreverence"* in touching the Ark, Uzzah died there, even though he was a priest and likely the grandson of Abinadab (2 Samuel 6:6). This frightened David. Why did this happen? God had given very specific details about carrying the Ark of the Covenant, the central item in the Tabernacle that spoke of the heart-to-heart covenant between the LORD and Israel. The Ark was to be carried on the shoulders of certain priests and no one was to touch it (Exodus 25:14; Numbers 4:5–6, 15; 1 Chronicles 15:15).

When all obeyed, everyone rejoiced as the priests carried the Ark into Jerusalem (2 Samuel 6:12–15, 17–19; 1 Chronicles 15:25–28; 16:1–3).

After the display of God's anger near the house of Obed-edom, David and others searched the Scriptures and found the details of how God said to carry the Ark, not on a cart, but on poles on the shoulders of certain priests. David made sure the priests and Levites were cleansed, consecrated, and prepared to move the Ark. With many singers, instruments, and much rejoicing, David, the leaders, and the priests carried the Ark in a procession to Jerusalem and placed it in the Tent David had prepared. It was a glorious and joyous day as David worshiped the Lord in humility, celebrating with offerings and distributing food to all the people, *"a cake of bread and one of dates and one of raisins."* The people rejoiced greatly and then went to their homes. However, this was not the end of the matter of God's dwelling place.

📖 Record your thoughts about David's comments in 2 Samuel 7:2. What did David want to do?

DID YOU KNOW?
What About Tyre?

Where was *Tyre*? It was a coastal city north of Israel (about 35 miles from Mount Carmel) and south of the city of Sidon in the land of Phoenicia on the Mediterranean coast, bordering the Lebanon mountains. Hiram became king of Tyre around 980 BC. One of his first moves was to build *"a house"* or royal residence for David in Jerusalem using local cedar from around Tyre along with offering his best craftsmen. Many see this as a political move seeking Israel's favor. David received this gesture as from the Lord and saw in it His workings to *"exalt"* the kingdom for the sake of Israel, God's covenant people (2 Samuel 5:11–12; 1 Chronicles 14:1–2).

David spoke of his palace in Jerusalem, *"a house of cedar,"* which would have been beautiful, sturdy, and long-lasting. David wanted to build a dwelling for the *"ark of God"* rather than letting it remain *"within tent curtains."*

📖 How did the prophet Nathan respond to David's desires to build a house for *"the ark of God,"* according to 2 Samuel 7:3?

Based on 2 Samuel 7:4–7, how did the Lord respond to Nathan's words to David?

What two questions did God ask David through Nathan?

Apparently, Nathan enthusiastically encouraged David to *"go, do all that is in your mind,"* even declaring *"for the LORD is with you."* God did not share Nathan's mindset or enthusiasm. Instead, He spoke to Nathan that *"same night"* to return to David with different words. The Lord had two questions for David through Nathan: first, about David—*"Are you the one who should build Me a house to dwell in?"* Then, the Lord explained that He had dwelt in a portable tent since Israel's days after fleeing Egypt to that day, over four hundred years. After stating that, He posed the second question: *"Wherever I have gone with all the sons of Israel, did I speak a word with one of the tribes of Israel, which I commanded to shepherd My people Israel, saying, 'Why have you not built Me a house of cedar?'"* The obvious answer is "No," God had never requested or commanded a new dwelling. The Lord had some more important matters to reveal to David.

First, what did God say about David in 2 Samuel 7:8–9?

What did the Lord say about Israel in 2 Samuel 7:10–11a?

DID YOU KNOW?

Five Covenants

The Davidic Covenant (2 Samuel 7:5–17; 1 Chronicles 17:4–15) is one of *Five* major covenants in Scripture. The first, the Noahic Covenant (Genesis 9:8–17), is followed by the Abrahamic Covenant (Genesis 15:1–21; see also 12:1–3; 13:14–17; 17:1–8; 18:9–14; 22:15–18). The Sinai Covenant in Exodus 19:3–8; 20:3–17, 22–26; 21:1—23:33; 24:1–8; 31:12–18 includes the Priestly Covenant or Priestly Regulations (Numbers 3:1–18; 18:1–20; 25:10–13). The Davidic Covenant is fulfilled in the birth and reign of Messiah Jesus (Luke 1:32–33, et al). God promised the New Covenant (Jeremiah 31:31–34), fulfilled in the life, death, resurrection, and eternal enthronement of Jesus Christ (Messiah), our Lord, Savior, and High Priest (Matthew 26:26–29; Hebrews 7:18–22; 8:1–13; 9:1–28; 10:1–18) *and* in the birth and growth of the Church (Acts 2, et al) made up of born-from-Above believers (John 1:12; 3:3–8, 16; 14–17, et al).

"The LORD of hosts" focused first on David, reminding him that He is the one who took him from keeping his father's sheep to become *"ruler over My people Israel."* In addition, God spoke of being *"with"* David *"wherever"* he had gone. That would have included all the places David hid in running from Saul as well as the places he traveled as king conquering nations surrounding the land of Israel. God is the one ultimately responsible for giving David his victories—He had *"cut off all your enemies before you."* Now, God promised, *"I will make you a great name, like the names of the great men who are on the earth."*

After reminding David of His work and affirming him in his office as king, the Lord spoke of His promises for *"My people Israel,"* assuring He would *"appoint a place"* as well as *"plant them"* securely in that place. Not only that, He would also give them peace, a *"rest from all your enemies."* God would not forget His covenant promises to Abraham. The Lord had more to give and to say.

Day Four

God's Promises and David's Prayer

After David heard from the prophet Nathan all that God had revealed, he took time to talk to the Lord. What God had revealed was heart-touching and mind-boggling. This was no ordinary cluster of promises, nor did it mean an ordinary conversation. God's promises affected everything—David's present, his future, his family, the people of Israel, even the world and eternity. We can learn and apply some things to our lives as well. Read carefully and prayerfully.

Read 2 Samuel 7:11b–12. What did the Lord promise about David's *"house"* or family line?

What did the Lord reveal about an actual *"house"* or dwelling place in 2 Samuel 7:13a?

Other matters were attached to what the Lord promised David. What did He speak about in 2 Samuel 7:12b and verse 13b?

God promised David that He would *"make a house for you,"* indicating that his family line would remain strong and secure. His descendants would rule in the kingdom established by the Lord Himself. This would apply first to his immediate descendant after him. In addition, this son who would be the next king would *"build a house for My name,"* an actual building for the Ark of the Covenant.

God's plans went beyond David's plans or thoughts. God promised that the kingdom of David's son would be established by the Lord, but more than that, He would *"establish the throne of his kingdom forever."* This kingdom would go beyond his son, even past many descendants; it would be *"forever."* This was no ordinary kingdom; God began talking about an eternal kingdom, something beyond comprehension.

WORD STUDY
"House"

In David's prayer, seven times he used the Hebrew word *bayith* (Strong's #1004), translated *"house"* or *"family,"* referring to his lineage or dynasty (2 Samuel 7:18, 19, 25, 26, 27, 29 [2x]). He was thankful and trustful for what God promised for the present and into eternity. His son Solomon used that same word when he penned Psalm 127:1a, *"unless the LORD builds the house, they labor in vain who build it."*

📖 That was not all God had in mind. He had some practical concerns about the next king in David's line. Read 2 Samuel 7:14–15. What did God promise to do with this next king?

📖 God made clear to David that He would secure David's kingdom. What do you discover in 2 Samuel 7:16? What *three* descriptive terms does God refer to in this verse and what did He promise?

God saw His relationship to the next king as personal; He would *"be a father to him and he will be a son to Me."* In this Father-son relationship, God would train him, including chastening him for his wrongs, sometimes using others to deal with him. *"When he commits iniquity, I will correct him with the rod of men and the strokes of the sons of men."* God would treat this relationship seriously and personally. He also spoke in light of His great love; His mercy or lovingkindness would be constant, promising to never take that from David's son as He had taken away His Spirit and the kingdom from Saul.

The Lord spoke of David's lineage and legacy as 1) his *"house,"* 2) his *"kingdom,"* and 3) his *"throne."* Each name referred to a present reality as well as an eternal relationship between God and David's *"house."* These three terms pointed to the people related to David, their future position of reigning, and the power they would exercise. God would guarantee this *"kingdom,"* promising that it would *"endure before Me forever."* That went beyond any earthly vision, any group's plans, or any man's ability. Nathan and David likely were in awe of this revelation.

DID YOU KNOW?
Remembering the Davidic Covenant

Several times Scripture makes mention of *God's covenant promises to David*. The prophet Nathan *spoke* these (2 Samuel 7:8–17; 1 Chronicles 17:7–15). David *prayed* based on those promises (2 Samuel 7:18–29; 1 Chronicles 17:16–27). David *told* those promises to Solomon (1 Chronicles 22:9–10, 12–13; 28:6b–9) who spoke of them at the *Dedication* of the Temple (2 Chronicles 6:10, 16–17). God reminded him of His promises at the *Feast* celebrating the new Temple (2 Chronicles 7:17–18). King Abijah (of Judah) reminded King Jeroboam (of Israel) of the *Davidic covenant* (2 Chronicles 13:4–5). The Chronicler noted *God's covenant promises* in 2 Chronicles 21:7. David as a *"lamp"* carrying the promises is recalled in 2 Samuel 21:17; 1 Kings 11:36; 15:4–5; and 2 Kings 8:19. The Angel Gabriel told Mary the *Messiah Jesus* would reign on the *"throne of His father David"* in a forever *"kingdom"* (Luke 1:32–33).

STOP AND APPLY—God Keeps His Word—Just as David trusted and prayed God's word to him about himself, his kingdom, and his family, including an eternal kingdom, so we can trust God (2 Samuel 7:25–29; 1 Chronicles 17:23, 25–26). Using the Hebrew idea of the number seven pointing to perfection, David penned Psalm 12 in which he declared, *"The words of the LORD are pure words; as silver tried in a furnace on earth, refined seven times. You, O LORD, will keep them..."* (Psalm 12:6–7a). There is nothing purer and nothing surer than God's words. David heard God's promises and prayed according to them. You and I can trust God and pray His Word as we journey through life following Him.

📖 What attitude do you find in David in 2 Samuel 7:18? What two matters did David focus on?

📖 Read 2 Samuel 7:19–22. What was David concerned with as reflected in these verses?

What did David say about himself? About the Lord?

As David *"went in"* before the Lord, he appears to have sat in reverence and awe. Looking at himself and his family, he humbly asked, *"who am I, O Lord GOD?"* He also asked, *"what is my house?"* pointing to the many ways God had worked to bring him *"this far."* David realized that God had been working in his life and in his family, but now was promising far more than David could imagine or comprehend. It also appears that David was not sure about what to say, but he quickly acknowledged to the Lord, *"You know Your servant, O Lord GOD."* The heart for God he had as a shepherd boy still comes through in his words as the shepherd king.

DID YOU KNOW?
Postures in Prayer

Second Samuel 7:18 states that David *"went in"* and *"sat before the LORD"* in a time of worship, reverence, and awe. Daniel prayed three times daily, *"kneeling on his knees"* at *"windows open toward Jerusalem"* (Daniel 6:10). Ezra prayed *"on my knees and stretched out my hands to the LORD my God"* (Ezra 9:5). Luke 18:11 points to a Pharisee standing, praying, whereas a *"tax-gatherer"* stood at a distance *"beating his breast"* as *"the sinner"* seeking God's mercy, *"unwilling to lift his eyes to heaven"* (18:13). Jesus often stood *"lifting His eyes to heaven"* as He did before feeding the 5000 (Matthew 14:19), at Lazarus' tomb (John 11:41), and on His way to Gethsemane (John 17:1). During His prayer time in Gethsemane, Jesus *"fell on His face and prayed"* (Matthew 26:39). What posture should we have in prayer? That which expresses the heart (and sometimes that which will better direct the heart in humility and love).

It is worth noting that when praying, David used the Hebrew words *Adonai Yahweh* seven times. Translated *"Lord GOD"* or *"Sovereign LORD,"* David focused on the Lord as the Ruler and the personal covenant God (7:18, 19 [2x], 20, 22, 28, 29). David praised God for His *"greatness"* in making this revelation and these promises to him; he also spoke of God as *"great"* in that there was *"none like"* Him and none *"besides"* Him.

📖 What did David note in 2 Samuel 7:23?

📖 Perhaps David recalled Deuteronomy 4:32–39. Read that account and summarize what Moses said about the Lord and Israel.

📖 According to 2 Samuel 7:24, what conclusions did David make as he thought about God's historic works?

David noted that it was God who initiated the relationship with Israel; He *"went to redeem for Himself"* the people of Israel and *"to make a name for Himself."* David's words are very similar to what Deuteronomy records. Just before the people entered Canaan, Moses recounted Israel's relationship with the Lord. He looked back to Creation and then forward to when the LORD took the nation of Israel out of Egypt. Like David, Moses stated, *"there is no other besides Him."* God revealed *"His great power"* out of His great love for Israel and their fathers. David could have prayed what Moses said, *"know therefore today, and take it to your heart, that the LORD, He is God in heaven above and on the earth below; there is no other"* (see Deuteronomy 4:32–39). David focused on how God *"established"* for Himself the people of Israel *"as Your own people forever"* and the Lord as *"their God."*

📖 In 2 Samuel 7:25, David began focusing on praying for the fulfillment of all God had said. Read and summarize 2 Samuel 7:25–27. What is the basis of David's prayer here?

📖 What three specific things did David state in 2 Samuel 7:28?

📖 What specific insights do you see in David's request for *"blessing"* in 2 Samuel 7:29? Note any other insights in David's prayer in verses 28–29.

IN THEIR SHOES

"Your Servant"

In his prayer, after God revealed His covenant promises to David about his *"house"* and his *"kingdom,"* David referred to himself as God's *"servant"* ten times using the Hebrew word *ebed* (Strong's #5650) (2 Samuel 7: 19, 20, 21, 25, 26, 27(2x), 28, 29(2x)). The Septuagint (LXX) (Old Testament Greek translation) uses the Greek noun *doulos*, referring to a slave or servant; in Acts 13:36, the Apostle Paul uses the Greek verb *hupereteo* (Strong's #5256) translated *"served."* He spoke of David serving *"the purpose of God in his generation."* The noun form *huperetes* referred to an "under rower" serving in a Greek or Roman ship, the lowest of servants. Each word reveals David's servant's heart, his humble attitude as the Lord's servant.

David based his prayer in verses 25–29 on *"the word"* God spoke to him. He asked God to *"do as You have spoken"* so that the name of *"the LORD of Hosts"* might be *"magnified forever"* and that the *"house"* of His *"servant"* David might be *"established before You."* It is noteworthy that years before David also spoke of *"the LORD of Hosts"* when he faced and defeated Goliath (1 Samuel 17:45). In this current prayer, David acknowledged it was *"the LORD of Hosts"* who *"made a revelation,"* literally, "uncovered the ear" of His servant concerning building his *"house."*

David zeroed in on three factors: 1) The Lord God is God, 2) His words are true, and 3) He has communicated His promises. Because God is God and His words *"are truth,"* He and His words are trustworthy. When God revealed and *"promised this good thing,"* certainty and encouragement filled David's heart. The phrase *"this good thing"* was sometimes used as a covenant term. These words to David were far more significant than simple information or good counsel. Just as David took seriously his covenant relationship with Jonathan and his descendants such as Mephibosheth, so David knew that God's promise here was to be taken seriously for himself and his descendants.

One of the marks of covenants in the Old Testament are God's blessing, His supernatural activity. Tom Elliff has spoken of the "blessing" of God, meaning receiving more supernaturally than is naturally possible.1 For David, because the Lord had given him covenant promises, he sought God's "blessing" for his "house." Two times David prayed for God's "blessing" to be applied "forever," seeking God's activity of supernatural blessing for David then and for the generations to come, even into eternity.

---

1. See Thomas D. Elliff, *Praying for Others* (Nashville: Broadman Press, 1979), p. 79.

STOP AND APPLY—Praying for Blessings—When Jacob *"blessed"* Joseph, he spoke of Ephraim and Manasseh growing into a *"multitude"* (Genesis 48:15–20). In other words, he desired God's work in them—that they do more supernaturally than is naturally possible. After Jesus *"blessed"* the five loaves and two fish, He fed five thousand men plus women and children (Matthew 14:19–21). What could God do with Spirit-led, Word-based prayers for His blessing?

Day Five

Following My Shepherd

New pastures can mean new adventures. David certainly found out this truth. That did not mean his problems or temptations were over. It meant he had to continually look to and follow the Lord as his shepherd, to lead him, to give him wisdom, and to do things David could never accomplish on his own. We can learn much from David and the way he faced these days. Ask the Lord to give you His Wisdom as you ponder the Scriptures in today's Scripture Adventure.

📖 *"A Heart for God"*—That is what we read about David in his youth. That mindset—or "heart-set"—did not go away. Yes, David stumbled some of the time. At times, he rebelled against the Lord and went his own selfish, stubborn way, but he came back to the Lord, to focus on Him and His will His way. Look at these verses, what David said or did or thought at various ages and stages in his life. Note your insights.

2 Samuel 8:11–12 (possibly age 43–44?)

2 Samuel 21:1, 3 (probably age 45–47?)

2 Samuel 12:18–23 (possibly age 50?)

Psalm 51:1–10 (around age 50)

2 Samuel 5:12 (also in 1 Chronicles 14:2) (probably age 60)

1 Chronicles 13:2–5 (possibly age 63?)

Decade after decade in David's life, Scripture affirms that David looked to the Lord and considered his victories and wise steps to be from the Lord. He continued to have a heart sensitive to the Lord, though he turned away from God and His word for a very brief season. After his horrendous, sinful choices about Bathsheba and Uriah, David responded to the truth spoken to him by the prophet Nathan and sought the Lord anew. After Hiram built David his new palace, David knew it was the Lord who had *"established him"* as king and had *"exalted his kingdom"* for the sake of His covenant people Israel. While far from perfect or sinless in his life and reign, even in his 60s, David does not seem to have any sense of "I have arrived," but a sense of dependence on the Lord and the desire to follow and obey Him.

A Heart *Toward* the Lord. Think about David from his earliest days tending sheep in the open fields around Bethlehem. He had a *"heart for God"* then. He kept that heart for the most part. How? In many ways, his heart was tuned *toward* the LORD. David wrote Psalm 19 in which we see his observations and his prayer for a heart tuned to the Lord.

DID YOU KNOW?
"The Stars Also"

Genesis 1:16 notes that God created ***"the stars also."*** Analysts report that there may be as many as two trillion galaxies with around 100 billion (or more) stars in each. There are many stars! God knows each star by name and where each is located (all of them), something no scientist or group or institute can do to this day (see Psalm 8:1, 3-4; 147:3-4; Isaiah 40:26). On a clear night, David could have seen several thousand stars. There were far more, but it was enough for him to be in awe of the Creator and worship Him. He praised the LORD, His care, and pondered the place of people, remembering those *"stars, which You have set in place"* [Psalm 8:3b; see 8:4 also (ESV)].

📖 Read Psalm 19:1–14 and consider the following questions...

David observed the bright sunny days and the night skies for years. Reread Psalm 19:1–6. Note verse 1. What are some ways *"the heavens"* could tell about *"the glory of God"?* Record your conclusions.

What story do verses 2–6 tell?

The created sun, moon, and stars speak of the Lord. He also speaks through His Word. How is the Word described in Psalm 19:7–9? Note the six different descriptions of the Scripture, their character and what they do.

What further word pictures and exhortations do you find in Psalm 19:10–11?

In what ways could David's prayer in Psalm 19:12–14 help him (or you or me) stay more tuned *toward* the Lord?

The Lord's Heart. Jesus is the greater Son of David, and He is God. What did *He* say about hearing and obeying *His* words? Read Matthew 7:24–27. What are the two foundations given by Jesus?

What are the two responses of people to Jesus' words? How did Jesus describe the two different individuals based on their response to His words?

What occurs to both kinds of houses? What different results came to each house?

Jesus spoke of two foundations: rock or sand. He noted that both kinds of individuals heard his words, but the response of each was different. Therefore, each experienced a different result, and each was labeled differently. One is considered *"wise"* because he acted upon or obeyed Jesus' words and the other who did not obey is labeled *"a foolish man."* Note that the storm is the same for both—*"the rain descended, and the floods came, and the winds blew, and burst against that house."* The building materials, appearance, and workmanship of each house could have been the same, but each had a different foundation. The one who obeyed was like one who built his house *"upon the rock;"* that house *"did not fall."* The disobedient man, and thus *"foolish,"* was like one who *"built his house upon the sand;"* that house *"fell, and great was its fall."* Hearing and obeying matter. It's a matter of life and death, of construction versus destruction.

TAKEAWAYS—
The Shepherd King in New Pastures

1) Life issues and Family continue to matter, even after tragedies strike.
2) Wrongs between family members (or any people) need to be dealt with God's way, not ignored.
3) Personal Vengeance is never the answer to an offense.
4) God does not change. Keep focusing on Him.
5) The Heart matters all life long, so matters of the Heart must be primary.

Lord, David received many blessings, and he faced many challenges. The same can be said of my life. I ask that You bless me most of all with a heart tuned to You. May I grow in having a *"heart for God,"* experiencing the many facets of Your character and Your will, realizing more about the many ways You work. Like David, may I continually humble myself under Your Mighty Hand, listen carefully to and learn more fully from You and Your all-sufficient Word. May I seek Your will and ways day by day, whatever the blessing or challenge that comes. In the Name of Jesus, our Savior and the ever-amazing *"Shepherd of our souls."* Amen.

Lesson 5

The Final Season

THE LEADERSHIP AND LEGACY OF KING DAVID

David lived until age 70, dying around 970 BC. David became king of Judah at the age of 30, reigning for forty years, 1010-970 BC. He did not have a perfect reign, but he remained faithful to the Lord for most of those years. God continually dealt with him about wrongs and guided him in the challenges he faced. God's purposes moved forward. David knew some of those, was amazed at some of what God revealed to him, and stayed perplexed about some matters, some things left unanswered.

Intrigue filled the last decade of his reign (980-970 BC). What occurred during these days reveals his heart for God, some of his failures, his humble attitude, and his strong leadership skills, all part of his life as "The Shepherd King." He dealt with matters at hand, and he made preparations for the coming days.

What can we learn from David in his final season as king, from about age 60 to age 70? We have seen some of what occurred, but God was not finished with David or his reign over Israel. The Lord continued to work, to give David guidance, and to place before him faith-challenges that required him to seek the Lord, to pray, search His Word, and deal with all kinds of people. The same can be said of us in our days.

We, too, need God's guidance, wisdom, and perspective. We need to know both "what now?" and "what next?" Also, we need to grasp "what not?"—what to stop or walk away from or throw away. In addition, we face "what's new?" What new things is God establishing, what new people is He working in or working through. He will always be true to His character and His Word, but He will often be very creative in how He deals with day-to-day matters, whom He uses, or how He fulfills His purposes in each generation. This is certainly seen in David's generation and thereafter.

Every person has some sort of challenge to deal with, no matter what age or stage of life, no matter what nation or location on planet earth. What can we learn from David? What is God saying to him that could easily be said to one of us? David shows us that people are people no matter what area or era they live in. Many of the things David learned then, we need to learn today. As David did long ago, we, too, need to look up, listen up, and follow closely. Remember, God remains the same, unchanging in His purposes and in His faithfulness. His Word is true; He never lies, and we are never not needy.

IN THEIR SHOES

David's New Palace

David lived in royal housing during his reign, but around 980 BC, Hiram became king of Tyre. Likely in an effort to properly align himself and his nation with David and Israel, Hiram offered to bring cedar timbers and skilled workers to Jerusalem to build David a palace. What was it like? The beautiful cedar wood would be resistant to rot or insect infestation. Doubtless, it was palatial, large enough to house David and his large family, along with several officials and servants needed in taking care of palace meals, household matters, as well as meetings with officials from Israel and other nations.

Day One

"...Absalom, O, Absalom..."

After the building of David's palace, relocating the Ark of the Covenant into Jerusalem, and his receiving the promises of God about the future, David's kingship hit rocky waters. Things were hectic in David's household; he had failed to deal with the wrongs of many of his children. Even though they were young adults, there were still wrongs that needed dealing with, and David failed to address those. Eventually, Absalom's coup occurred as a result.

At age 31, Absalom was still fuming about all that had occurred involving his sister Tamar, plus his many years of self-imposed exile, and his father David's responses. Absalom's anger soon became evident; he had more self-made plans. They were not plans revealed by God nor from God; they were out of his own selfish ambition and pride, and they were against his father David, now approximately 64 years old. We can learn from Absalom and David. How they responded or reacted reveals much for us to consider, some to avoid and some to receive and apply.

IN THEIR SHOES

Absalom's Chariots and Runners

After Absalom returned to Jerusalem and his father David indicated his forgiveness and acceptance, as a king's son he had access to several privileges including chariots and men to run before him like soldiers escorting him (1 Samuel 8:11; 2 Samuel 15:1). Most would not see this as unusual.

What do you discover in 2 Samuel 15:1-6? How did Absalom steal away *"the hearts of the men of Israel"*?

What did Absalom do to plot his enthronement? Read 2 Samuel 15:7–14, summarizing what Absalom did and the events that occurred.

Day after day, Absalom began to turn the hearts of the people of Israel toward himself. As people came to Jerusalem to have their concerns settled, he stood at the city gates and spoke to them of the need for each concern to be heard. More and more people became attracted to him, even wanting him as their leader.

Even with his father's forgiveness and acceptance, Absalom (age 31) still acted in an independent way. He began maneuvering to become king, perhaps desiring to live in the "new" palace. Unaware of Absalom's scheme, two hundred leading men of Judah accepted his invitation to join him in Hebron, Absalom's birthplace and the location where David began his kingship. When all arrived in Hebron, Absalom's plans began to come together. He even sent *"spies"* into the twelve tribal regions to ready people to accept him as the new king. Someone ran back to Jerusalem and informed David that Absalom had turned the hearts of many to himself. David prepared to escape the city lest warfare there destroy him and all he had done.

DID YOU KNOW?

Cherethites, Pelethites, and Gittites

When David escaped Jerusalem, the six hundred men who had followed him for several years stayed with him. Many of these were foreigners, including the Cherethites, possibly from Crete, the Pelethites, and the Gittites, Philistines from Gitti near Gath. Ittai, one of the Gittites, led them, remaining loyal to David throughout the ordeal caused by Absalom. Later, during David's exile, Ittai was leader of one-third of David's army (2 Samuel 18:2).

Based on the account in 2 Samuel 15:15–18, who joined David in escaping Jerusalem?

What do you learn about Ittai the Gittite in 2 Samuel 15:19–22?

David had reigned for 34 years, and many remained loyal to David during Absalom's attempt to become king. David's servants in Jerusalem pledged their loyalty no matter what occurred. This included the six hundred men who had followed him for several years and stood by him as his fighting force. The Gittites (Philistines) led by Ittai were part of that force. Though from Philistia, it appears that Ittai had turned to the Lord as his God; when he pledged his loyalty to David, he stated his choice with a faith statement, *"as the LORD lives."*

IN THEIR SHOES
David's Heart for God

When David fled Jerusalem during Absalom's coup, he continued to show his heart for God and surrender to His will. He told Zadok the priest, *"If I find favor in the sight of the LORD, then He will bring me back again...But if He should say thus, 'I have no delight in you,' behold, here I am, let Him do to me as seems good to Him"* (2 Samuel 15:25b–26).

📖 David showed his heart for God, for the priests, and for worship in his response to Zadok and Abiathar. Summarize what you discover in 2 Samuel 15:24–29.

📖 Read 2 Samuel 15:30–37. What further developments occurred?

When Zadok, the Levites, and Abiathar came bringing the Ark of the Covenant out of Jerusalem, David stopped them and ordered them to return for the sake of worship and as a help to him. Their loyalty to him could prove helpful in future days with Absalom in Jerusalem. David revealed his heart, looking to God to restore him to Jerusalem if He would, if it seemed *"good to Him."* He and many others continued the journey out of Jerusalem over the Mount of Olives, weeping as they traveled. David told Hushai to return to Jerusalem to act as a counter-advisor to Ahithophel, who had often wisely advised David. As *"David's friend,"* Hushai would be in league with the priests Zadok and Abiathar to inform David when needed.

DID YOU KNOW?
Psalms 3 and 63

Psalms 3 and 63—The subtitle for Psalm 3 states, "A Psalm of David when he fled from Absalom his son." Some consider Psalm 63 to be penned by David during his time in the wilderness fleeing from Absalom. This possibly refers to the hill country west of the Jordan River before David and those with him crossed the Jordan and went into the city of Mahanaim.

David encountered Mephibosheth's servant Ziba with food supplies for David and those fleeing with him. Seeking to gain for himself, Ziba lied to David about Mephibosheth, and David believed him. Then Shimei, one of the family of Saul, met them and began accusing and cursing David. Instead of defending himself, David spoke of looking to the Lord to take care of him in His way.

📖 What do you discover in 2 Samuel 16:19–23?

📖 What occurred in 2 Samuel 17:1–14? Note your insights about these interactions.

📖 What did Hushai do at this critical juncture, according to 2 Samuel 17:15–16?

📖 What occurred next? Read and summarize 2 Samuel 17:17–22, 24, 27–28?

Ahithophel began advising Absalom when they arrived in Jerusalem. It is very possible that Ahithophel was acting in vengeance against David, since Bathsheba was his granddaughter (2 Samuel 11:3; 23:34). His counsel to strike David could have destroyed David and his household, but Hushai, in his loyalty to David, made sure David knew to cross the Jordan River and escape Absalom's attack. In these interactions, God was working against Absalom and his selfish scheming to be king.

Hushai's warning reached David after Jonathan and Ahimaz, sons of Zadok and Abiathar, went through an intriguing series of events that included hiding like spies in a covered well. David and those with him escaped across the Jordan River and eventually reached the city of Mahanaim in Gilead in the tribal allotment of Ephraim, about forty miles north of Jerusalem.

DID YOU KNOW?
Mahanaim

Where is Mahanaim?—When David fled Jerusalem and Absalom's coup, he and his followers went to *Mahanaim*, a city in Gilead on the east side of the Jordan River, about forty traveling miles north of Jerusalem (2 Samuel 17:24–28; 19:32). It was one of the 48 Levitical cities and served as the capital of Israel for Ish-bosheth during his two years as king of Israel when David was king of Judah (2 Samuel 2:8–10).

Because Absalom and his men did not follow the counsel of Ahithophel, Ahithophel traveled back to his home in Giloh near Hebron. There Ahithophel took his life. Perhaps guilt overtook him, or it could be he realized that because Absalom did not follow his counsel, he would soon face defeat, in which case Ahithophel would have to give David an account for his treason.

Absalom pursued David and those with him, crossing the Jordan River, and camping in Gilead. Several loyal to David, brought supplies of food, drink, and other essentials to David and his followers at Mahanaim.

📖 What did David do in Mahanaim, according to 2 Samuel 18:1–4?

📖 According to 2 Samuel 18:5, what significant order did David give concerning Absalom? Summarize what occurred next, according to 2 Samuel 18:6–8?

📖 What occurred with Absalom, according to 2 Samuel 18:9–17?

📖 There were many reactions to Absalom's death. Read 2 Samuel 18:19–33 and summarize what you find.

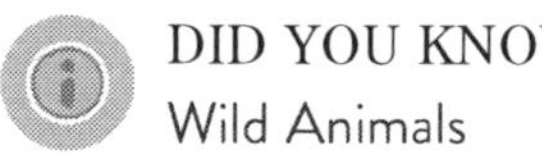

DID YOU KNOW?
Wild Animals

In the battle between David's forces and the Israeli army loyal to Absalom, twenty thousand of the Israeli army died. According to 2 Samuel 18:8, more were *"devoured"* by the wild animals of the forest of Ephraim than by *"the sword"* of David's forces. Animals known to be in the forest at that time included lions and bears.

Apparently, several thousand stood with David. He numbered them and divided his army into three divisions with three commanders, Joab, Abishai, and Ittai, each leading a third. He gave orders not to harm Absalom and sent his army out. In the extensive forest of Ephraim east of the Jordan River, David's forces encountered Israel's army under the command of Amasa, loyal to Absalom. During the fighting, twenty thousand Israelis died, a number by *"the sword"* but even more *"devoured"* by the forest and its wild animals.

Riding his kingly donkey, Absalom became tangled in some tree limbs when the donkey passed under it. Someone told Joab who quickly went and stabbed him with three spears. The soldiers took his body, threw it into a forest pit, and covered it with stones. Two runners rushed to tell David of Absalom's death.

When David heard about Absalom's death, he began to weep and mourn. Those loyal to David felt shame and reproach. Joab then rebuked David for his response and warned him to quickly show his regard for those who fought on his side, saving him and his family from destruction. David did so, then returned to Jerusalem, making Amasa his new army commander, likely seeking to gain the loyalty of Judah at this crucial juncture.

STOP AND APPLY—Which Kind of King?—When we look at David and Absalom, we see *two kinds* of kings. One came from being a shepherd boy and had a humble *"heart for God."* The other came from the palace as a prince and appears to have had a lot of pride and no heart for God. Which kind of king would you rather follow? Which kind of person are you? Consider their lives—neither perfect, but each proven, with clear direction or lack of good direction in life. Pause and pray. Talk to the Lord about these men and about your own attitudes and heart. Follow the Lord as *your* King.

Day Two

Pride Never Rests

Sometime after Absalom's attempted coup, around the age of 65, David settled into reigning as king in Jerusalem, but he still had battles to fight—internal battles from which none of us are immune. How would he handle these days? By the Lord's strength, wisdom, and blessing, David had conquered his enemies all around Israel, to the north, east, south, and west. The land had peace, and the kingdom of David was prospering. How would David and the nation respond to this? What did this mean for David and Israel? What does it mean for you and me?

DID YOU KNOW?
Numbering the Nation

In David's day, nations numbered the men in order to surmise the numbers eligible for warfare, one indication of military might. The census and the calculation of numbers of troops were not wrong in itself, but asking for this census obviously stemmed from feelings of personal or national pride. God hates selfish pride; such pride is at the heart of every sin (Psalm 18:27; 101:5; Proverbs 6:16–17; 21:4; James 4:6; 1 Peter 5:5). Leviticus 26:14–20 speaks of God dealing with sinning and proud Israel. Ezekiel 16:49–50 speaks of the sins of Sodom as rooted in pride or arrogance. Such was the sin of Satan himself when he fell (Isaiah 14:12–14; Ezekiel 28:12–15; 1 Timothy 3:6).

Immediately after returning to Jerusalem, David had to deal with Sheba and his revolt. How is Sheba described in 2 Samuel 20:1?

What did Sheba do, according to 2 Samuel 20:1–2?

According to 2 Samuel 20:6–7, what did David say about Sheba and his revolt? What did he order?

What occurred in the pursuit of Sheba, and who led the pursuit, according to 2 Samuel 20:13–22?

Sheba, one of the Israelites of the tribe of Benjamin, is described as *"a worthless fellow,"* a translation of the Hebrew phrase *ben belial* or "son of Belial," referring to emptiness or worthlessness. He called for the men of Israel to turn away from David. Many began to follow him. David ordered Abishai and *"Joab's men"* to pursue Sheba and deal with him. Joab and his men pursued Sheba to the town of Abel Beth-maacah, where the people eventually cut off his head, effectively bringing the revolt to a sudden end. Joab, who had killed Amasa, returned to Jerusalem.

Apparently, soon after David returned to Jerusalem upon dealing with Sheba's revolt, David organized a census of Israel. What do you discover in 1 Chronicles 21:1–2?

📖 According to 2 Samuel 24:1, what other factor appears to be involved in this situation?

📖 How did Joab and the other army commanders respond to David's orders, according to 1 Chronicles 21:3, 6 and 2 Samuel 24:3–4?

In a mixture of motives and methods, David decided to number Israel. In 1 Chronicles 21:1, we discover that Satan tempted David *"to number Israel,"* apparently a temptation of personal or national pride or perhaps concern over the kingdom that Solomon would eventually govern. It is likely he was seeking to assess what kind of military might Israel possessed. At the same time, we read of the Lord's *"anger"* burning against Israel—both David and Israel were out of line in God's eyes.

David's army chief, Joab, and fellow commanders were against this move, and Joab told David this. Joab even noted that this would be wrong in the Lord's eyes. Joab continued to consider David's command *"abhorrent."* Yet David persisted in his demands. It took nine months and twenty days to complete the census, and at its completion, Joab reported the results to David.

IN THEIR SHOES
God's Chastening

The Scriptures give many instances of the Lord dealing with His people as a father chastening or disciplining His child. David and the nation of Israel experienced chastening over the prideful census (2 Samuel 24:1–25). God's use of chastening as correction is mentioned in Deuteronomy 8:1–6; 2 Samuel 7:14; Psalm 89:30–37; Proverbs 3:11–12; 13:24; 19:18; 22:15; 23:13–14 and 29:15, 17. In the New Testament, Paul speaks of God's chastening in 1 Corinthians 11:28–32. Quoting Proverbs 3:11–12, Hebrews 12:5–11 speaks about God's disciplining His children as part of His love so that each believer might better *"share His holiness"* and experience *"the peaceful fruit of righteousness."*

Second Samuel 24:3–8 and 1 Chronicles 21:4–5 give the details of Joab and his officers as they traveled throughout the land, numbering the people. They discovered over one million men *"who drew the sword"* (eligible as soldiers) in Israel and Judah, not including the men of the tribes of Levi and Benjamin.

📖 How did God view this census, according to 1 Chronicles 21:7?

📖 Based on 2 Samuel 24:10 and 1 Chronicles 21:8, how did David view what he had ordered? What occurred next, according to 2 Samuel 24:11–14 and 1 Chronicles 21:9–13?

📖 What happened after David chose the *"three days pestilence,"* according to 2 Samuel 24:15? How many men died in this pestilence?

📖 What further actions do you discover in 2 Samuel 24:16–17 and 1 Chronicles 21:15–17?

God saw David's actions along with some other offense(s) in the nation of Israel as wrong. He prepared to deal with David and the nation. God sent the prophet Gad to David with three punishment options. David chose the punishment of *"three days pestilence,"* noting that to fall into the hands of God would be better (and hopefully more merciful) than to face the ways of humanity. The pestilence came driven by the Angel of the LORD. Seventy thousand men of Israel died.

📖 Read 2 Samuel 24:18. What remedy did God give through the prophet Gad (also in 1 Chronicles 21:18)? How did David respond, based on what you read in 2 Samuel 24:19–25?

DID YOU KNOW?
The Angel of the LORD

The name *"the Angel of the LORD"* is found in one form or another about thirty-five times in the Old Testament. He is far more than an "angel." Each appearance (or sometimes simply the hearing of His Voice) is a "Christophany"—a manifestation of the pre-incarnate Christ. When He appears or speaks, He reveals Himself as a Warrior fighting for His people and His purposes. He always wins.

What further details do you find in 1 Chronicles 21:19–26a? According to 1 Chronicles 21:26b–27, how did God respond?

What did David declare about this site, according to 1 Chronicles 22:1?

What further information do you discover in 2 Chronicles 3:1? [You may want to read Genesis 22:1–18 for further clarification about this site.]

STOP AND APPLY—Making the Connections—Facing difficulties or perplexing situations in life does not always point to personal sin. It is true that sometimes what we face are the consequences of personal sin or someone else's sin. It is always appropriate to try and make the connections, even to ask the questions: "Have I sinned in some way?" or "Lord, is there something I am not understanding or not aware of in this situation?" By His Word and through His Holy Spirit, He will guide us into the right perspective, either to deal with personal sin, to deal with others' sins, or to simply deal with life on a fallen and cursed earth. For further guidance see the Chart HOW TO DEAL WITH SIN at the end of this Lesson.

DAY THREE

KINGDOM PREPARATIONS AND TEMPLE PREPARATIONS

As David's reign came close to its end, he began preparing for building the Temple. What we read in Scripture describes the preparation of his and the nation's heart as well as the preparation for his son Solomon to take the reins of leadership. In addition, David also began preparing Solomon for building the Temple. At the same time, not everyone was focused on God's designs; some were still seeking to manipulate matters. What David prayed, said, and did give us tracks to run on in following God's will in our lives.

📖 David was in his last days; he planned for his son Solomon to reign as the new sole king. However, another son of David, Adonijah, had his eyes on the throne. What do you discover about Adonijah in 1 Kings 1:5–10? Note those who chose not to follow Adonijah.

As David remained in his declining condition, his son Adonijah desired to be the next king, instead of Solomon. As David's oldest living son (about age 35 or 36), Adonijah's desire would have been seen as natural and expected, but there is no indication Adonijah had sought the Lord about this. David had never *"crossed him at any time,"* never calling him to account for his actions. It seems David let him run free (and perhaps errant). In any case, Adonijah showed his independent spirit, making his own arrangements for becoming king. He sought the aid of both Joab, the infamous military leader, and Abiathar the priest.

Several did not follow Adonijah. These included Zadok the priest, Nathan the prophet, along with David's *"mighty men."* Adonijah pushed forward, inviting his brothers and the men of Judah to En-Rogel for the sacrificing of several animals and a feast at his self-made inaugural gathering. It is noteworthy that he did not invite David's *"mighty men"* nor *"Solomon his brother"* among others.

📖 Read 1 Kings 1:11–31. What allegiance do you find in Nathan and Bathsheba? What did they do about Adonijah's actions?

📖 According to 1 Kings 1:32–37, what counsel did David give concerning the crowning of the next king?

The prophet Nathan spoke to Bathsheba concerning Adonijah's actions to make himself king. Not knowing about this, at Nathan's urging, she went to King David and spoke to him about Adonijah seeking to be king and about the promise of Solomon being king. As planned, Nathan entered and confirmed her words.

David responded to the words of Bathsheba and Nathan, affirming that he had certainly stated that Solomon would be king after him. David ordered, *"call to me Zadok the priest, Nathan the prophet, and Benaiah the son of Jehoiada."* They obeyed; the king then ordered them and his other servants to set Solomon on David's mule and go to the Spring of Gihon there in Jerusalem. There, Zadok and Nathan were to anoint Solomon as king, blow the shofar trumpet and proclaim, *"Long live King Solomon!"* They followed David's orders. This somewhat private ceremony at Gihon Spring gave Solomon the legitimate credentials as king under David's orders. After this, Solomon came from Gihon and sat on David's throne as co-regent with his father David.

DID YOU KNOW?
Who Was Benaiah?

"*Benaiah the son of Jehoida*" first appears as the leader over *"the Cherethites and the Pelethites,"* part of the men loyal to David (2 Samuel 8:18; 15:18). David appointed Benaiah, a warrior renowned for his many exploits *"over his guard"* (personal bodyguard, 2 Samuel 23:20–23). Listed with Zadok the priest and Nathan the prophet in matters pertaining to Solomon's becoming the new king of Israel after David (1 Kings 1:8, 10, 26, 32, 36–37, 38, 44), he became Solomon's chief army commander after the execution of Joab (1 Kings 2:34–35).

📖 What occurred in Jerusalem after David gave orders concerning the crowning of Solomon as the next king? Review 1 Kings 1:38–40 and summarize what happened.

📖 How did Adonijah and those with him respond to the noise of the shofar trumpet and the roar of many people, according to 1 Kings 1:41–50?

📖 Read 1 Kings 1:51–53 and record your insights about the interaction between Adonijah and Solomon.

Zadok, Nathan, Benaiah, all loyal to David, along with the Cherithites and Pelethites, went with Solomon as Solomon rode on the king's mule. At Gihon, Zadok the priest anointed Solomon as the next king. The shofar trumpet sounded, and many people shouted, *"Long live King Solomon!"* When Adonijah and those with him heard the shofar and the great noise along with the news from Jonathan that King David had made Solomon the new king, those with Adonijah became *"terrified"* and left that place. In great fear for his life, Adonijah ran to the altar at the Tent and *"took hold of the horns of the altar,"* seeking to save his life from execution. Solomon responded, willing to let Adonijah live if he would do right going forward, but if he acted in *"wickedness"* he would die. As king, Solomon ordered him to go to his house.

Solomon was in place as co-regent to David his father; several matters needed to be clear in Solomon's mind as David prepared him to be the next king and the one to build the Temple in Jerusalem. David did several things in putting together the labor force and the materials for the upcoming Temple (see 1 Chronicles 22:1–5). Most importantly, David had instructions for Solomon, whom he described as *"young and inexperienced"* (1 Chronicles 22:5a).

📖 Read 1 Chronicles 22:6–13. Summarize the charge of David to his son Solomon concerning the Temple.

📖 According to 1 Chronicles 22:17–19, what did David say to the leaders of Israel and to Solomon?

DID YOU KNOW?

David's Preparations for the Temple

David gathered materials for the construction of the Temple, including stones (plus stonecutters and skilled craftsmen), iron, and bronze (*"more ... than could be weighed"*). He gathered cedar logs like those used for the palace. David also provided *"100,000 talents of gold and 1,000,000 talents of silver"* as well as immeasurable quantities of iron, bronze, timber, and stone. (1 Chronicles 22:2–5, 14–16).

David reminded his son Solomon that he had *"intended to build a house to the name of the LORD my God,"* but God stopped him. He also told Solomon how God promised him that a son would be born to David. (This revelation about a son could have come many years earlier.) This son would reign and be a *"man of rest,"* not a man of war as David had been. God also promised the nation of Israel would be marked by *"peace and quiet"* in his reign. God even gave David the name of this son, "*Solomon*," similar to the Hebrew word *shalom* ("peace"). David charged Solomon that he must build the Temple, "*a house for the* L*ORD God of Israel.*"

David charged and encouraged Solomon, exclaiming "*the* L*ORD be with you that you be successful*" in building the Temple. He made it clear that Solomon must receive "*discretion and understanding*" to do this and must obey the law of God. With this challenge, David gave Solomon words like those God gave Joshua as he was on the verge of conquering Canaan, "*be strong and courageous, do not fear nor be dismayed*" (see Joshua 1:6–9).

David recognized that his son Solomon would need much help and wise advice along with adequate preparation in order to reign and to build the Temple that David described as "*exceedingly magnificent, famous, and glorious.*" David's focus remained on the Lord and worship of Him. He charged those ready to help, "*arise and work, and may the* L*ORD be with you*" (1 Chronicles 22:16). David charged the leaders to focus on the presence of "*the* L*ORD your God,*" pointing to how the Lord had given him and Israel victory throughout the land and in the nations surrounding Israel. This was more than a construction project; it was an honor to the Lord and a way to lead others in worshiping Him.

DID YOU KNOW?

Organizing the Temple Priests

Led by God, David organized the Temple priests, Levites, and other servants (1 Chronicles 23:3–32; 24:3–5, 19, 31), dividing the priests into 24 courses or divisions; sixteen as descendants of Eleazar and eight as descendants of Ithamar. This matched what the Lord had commanded Aaron, "*according to the sons of Levi: Gershon, Kohath, and Merari.*" Some served as "*officers and judges;*" others served as "*gatekeepers.*" Revealing his heart for God, he spoke of the many "*instruments*" he "*made*" "*for giving praise*" and continued to focus everyone on the Lord Himself—"*the* L*ORD God of Israel has given rest to His people, and He dwells in Jerusalem forever*" (1 Chronicles 23:25).

📖 What further instructions do you find in 1 Chronicles 25:1–8?

📖 What do you discover about "*gatekeepers*" (Temple security measures) in 1 Chronicles 26:1, 12–13?

📖 What did David do regarding the Temple *"treasures"* in Jerusalem along with matters outside the confines of Jerusalem, according to 1 Chronicles 26:20, 29–32?

📖 What details did David care for regarding the army and other areas of national concern. Read and summarize what you discover in 1 Chronicles 27:1–34.

In addition to the various priestly and Levitical duties, David and several of his army commanders directed *"the sons of Asaph and of Heman and of Jeduthun"* as musicians in their various functions. There were 288 *"trained in singing to the LORD"* alongside skillful musicians. They served in prophesying *"with lyres, harps, and cymbals"* as well as in other areas as directed by the king, some focusing on *"giving thanks and praising the LORD."* Split into twenty-four divisions, duties were assigned to each person, *"the small as well as the great, the teacher as well as the pupil."* These were assigned based on casting "lots," trusting that the Lord Himself would direct (see Proverbs 16:33).

Three noteworthy men served as spiritual leaders alongside David. Asaph *"prophesied under the direction of the king"* and directed his sons in Temple service. It is noteworthy that the twelve *Psalms* listed as "Psalm[s] of Asaph" could have been authored by him or his descendants or been penned or used under his influence. Jeduthun led his sons in their service in the Temple. Heman served as *"the king's seer"* or prophet. Heman had fourteen sons and three daughters, all of whom *"were under the direction of their father to sing in the house of the LORD"* accompanied by various instruments.

In his reign, David took care of many details. His administration included not only the various upcoming Temple duties, but also the detailed service of the Temple *"gatekeepers,"* as well as assigning some to oversee the various *"treasures of the house of God."*

In addition, using *"capable men,"* David took care of matters in other parts of Israel beyond Jerusalem. Concerning the army, twelve divisions served in Jerusalem, one for each month with twenty-four thousand soldiers in each division. Each tribe had a *"chief officer."* Additionally, David made sure there were supervisors over the storehouses scattered throughout the land, over the farm fields, the vineyards, the olive and sycamore trees, and the livestock.

STOP AND APPLY—Details Matter—David took care of many details in the administration of the nation of Israel, partly focused in his duty to Israel and to God and partly focused in preparation for Solomon's reign. Details matter to God. Hundreds of years later, we read of people giving to Jesus' ministry that included many details (see Luke 8:3; 10:7; Mark 15:41). Paul spoke of supporting those who served in *"spiritual"* matters (1 Corinthians 9:4–11; Galatians 6:6; 1 Timothy 5:17–18). He also made sure that any details were well taken care of, noting *"we have regard for what is honorable"* in God's sight and man's sight (2 Corinthians 8:16–21).

Day Four

Final Days and New Days

The final days of David led to new days for Solomon as the new king. What David did and said to prepare for the days ahead, for the Temple building, and for Solomon to reign are instructive to us for daily life as well as the new days, new challenges, or new opportunities each of us might face. Read carefully and apply as you see application points.

📖 Read 1 Chronicles 28:1–8. Summarize David's address to the various leaders of Israel concerning the building of the Temple.

📖 Upon what main issue did David focus the leaders, according to 1 Chronicles 28:8? What did David say to Solomon in 1 Chronicles 28:9–10?

David gathered leaders from throughout the land to address them concerning the Temple and his son Solomon. Though David desired greatly to build the Temple, God did not accept this desire, stating, *"because you are a man of war and have shed blood."* Of all the sons of David, Solomon was God's choice as king and the one who would build the Temple. David emphasized God's call for Solomon to obey the Lord in order to continue enjoying the good land God had given them.

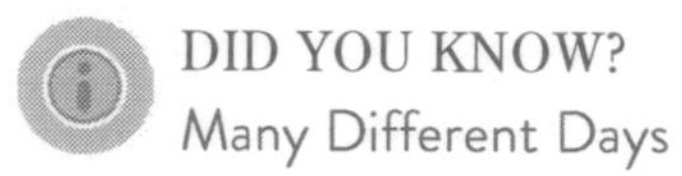

DID YOU KNOW?
Many Different Days

God gave the nation of Israel several different unique days in the yearly calendar with certain offerings for each of the unique days—the weekly Sabbath, each month's new moon, and the Seven Feasts (Passover, Unleavened Bread, First Fruits, Passover, Trumpets, Day of Atonement, Tabernacles), all to be offered as *"before the LORD"*—it was personal. The priests and Levites had specific duties to fulfill in keeping these calendar days and offerings.

David focused Solomon on the Lord, on serving Him *"with a whole heart and a willing mind."* David noted a fact that applies to every age and every person: *"the LORD searches all hearts, and understands every intent of the thoughts."* Solomon needed to know that, as do each of us. How we respond to Him, either seeking Him or forsaking Him, matters now and forever. Knowing there would be many challenges, David urged Solomon to take seriously the task of building the Temple—*"be courageous and act."*

📖 Where did David find the plans for the Temple? Read 1 Chronicles 28:11–19 and note where David found the plans for the Temple and what other instructions he received.

The plans David gave to Solomon came from the Lord Himself. David testified that the Lord *"made* [him] *understand in writing by His hand upon* [him], *all the details of this pattern."* This included all the intricate details of *"the porch..., its buildings, its storehouses, its upper rooms, its inner rooms, and the room for the mercy seat,"* also known as "the Holy of Holies." God also gave David clear plans for the priestly divisions and for the various instruments used in the Temple, including their weight and design.

📖 Read 1 Chronicles 28:20–21. What encouragement did David give Solomon?

📖 What did David say to *"the entire assembly,"* according to 1 Chronicles 29:1–5? According to 1 Chronicles 29:6–9, how did the people respond to David's testimony and challenge?

IN THEIR SHOES
God's Call to Courage

Concerning entering Canaan, Moses commanded Joshua to *"be strong and courageous"* (Deuteronomy 31:7, 23). In calling Joshua to lead, God said, *"be strong and courageous,"* identical to David's words to Solomon about building the Temple (Joshua 1:6, 7, 9, 18; 1 Chronicles 22:13; 28:20). Joshua told the leaders of Israel the same as they continued conquering (Joshua 10:25). *"Courageous"* is a translation of the Hebrew word *amats* (Strong's #553), meaning "to be alert" mentally. God calls us to be alert to Him, His Word and His will, obeying in His strength. This is part of trusting Him.

To Solomon, David's co-regent during the final months of his life, David commanded, *"be strong and courageous, and act; do not fear nor be dismayed."* He could say this because his focus was on the Lord who would be *"with you,"* not failing him or forsaking him at any point. He would lead Solomon to the finish of the *"house of the LORD."* Skilled workers would be ready for *"all kinds of service."* Along with the *"officials"* and *"the people,"* the priests and Levites would be ready for the various services of the newly built Temple.

David focused the people on encouraging his son Solomon as God's choice as king. Though Solomon was *"still young and inexperienced"* facing *"the work that is great,"* David wanted Solomon's goals to be God-centered, not Solomon-centered. Solomon and his subjects needed to know that *"the Temple is not for man, but for the LORD God."* David himself had given much for the Temple in vast amounts of gold and silver, plus bronze, iron, wood, as well as various precious stones.

After David spoke of his offering, the leaders and people *"offered willingly"* much gold, silver, brass, and iron, along with many *"precious stones."* Exuberant rejoicing marked this assembly and the offering; the people and King David *"rejoiced greatly."* David then began to pray and bless the Lord.

📖 Summarize David's prayer in 1 Chronicles 29:10–19—his words to God (10–13), his words about the people (14–15), his words about the offering (16–18), and his words for Solomon (19).

David remained God-focused, blessing *"the LORD"* before all the people. He praised the Lord for His greatness, power, glory, victory, and majesty. The Lord is ever God over all *"the heavens and the earth,"* exalted *"over all"* and the one who provides everything, all *"riches and honor,"* all *"power and might"* and every measure of strength.

David acknowledged that anything and everything they had given had first come from God's hand. All the people, himself included, were *"sojourners before"* God, even *"tenants"* whose lives are like a fleeting *"shadow."* Apart from the Lord, there is *"no hope."* David honestly spoke before the Lord, admitting that God knows the heart of each person, delighting in *"uprightness."* He prayed that God would keep the peoples' hearts focused on the Lord, ever surrendered, and *"willingly"* giving as they were that day.

🕮 Note your insights about David's words to the people in 1 Chronicles 29:20. Based on 1 Chronicles 29:21–22, what occurred the next day? How did the people respond?

David worshiped the Lord. He wanted the same worship in the hearts of the people. Therefore, he called them to *"bless the LORD your God."* They readily did so, bowing before the Lord and paying *"homage"* to the Lord and David their king. On the next day, the priests and people sacrificed many animals as burnt offerings and other sacrificial offerings. With hearts surrendered and their focus on the Lord, their relationship with Him as it should be, they rejoiced in a day of feasting. Everyone *"ate and drank... before the LORD with great gladness."* That day, in a very public ceremony, Solomon was anointed king *"a second time,"* while Zadok was anointed as High Priest. From this point, Solomon further carried out his reign as his father David had directed (see 1 Chronicles 29:22b–25).

WORD STUDY
"Gladness"

According to 1 Chronicles 29:22, David and the people feasted with *"great gladness"* over preparations for building the Temple. *"Gladness"* is a translation of the Hebrew word *simchah* (Strong's #8057), appearing 93 times in the Old Testament. *"Gladness"* marks the presence of God (Psalm 21:6); He desires that for His people (Isaiah 9:3). Moments of *"gladness"* mark the presence of the Lord in the present. Eternity will be marked with *"fullness of joy"* and *"gladness in Your Presence"* (Psalm 16:11; 21:6). *"Gladness"* marked Jesus' life (Hebrews 1:9). New Testament believers experienced *"gladness"* and *"joy"* (Acts 2:46; Galatians 5:22).

STOP AND APPLY—*Your* Focus—Where is *your* focus? On the Lord? On yourself? On others? On your circumstances? David continually focused the people's attention on the Lord; that was one of the marks of his *"heart for God."* What he did and said revealed this in numerous ways. Pause and pray. Evaluate—ask God to show you where you are, what your focus is, ask whether any changes are needed, and ask for any encouragement for today.

📖 What was David's condition in his final days, and how was he cared for, according to 1 Kings 1:1–4?

📖 Note David's final words in 2 Samuel 23:1–7. What four descriptive phrases are used of David in verse 1?

What three designations did David give to God in verses 1 and 3?

How did David describe the rule of a righteous king, according to verse 4?

In his waning days (around age 70), David stayed cold much of the time. His attendants chose Abishag, a young maiden, to care for him in these days.

David had some significant final words for all to hear. The writer of 2 Samuel noted David as *"the son of Jesse,"* a reminder of his simple lineage. David was also the one *"raised on high"* as *"the anointed of the God of Jacob,"* none higher. He was also known as *"the sweet psalmist of Israel,"* pointing to his honest and humble heart, his skill and sensitivity to the Lord as a poet and musician, and perhaps to his being a *"man after His* [God's] *own heart."*

David focused on the Lord, referring to Him as the promise-keeping and gracious *"God of Jacob."* David also identifies God as the *"God of Israel"* and the *"Rock of Israel,"* names denoting His faithfulness and strength. One must follow Him to rule *"righteously"* in *"the fear of God."* That ruler would be refreshing and helpful like the morning sunrise and stable as the covenant-keeping God (2 Samuel 23:4). Any who did not follow Him would be considered *"worthless"* or empty and vain, doomed to judgment (2 Samuel 23:6–7).

David died in Jerusalem, *"in a ripe old age, full of days, riches and honor, and his son Solomon reigned in his place"* (1 Chronicles 29:28). He was *"buried in the city of David,"* Jerusalem (1 Kings 1:10). Life continued in Jerusalem as Solomon consolidated his reign.

DID YOU KNOW?
Adonijah's Request

Adonijah asked Bathsheba to make his request to marry Abishag known to King Solomon, acting presumptuously at best and treasonous at worst. Marrying Abishag, David's nurse in his final years, would have placed him in a position of rulership in most eyes, tantamount to asking to reign as king and thus an act of treason, an offense punishable by death in Solomon's day.

According to 1 Kings 2:13–18, what did Adonijah request of Bathsheba? How did Solomon respond to Adonijah's request, according to 1 Kings 2:22–25?

Using Bathsheba as a go-between, Adonijah requested that David's nurse Abishag be given to him as his wife. This was equivalent to asking to be king since having the king's *"nurse"* would appear as being treated as king. Solomon knew this request from his older half-brother was tantamount to a request to be king. And Adonijah would not stop with this request. More brazen requests like this one would come. Solomon responded with swift justice and ordered Adonijah to be executed, thus establishing himself as the legitimate king.

Scripture reveals many ways in which Solomon continued to consolidate and establish his kingship. According to 1 Kings 2:26–27, what did Solomon order?

How did Solomon's actions toward Abiathar fit in with the prophecy of the *"man of God"* in 1 Samuel 2:30 36? Note that Abiathar was a descendant of Eli. Who served as the High Priest under Solomon, according to 1 Kings 2:35?

Abiathar had sided with Solomon's brother Adonijah and his bid to be the next king. As a result, Solomon ordered Abiathar to return to his village of Anathoth, cutting him off from being a priest. This fulfilled the prophecy given to Eli by an unnamed *"man of God."* After this, Solomon *"appointed Zadok the priest in the place of Abiathar."* Zadok is also mentioned in the anointing ceremony of 1 Chronicles 29:22. He was a descendant of Eleazar, the son of Aaron (1 Chronicles 6:1–8).

DID YOU KNOW?
Zadok's Lineage

Zadok's Lineage and Descendants—Zadok's lineage can be traced back to Aaron (1 Chronicles 6:1–8). His descendants would serve as priests in those days as well as in the Millennial Reign of Christ. Ezekiel 40:46; 43:19; 44:15 and 48:11 mention Zadok's descendants serving in the Millennial Temple.

STOP AND APPLY—Final Words Matter—Often a person's final words are recorded for their uniqueness, seriousness, or even foolishness. David's final words to Solomon are noted throughout history for their grandeur, wisdom, and challenging nature (2 Samuel 23:1–7). Jesus noted that one's words reveal the heart (Mark 7:21). Think about it: what might your final words be?

Day Five

Following My Shepherd

The Lord is always the Good Shepherd and always worthy of following. He is ever able to lead and reveals that throughout Scripture. David discovered this in his life, throughout each year, each decade. In his final years, he continued to trust and follow the Lord, even amid some very challenging days, that included being betrayed by his son Absalom and several others. We may not relate to everything David faced, but each of us has unique challenges that call us to trust the Lord, perhaps in a new way. Look over the questions and verses given below and look to the Lord for the precise applications to your life.

WORD STUDY
"Proud"

"Proud" is a translation of the Hebrew word *ge'eh* or *ge'* (Strong's #1343 or #1341) meaning "arrogant" or "haughty." Both words are rooted in *ga'ah* (Strong's #1342) meaning to rise or exalt. *Ga'ah* is used most often of God who is truly highly exalted, ever right in revealing Himself as the highest. When revealed in a person, pride is usually a sin, a wrongful attitude and action since it most often refers to one's selfish self-effort or self-exaltation. God deals with people's pride.

David knew his share of proud people. "Pride" most often refers to how one thinks highly of self—more highly than is warranted. What does God think of selfish pride? Read the following verses and record your insights about each.

Psalm 39:45 (David wrote this psalm.)

Proverbs 6:16–19

Proverbs 16:18 and 29:23

God honors humility. Read the following verses and note your insights and any applications to daily life.

2 Chronicles 7:14

Psalm 53:23

James 4:10

1 Peter 5:5–7

📖 In the long run, what matters in life? Read the verses below and note what is considered a priority in life. Record your thoughts or insights.

Mark 12:28–31

Luke 10:38–42

Philippians 3:7–14

TAKEAWAYS

David's Final Season

There are four takeaways from David's final season. 1) God's Plans go beyond what we can see, understand, or experience. 2) Rebellion is never the solution. 3) Pride never brings benefits. 4) We need one another; we can never live life alone

Lord, You are greater than all, understanding every thought, motive, and action of all people. You raise up kings and put down kings for Your larger purposes (Daniel 2:21). You raised up David from shepherding a relatively small flock of sheep and made him a great king over a powerful kingdom. In Your sight, what mattered was his heart for You. May I have the same kind of heart. Show me where my heart is failing to focus on You and Your Word as it should. Reveal any pride and show me how best to humble myself in Your sight, under Your hand. In the name of Jesus, our Lord and Savior, Amen.

The Angel of the LORD

Christ Revealing and Accomplishing His Will
The Angel of the LORD is considered a Christophany,
a pre-incarnate appearance of Christ in the Old Testament

Scripture	Event	Place
Genesis 16:1; note verses 7-13	The Angel of the LORD found Hagar and Ishmael in the wilderness running from Sarai's harsh treatment. He delivered them and instructed Hagar to return to Sarai.	Wilderness near Shur
Genesis 17:1–22, note verses 1, 22	"*The LORD appeared to Abram*" in some form when he was ninety-nine years old and promised him a son Isaac. After meeting with him, He "*went up from Abraham*."	By the oaks of Mamre near Hebron
Genesis 18:1–33	The Lord came to the home of Abraham in the form of a Man along with two angels also in the form of men. He spoke to Abraham and Sarah about their coming son Isaac and to Abraham about the coming judgment of Sodom.	By the oaks of Mamre near Hebron
Genesis 21:8–21, note verses 17-19	The Angel of God knew about Hagar and Ishmael and heard Ishmael crying. He spoke to her and provided water for them.	Wilderness of Beersheba
Genesis 22:1–19, note verses 11-19	As Abraham was offering up Isaac on Mount Moriah, the Angel of the LORD stopped him, spoke to him, and gave him many promises.	Mount Moriah (modern Jerusalem)
Genesis 28:10–22; 31:11, 13	The Lord appeared to Jacob in a dream at Bethel promising him the land, many descendants, and a seed through whom the earth would be blessed. This same Lord appeared as the Angel of God twenty years later.	Bethel
Genesis 31:10–13	The Angel of God spoke to Jacob in a dream instructing him to leave Haran and return to Canaan.	Haran

Genesis 32:22–32; Hosea 12:4–5	The Angel of the LORD wrestled all night with Jacob and blessed him at the Jabbok River.	Jabbok River
Genesis 48:3, 16	In Egypt, while blessing the sons of Joseph, Jacob testified before his family of "*the Angel who has redeemed me from all evil*" (NKJV). Only God can redeem. He invoked this "Angel" to "*bless the lads*," something only God could do.	Testimony in Egypt
Exodus 3:1–6, note verse 2; Deuteronomy 33:16; Acts 7:30–36; Mark 12:26; Luke 20:37	The Angel of the LORD appeared to Moses in a flame of fire in the midst of a bush at Mount Horeb in the desert of Midian.	Mount Horeb (also known as Mount Sinai)
Exodus 4:24–26	The Lord met Moses and sought to kill him for failing to circumcise his son. This was possibly the Angel of the LORD.	On the way to Egypt
Exodus 14:19–20; Psalm 78:12–16; Isaiah 63:9	The Angel of God appeared in the Pillars of Cloud and of Fire guiding and protecting the children of Israel from Pharaoh's army.	At the Red Sea
Psalm 78:52–53	The Lord "*led forth His own people like sheep, and guided them in the wilderness like a flock*" (Psalm 78:52).	From Egypt to Canaan
Exodus 19–20; 24:12–18; Acts 7:38	The Angel of the LORD gave the Law to Moses on Mount Sinai.	At Mount Sinai
Exodus 24:1–11	The Lord invited Moses, Aaron, Nadab, Abihu, and the Seventy Elders to come up to Mount Sinai where He spoke and appeared to them. This was possibly the Angel of the LORD whose appearance mirrors that of the Lord in Ezekiel 1:26-28; Daniel 7:9-10, and of Christ in Revelation 4:2-3	At Mount Sinai
Exodus 23:20–23 Acts 7:35–36	Moses received God's promise that He would send the Angel of the LORD to guide Israel into Canaan. "*My name is in Him.*" "*My Angel will go before you.*" (NKJV).	At Mount Sinai

Exodus 32:34 33:1–6, 12–16	The Lord told Moses He would send a representative angel before them, not the Angel of the LORD. He Himself would not go with them because of their sin. Moses interceded and God promised, "*My presence shall go with you.*"	At Mount Sinai
Numbers 22—24, note 22:22-39	On Balaam's journey to meet Balak with the leaders of Moab, the Angel of the LORD met Balaam and his donkey.	The Plains of Moab
Joshua 5:13–15; 6:1–5	A Man, the Commander or "Captain of the Host of the LORD," met Joshua near Jericho and instructed him in how to conquer the city.	Near Jericho in the land of Canaan.
Judges 2:1	The Angel of the LORD rebuked Israel for disobeying Him in not dealing with the Canaanites as He had commanded.	Bochim (means "Weeping")
Judges 5:23	The Angel of the LORD cursed the people of the town of Meroz for not fighting with the people of God against the Lord's enemies in northern Israel.	Meroz
Judges 6:11–24, 25–27	The Angel of the LORD appeared to Gideon calling him to lead Israel against the Midianites.	Ophrah
Judges 13:1–24	The Angel of the LORD, also called "*the Angel of God*" (13:6, 9) appeared to Manoah and his wife promising them a son and then ascended in the flame of their burnt offering.	Zorah
Psalm 35:5-6	David prayed for the help of the Angel of the LORD against an enemy who was against him without cause.	Israel
2 Samuel 14:17, 20	A woman of Tekoa spoke to David about the Angel of God "*discerning good and evil*" and being marked by "*wisdom...to know everything that is in the earth*" (NKJV).	Jerusalem

2 Samuel 24:10–25; 1 Chronicles 21:1–30, note verses 12–20, 27, 30	The Angel of the LORD was involved in judging David's sin of numbering the people (probably to enhance his military might or perhaps out of pride in his military potential).	Israel and Jerusalem
Psalm 34:7 (with 1 Samuel 21:10–15)	David celebrated the protection of the Angel of the LORD in the danger he faced from Abimelech—King Achish of Gath.	Gath, city of the Philistines
1 Kings 19:5, 7	The Angel of the LORD touched Elijah twice, instructing him eat and drink in preparation for the journey ahead.	Wilderness south of Beersheba
2 Kings 1:2–17, note verses 3, 15, 16	The Angel of the LORD instructed Elijah to go and deliver a message to Israel's king Ahaziah.	Samaria
2 Kings 19:35–36; Isaiah 37:36	The Angel of the LORD struck 185,000 Assyrian troops bringing Sennacherib's threats to naught and delivering Hezekiah and the people of Jerusalem.	Near Jerusalem
Daniel 3:19 Daniel 3:19–30, note verse 28	God "*sent His Angel*" and delivered Shadrach, Meshach, and Abed-nego from the fiery furnace. To Nebuchadnezzar this fourth Man in the furnace appeared "*like the Son of God*" (or margin, "a son of the gods") (Note: 3:25, 28-NKJV).	The Plain of Dura in the province of Babylon
Daniel 6:1–28, note verse 22	When rescued from the lion's den, Daniel testified, "*My God sent His angel and shut the lions' mouths...*" That phrase is the same as that found in Daniel 3:28.	The city of Babylon
Zechariah 1:7–17, note verses 11, 12	The Angel of the LORD appeared in Zechariah's first vision as the Commander-in-Chief of the angelic hosts riding on a red horse of judgment seeking to bring mercy and restoration to Israel.	Israel and the Earth

Zechariah 3:1–10, note verses 1–2, 3–4, 6	The Angel of the LORD appeared in Zechariah's fourth vision rebuking Satan and declaring Jerusalem and the nation (represented by Joshua the High Priest) as the cleansed and restored people and priesthood of God. With that is the promise of the coming Messiah (Servant, Branch, Stone).	Israel
Zechariah 12:8	Zechariah prophesied about the future of Israel when the nation will be strong like David or like a nation with the Angel of the LORD leading them.	Jerusalem and the area surrounding it

How to Deal with Sin

Dealing with Your Personal Sin

God is Faithful to Convict. As you read the Word of God, study with a small group, or listen to a message being preached or taught, God will often convict of some sin. He wants us to come to Him, agree with Him about the sin, agree to turn from that sin, agree to turn to what is right in that area or in that relationship, and by faith receive His forgiveness and cleansing for that sin (1 John 1:5–9).

Ask God. If you think there is a fellowship break between you and the Lord, go to Him in prayer asking Him to show you what is displeasing to Him. Ask Him to reveal anywhere you have stepped over the line of His Word, anywhere you have grieved or quenched His Spirit. He promises to show us where there is sin (John 16:8–11).

Watch Out for False Guilt and Lies. The enemy, the evil one, is also called the adversary—he is against God, against God's people, and against God's purposes. He is also the accuser against God and *"the brethren"*—all believers (Revelation 12:10). He is the father of lies and spreads untruth anywhere he can—lies about God, about God's Word, about God's people, about anything—to create division, discord, and distrust. When it comes to the lives of individual believers, he shoots "thought darts" to accuse—either of sin we have committed or even of sin which we have faced in temptation but have not committed—anything to confuse, frustrate, condemn, and make us feel guilty. Remember, to be tempted is not a sin, to have a tempting thought is not sin. It is not a sin until we act on that temptation or continue to cradle a thought such as lust or anger. When we do, we need to confess it and make it right.

The Spirit is Specific. When the Holy Spirit convicts of sin, He is specific so we can confess specifically—"Lord, here is what I did, when I did it. I was wrong. I turn from it. I want to do the right thing. Thank You for forgiving me." Satan is often general, condemning and confusing—"you are bad, weak, foolish, etc." Trust God to guide in truth. *"The wisdom from above is first pure, then peaceable, gentle, reasonable, full of mercy and good fruits, unwavering, without hypocrisy"* (James 3:17).

God Does Not Remember Sins so as to Use Them Against Us. The Holy Spirit does not bring up old sins. Those are removed, forgiven and forgotten. Satan uses instant replay to remind us, hassle us, depress us, defeat us. He nags at us—"Remember how many times you've done that. You will never change. You cannot do anything right. Remember." Simply remember the promises of the Word of God and hold to them (Hebrews 10:17–18).

Receive Forgiveness by Faith Not Feeling. Trust the Word of God to be true, as true as the God of the Word. Deal with bedrock facts, not shifting-sands feelings. Jesus died to forgive, not condemn.

Dealing with Your Personal Sins Against Others

When Someone Has Something Against You. First, if someone has something against you, you need to go to that person (or persons)—face to face, if possible, by a phone call if not face to face (Matthew 5:23–24). If you cannot reach them either way, seek the next best way, the fastest way possible. Ephesians 4:26 says, *"Do not let the sun go down on your anger."* In other words, deal with any sin, especially anger, on the day you face it. It is like household garbage; the longer you wait to get rid of it, the worse it stinks. What if he or she does not receive you or your attempt to get things right or does not forgive you? You are responsible for you. Let God deal with that person.

The Circle of Confession is as big as the circle of offense. If your sin is against God, confess it to Him. If you have sinned against an individual, go to that individual, confess, and make it right. If you have sinned against a group, make it right with the group.

Restitution. If there is need for restitution—financial, material, property lost or stolen, whatever—make it right as much as is possible. The burden may seem heavy now, but making it right makes the burden on your heart turn into wings for your soul.

Dealing with Others Who Have Sinned Against You

When Someone Sins Against You, first have a forgiving, kind attitude toward that one, *"forgiving each other, just as God in Christ also has forgiven you"* (Ephesians 4:32). What if he or she does not ask for forgiveness? You are responsible for you. Obey God. Show love. Let God deal with that person.

Two Options. To get things right, you have one of two choices. Forget it and do not mention it. The person may be unaware he has offended you in some way. *"Love covers a multitude of sins"* (1 Peter 4:8) *OR*...Go to him or her and point out the offense in order to restore the relationship (not in order to make the person feel bad or feel guilty) (Matthew 18:15–20; Galatians 6:1; 2 Thessalonians 3:15). God's goal is oneness with Him and with one another—walk in harmony, peace—real love toward one another (1 Peter 3:8–18). *"As much as depends on you, live peaceably with all men"* (Romans 12:18).

Lesson 6

Jesus Christ, "Son of David"

JESUS, THE GOD-MAN, BORN INTO THE LINE OF DAVID, REVEALING HIMSELF AS KING, LORD, MESSIAH, AND SAVIOR

For centuries, God's people waited on the fulfillment of the many promises of a Messiah, a Savior who would bring to fruition the many covenant promises God made to His people. One after another, great leaders came, each bringing certain leadership skills, heroic feats, and evidence of faith in the Living God. However, none of those proved to be *The* Leader. Enoch came, but a greater than Enoch would come. Noah came, but a greater than Noah would come. Abraham, Isaac, Jacob, Joseph, Moses, Joshua, Samuel, even David came, but none of these proved to be *The* Leader, the Messiah. People waited. The One to come would certainly be like these men, but greater.

When the Angel Gabriel came to Mary in the little town of Nazareth, he announced to her that she would bear the promised Messiah. How could this be? While veiled in much mystery, this One would be unique. There were clues; in one of Gabriel's statements, he said, *"the Lord God will give Him the throne of His father David"* (Luke 1:32b). David? He would be a descendant of David. The title *"Son of David"* or some connection between Jesus and David is found about twenty-five times in the New Testament.

When Jesus began ministering, many began asking if He was the *"Son of David,"* implying that this was a topic of conversation and an expectation in many hearts for many years. What did this expectation mean? How did Jesus respond to those who proclaimed Him as the *"Son of David"* and to those who questioned Him about that possibility?

When we look at King David and then at Jesus, we see similarities and obvious differences. What did *"Son of David"* mean to the people of Jesus' day and what does it mean to us? How does that title or name apply to each of us? What about Him was different? How can He be our Leader and Savior?

IN THEIR SHOES
Jesus' Genealogy

Jesus' genealogy in Matthew 1:1–17 focuses on Jesus' royal lineage from Abraham through David, revealing Jesus' legal status under Joseph, a descendant through David's son Solomon. Joseph, not Jesus' physical father, carried the legal status needed by the Messiah (Matthew 1:18, 23–25; Luke 3:23). In Luke 3:23–38, Luke began with Joseph as Mary's husband, thus Eli's (or Heli's) son "in-law," then tracing Mary's lineage through Eli (Heli) through David's son Nathan back to Adam. From both genealogies, Jesus is a *"son of David,"* in the legal royal lineage of the Jewish Messiah through Joseph and a physical descendant of David through Mary. Jesus came in the line of the *"seed"* of the woman through Seth, with no connection with the *"seed"* of the serpent (Genesis 3:15; 4:25–26; Luke 3:38).

Day One

Promises Made and Kept

From the days of Adam and Eve in the Garden of Eden to the birth of Jesus, God made many promises about the coming of the Messiah who would be the Savior. What did God promise? What would this "Messiah" be like? There are over three hundred promises about the first coming of the Messiah, with several others related to His second coming, and many of these are attached to the Messiah's relation to King David. What can we learn from this? How does this relate to us today?

Read Genesis 3:15. Summarize what you find—the setting, the characters in the Garden, the details of the promise.

Based on Genesis 4:25–26, noting that Eve referred to Seth as literally *"another seed in place of Abel,"* what focus do you discover in her words? Compare what you read in Genesis 4 with what you find in Luke 3:38.

WORD STUDY
"Seed"

When the LORD promised the coming of a *"seed"* of the woman, He used the Hebrew word *zera'* (Strong's # 2233) meaning "seed" or "child" rooted in *zara'* (#2232), meaning "to sow." The *"seed"* of the woman would be at *"enmity"* with the *"seed"* of the serpent; this has proven true throughout history and in the life of Jesus, the *"seed"* of the woman. Many longingly looked for this *"seed,"* some even focusing on the idea of the *"seed,"* the *zera'*, to the point of establishing religions. Zoroastrianism, a religion of the

Mesopotamian region has in its very name the Hebrew word *zera'*—*Zoro*astrianism. The promised *"seed"* Jesus came through the line of Abraham and David, a clear descendant of these two.

During the LORD'S meeting with Adam and the Woman over their sin, God promised a coming *"seed"* of the woman (*"her seed"*) who would always be at *"enmity"* with the *"seed"* of the serpent. This *"seed"* of the woman would be wounded by the serpent but would crush the head of the serpent. The Lord pointed to two seeds and two ways and the promise that evil would be crushed by the *"seed"* of the woman. Placed in the hearts of Adam and Eve, this promise awaited fulfillment. When Eve gave birth to Seth, she focused attention on him as the *"seed in place of Abel,"* implying that she thought of Abel as some connection to the *"seed"* to come; perhaps Seth was the *"seed."* After Abel's death, much changed. Eve saw in some measure that through Seth would come the Ultimate *"Seed."* Then, in Seth's line came his son Enosh. It appears significant that in the day when Enosh was born *"men began to call upon the name of the LORD,"* likely pointing to a measure of spiritual awakening and perhaps a greater longing for the coming of the *"seed"* of the woman. It is worth noting that Seth and Enosh are in the lineage of Jesus in Luke 3.

Fast-forward several centuries. In the annals of history in Scripture, we discover that God called Abram out of Ur of the Chaldees to follow Him. This occurred piecemeal. Abram's father Terah left Ur with Abram and Abram's wife Sarai along with several other family members. In Haran, after Terah died, the Lord called Abram to leave Haran and travel to Canaan.

📖 Genesis 12:1–3. Summarize what you find in those verses. In addition, what do you note about Abram's impact on *"the families of the earth"*?

📖 A few years later, God further clarified His call and His promises to Abram. What did God promise Abram about his *"seed"* or *"offspring"* in Genesis 15:1–5?

📖 How did Abram respond to the Lord in this encounter, according to Genesis 15:6?

📖 What else occurred in this encounter? Read Genesis 15:7–21 and summarize what occurred.

God promised Abram that He would *"bless"* him giving him the land He would reveal (the land of Canaan), many descendants to fill the land, and then through Abram God would bless *"all the families of the earth."* This sounded good, but it did not happen quickly. Years passed. Abram became discouraged or at least questioning about God's working. God came to him and promised His protection like *"a shield"* as well as provision, even seeing the Lord Himself as Abram's *"reward"* or treasure.

Abram still had questions about a literal son who would be his *"heir."* God promised that he would have an *"heir"* from "[his] *own body"* and that eventually Abram would have as many descendants as the stars he could see and count. To confirm this, God entered into a covenant with Abram. Abram provided the sacrifices, and God manifested His fire and spoke His promises—a land and many descendants who would be enslaved but one day freed, even coming out *"with many possessions."*

DID YOU KNOW?
The Record of Abraham and His Faith

Paul spoke of Abraham's faith and that of David in Romans 4:1–25, quoting Scripture about Abraham five times (see Romans 4:3, 9, 17, 18, 22) and David once (see Romans 4:7–8). In Galatians, Paul called him *"Abraham the believer,"* twice quoting Scriptures about him (see Galatians 3:6, 8, 9). James noted the evidence of Abraham's faith, showing him to be *"justified"* (Greek, *dikaioo*, Strong's #1344)—his *"works"* of faith revealed the faith he already possessed (James 2:21–24).

Still later, the Lord came to Abram again, instructing him to circumcise all the men of his household. He also changed his name to *"Abraham,"* meaning *"father of a multitude"* and changed Sarai's name to *"Sarah"* ("princess"). Soon after, the Lord appeared to Abraham and promised him that he and Sarah would have a son to be named *"Isaac,"* meaning *"laughter."* With their ages being 100 and 90 respectively, Abraham and Sarah at first considered this impossible, even laughable, but the Lord assured them stating, *"is anything too difficult for the LORD?"* (see also Romans 4).

📖 What did God promise Abraham in the encounter described in Genesis 18:1–14?

DID YOU KNOW?
Abraham's Seed

There are two focus points in *"seed"*—one plural referring to many descendants and one singular, referring to the *"seed"* God promised who would bless *"all the families of the earth."* God first spoke of Abraham's singular *"seed"* in Genesis 22:17b–18 which Peter quoted referring to Jesus (Acts 3:25). In agreement with this, Paul stated in Galatians 3:16, *"Now the promises were spoken to Abraham and to his seed. He does not say, "And to seeds," as referring to many, but rather to one, "And to your seed," that is Christ."* Then, he wrote, *"you are all sons of God through faith in Jesus Christ...and if you belong to Christ, then you are Abraham's offspring* (literally, *"seed"*), *heirs according to promise"* (Galatians 3:26, 29. See also 3:8). Abraham's *"seed"* was Jesus Christ, born as *"the son of David, the son of Abraham"* (Matthew 1:1).

📖 Abraham and Sarah gave birth to their son Isaac. Several more years passed, and at some point, God called Abraham to sacrifice Isaac on Mount Moriah. Read Genesis 22:15–18. What did God say about Abraham's *"seed"* in verse 17? What further revelation did God make in verse 18?

Much occurred in the lives of Abraham and Sarah in their remaining years, and these events shaped the next several hundred years to come and are still impacting life today. Abraham's *"seed"* or *"descendants"* did indeed number as *"the stars"* or *"the sand."* Through Isaac came Jacob and Esau. Then, through Jacob and his twelve sons, thousands were born. Those descendants experienced Egyptian slavery, but God led Moses in delivering them out of Egypt with the promised *"many possessions."* Eventually, Joshua led them into Canaan, the "Promised Land." There they grew into a great nation. Eventually, after several years of territorial rule by several *"judges,"* God gave them their first king, Saul. After him came King David.

📖 God had more in mind. He promised many things to David. What specific promises from God do you find in 2 Samuel 7:12, 16?

📖 According to 2 Samuel 7:25–29, how did David respond to these specific promises?

The Lord promised David that his *"seed,"* literally "descendant," would *"come forth"* from David and God would *"establish his kingdom."* This appears to refer to Solomon in the near fulfillment and to Jesus the Messiah in the far fulfillment. The Lord spoke about David's *"house"* or dynasty and his kingdom and throne being *"established forever."* In response, David prayed that the Lord would *"confirm"* forever what He had spoken about David's *"house,"* and that it would be *"blessed forever."*

📖 Read Matthew 1:1. What truths do you find in the first verse of the genealogy given by Matthew? What additional thoughts do you find in Matthew 1:6 and 16?

📖 Luke also gives the genealogy of Jesus, but from a different angle. Read Luke 3:23, 31, and 38. What differences do you discover in these verses? Summarize your insights.

📖 Note any further insights you glean from John 1:1, 14 and 1 Corinthians 15:45.

Hundreds of years after God's promises to David, we find the New Testament record giving the clear genealogies of Jesus. Writing from a Jewish perspective, Matthew noted the genealogy of Jesus from Abraham, through his descendants, then from David through his descendants beginning with Solomon, and tracing the line to Joseph, Mary's husband. With Joseph being the "legal" head of the home, Matthew gave the "legal" or "royal" genealogy of Jesus as fitting for a *"son of David."* Luke, on the other hand, traced the genealogy of Jesus through Mary with Joseph being considered the "legal" son or son "in-law," and thus the "legal" ancestor of Jesus. Luke traced Jesus' genealogy through Mary's blood line back to David through his son Nathan, then back to Abraham, ending with Adam, the man created by God.

Jesus is *"the Word"* who created all; He became a man. He is *"the Last Adam"* as well as the *"son of Abraham"* and the *"son of David."* While this remains a mystery in many ways, each of these titles or names reveals something of Jesus' lineage as the God-Man, the *"Word made flesh"* and the *"son of David"* who fulfills God's promises to David as well as His promises to others.

DID YOU KNOW?
"Faith" and the "Seed"

As Abraham placed faith in the Lord and received God's righteousness (Genesis 15:6; Romans 4:3, 20–22; Galatians 3:6), so each person who places faith in Jesus as Lord and Savior becomes *His* (John 1:12), a child of God, receiving God's righteousness and being marked as Abraham's *"seed"* forever (Galatians 3:6–9). God's *"seed"*—His nature in agreement with His *Word*—dwells in each believer, each one being *"born"* into God's family through the *"seed"* of the *"living and abiding word of God"* (1 John 3:9 and 1 Peter 1:2–25 with Ephesians 1:13–14

STOP AND APPLY—God and His Promises—God is ever true to Himself, to His nature, and to His Word. When He makes a promise, He keeps it. This is seen over and over throughout Scripture in the lives of countless individuals as well as in various nations of the earth. David spoke of God's Word being like *"silver"* refined *"seven times"*—the idea of seven-fold or *perfect* refining for the purest silver (Psalm 12:6–7). God is truthful, and His Word is pure. Consider His promises. Pause and pray to Him about *your* life.

Day Two

Whose Son Is He?

The Angel Gabriel came to Mary and told her she would bear a son who would be the Messiah. Mary received this revelation and expressed her trust in God. Almost from the start, questions and controversies arose over this child Mary carried. It started close to home, with her betrothed Joseph. How could this be? Joseph wondered, questioned, and was likely stunned by the whole matter. What does Scripture tell us? How did God explain this to Joseph? How has God explained this to us and how does this relate to us?

IN THEIR SHOES
"Put Her Away Secretly"

About Joseph and Mary, Matthew 1:19 states that Joseph *"desired to put her away secretly."* What does that mean? In the Jewish culture of that time, betrothal meant entering into a legal marriage agreement that only a legal divorce could end. *"A righteous man,"* Joseph lived by the Word of God (Deuteronomy 22:20–24; 24:1–4). Not wanting to make a public spectacle of Mary or her pregnancy, he chose to end the marriage *"secretly"* or quietly. God worked supernaturally; He sent an angel with new information. Joseph obeyed, keeping Mary as his wife and making sure he took care of the infant Jesus (Matthew 1:20–25).

📖 The angel Gabriel came to Mary in Nazareth, informing her that she would give birth to a unique son named Jesus. What connection between this child and David did the

Angel Gabriel note in Luke 1:32–33?

📖 What further revelation did the Angel Gabriel give Mary in Luke 1:35? What would this child be *"called"* according to Luke 1:32 and 35?

The Angel Gabriel came to Mary in the small town of Nazareth and revealed to her that she would bear and give birth to a son in the line of David. In fact, this son would be *"great"* and would be called *"the Son of the Most High"* and *"the Son of God."* God would give Him *"the throne of His father David,"* thus as a descendant of David, this child would forever rule over *"the house of Jacob"* and have a *"kingdom"* with *"no end."* Mary received this revelation, entrusting herself into the Lord's hands to fulfill these words.

📖 What was Joseph's first reaction to Mary's news, according to Matthew 1:18–19?

📖 Read Matthew 1:20–21. What did God do to clarify Joseph's understanding?

According to the angel, who was this *"Jesus"*?

📖 What further clarification do you discover in Matthew 1:22–23?

Joseph and Mary were betrothed to be married in a few months; only a legal divorce could separate them. That was the Jewish custom and law. When Joseph found out about

Mary's pregnancy, fear enveloped him, as he likely considered what this could mean. He assumed she had been unfaithful; the hurt and shame would have been great. Wanting to do the right thing and not wanting to openly shame Mary, Joseph considered a quiet, private divorce. That would avoid some, if not most, public shame to both of them and would allow Joseph to go on with life.

God intervened in the situation, sending Joseph an angel with a message in a graphic dream. The angel declared, *"Joseph, son of David, do not be afraid to take Mary as your wife; for that which has been conceived in her is of the Holy Spirit."* The angel told him that Mary would bear a son to be named *"Jesus"* and He would *"save His people from their sins."* Matthew recorded that this actually fulfilled a prophecy of Isaiah about a virgin conceiving, bearing a Son called "IMMANUEL," meaning "GOD WITH US."

📖 According to Matthew 1:24–25, how did Joseph respond to all God revealed to him?

Joseph believed the words of the angel, receiving the dream as from God. He obeyed, seeing the command as from the Lord Himself. Joseph took Mary as his wife but had no physical relations with her until after she gave birth to the Son Jesus.

📖 Fast-forward several years to Jesus' ministry days. The date is around the Autumn of AD 28 in the city of Capernaum. Read Matthew 12:22–23. What conclusion did the people of that area draw from what Jesus did?

In Capernaum, Jesus healed a demon-possessed man who was *"blind and dumb;"* he began to see and speak. The people were *"amazed."* Likely thinking of the many prophecies and expectations that the Messiah would be a descendant of David, even doing supernatural actions, people began to ask whether Jesus could be *"the Son of David."* He obviously had supernatural power; His healing of this man revealed that to all.

📖 It appears there were many different ideas and opinions about the Messiah to come and about Jesus in His day. Just a few weeks later, Jesus and His disciples were ministering in Nazareth. According to Matthew 13:54–58, what do you find in the reactions of some of His former neighbors in Nazareth?

"Astonished" at Jesus' teaching, people in Nazareth began to ask questions about Him, essentially asking, 'Isn't this the simple *"carpenter's son"*? Aren't his mother Mary and His brothers and sisters with us today and every day?' They became offended at Jesus and His teachings; no thought that He could possibly be *"the Son of David."* In their reactions, Jesus recognized their *"unbelief."* He also saw that a prophet in his *"hometown"* and *"in his own household"* was usually considered just another man, receiving no honor. Few were His miracles there.

📖 A few months later, around the Spring of AD 29, Jesus was back in Capernaum teaching. What further details do you find in John 6:42?

Just a short time before, Jesus had miraculously given bread to thousands of people. The people in Capernaum wanted more free bread from Jesus; at the same time, they would not receive what He taught. He knew this. They considered Him just another rabbi or teacher but showed no thought of Him being the Messianic "Son of David." According to their perspective, Jesus was simply *"the son of Joseph,"* not a man who had come out of *"heaven,"* and certainly not the Messiah.

Likely in the Autumn of AD 29, Jesus taught in Jerusalem at the Temple during the days of the Feast of Tabernacles. In a somewhat heated conversation, some of the Jewish leaders seemed to question Jesus' lineage. What do you find in John 8:31–47 (note verse 41)?

DID YOU KNOW
"My Day"

When Jesus spoke of Abraham rejoicing in *"My day,"* He was speaking of *"the Day of Christ"* mentioned in several other places in the New Testament. It is the Day of His coming, His Presence or *Parousia*, His rewards, and His reign, spoken of by the apostle Paul in 1 Corinthians 1:8; 3:13; Philippians 1:6, 10; 2:16; 2 Timothy 1:12, 18; 4:8. It is possible that the Lord revealed this *"Day"* of Christ's victory and reign to Abraham in his time on Mount Moriah (Genesis 22:1–18).

📖 During this same interaction, the Jewish leaders further berated Jesus. He revealed even greater truths. What further reaction do you discover in John 8:48–59, especially in verses 48 and 59?

In Jerusalem, several Jewish leaders confronted Jesus about His statements. In their scoffing, they accused Him of being *"a Samaritan"* and having *"a demon."* Both statements were false; Jesus focused their attention on His honoring His Father while they dishonored Jesus. Jesus went even further, speaking of one keeping His *"word"* never seeing *"death."* What a statement! They became infuriated, claiming Abraham as their *"father"* and focusing on his greatness. Jesus focused on knowing His Father, on their *not* knowing His Father and on Abraham rejoicing in Christ's *"Day."* It appears the Jewish leaders grew more indignant. Jesus stated in no uncertain terms, *"before Abraham was born, I am."* They saw this as His claim to being God and greater than Abraham and picked up stones to *"throw at Him"* intending to kill Him, but Jesus escaped. This was not the end.

📖 One other incident in Jesus' life reveals more of His connections as a *"son"* to David. It occurred after His triumphal entry into Jerusalem. Read Matthew 22:41–46. What did Jesus first ask the Pharisees? What did the Pharisees say about whose *"son"* the Christ would be?

📖 Jesus quoted David referring to the Messiah as his *"Lord."* How did the Pharisees (and anyone else at the scene) respond to Jesus' third question—If the Christ or Messiah is David's *"Lord,"* then *"how is He his son"*? Read Matthew 22:45–46 and note your insights.

When Jesus asked the Pharisees whose son the Messiah or Christ would be, they were quick to respond with *"the son of David."* Then, Jesus quoted David's words from Psalm 110:1 in which David called the Messiah "MY LORD." When Jesus asked how the Messiah could be the *"son of David"* and how David could call Him *"Lord," "no one was able to answer"*—not *"a word."* As a result, no one asked Him any further questions. No one seemed to grasp the full meaning of *"the son of David"* or the revelation of Psalm 110.

STOP AND APPLY—When We Don't Know All the Facts—Most (if not all) of the time, we do not know all the facts about what God is doing. That certainly occurred in the fulfillment of God's many promises about the Messiah. Even to this day, there remain numerous mysteries associated with the birth, life, death, and resurrection of Jesus. What about in daily life? Just as Mary and Joseph had to trust the Lord, so must we. Just as we trust Him for the things we do know, so in the matters we do not know or understand, we can still trust Him. He is a Father, ever mindful that *"we are but dust"* (Psalm 103:14).

Day Three

The Merciful Son of David

Often in Jesus' encounters with others, we read of people crying out *"Son of David, have mercy"* or words like those. What did this mean in Jesus' day? Why did people often say that? What do we find about the mercy of God and of Jesus in those encounters and in that statement?

> *The cry "have mercy" is addressed to Jesus as the "Son of David" eight times in the Gospel accounts (Matthew 9:27; 15:22; 20:30, 31;Mark 10:47, 48; Luke 18:38, 39). In addition, a father cried out to Jesus for mercy for his son (Matthew 17:15) and a repentant tax-gatherer cried out "God, be merciful to me, the sinner!" Luke 18:13).*

📖 What did people think of the mercy of God in the days of Jesus? Read Mary's prayer in Luke 1:46–55 and note when the word *"mercy"* is used.

📖 Read Luke 1:57–58 and 67–79. What insights about *"mercy"* do you discover in the words of Elizabeth's *"neighbors"* and *"relatives"*? What did Zacharias say about *"mercy"* in his words of prayer and prophecy concerning the birth of his son John?

Soon after the Angel Gabriel announced the coming of Messiah Jesus through Mary, Mary hurried to Elizabeth's house. The two greeted one another with great praise. Mary began to exalt the Lord for all He was doing in her life and likely in Elizabeth's life as well. Mary prayed Psalm 103:17 written by David: "His mercy is upon generation after generation toward those who fear Him." She knew that the Lord was working in mercy in her life and in those around her, bringing the Messiah at this time in history. She also praised the Lord for giving *"help to Israel"* through *"His mercy"* spoken to Abraham and to so many more through the ages.

When Elizabeth gave birth to her son, John, many *"neighbors"* and *"relatives"* rejoiced, seeing this as a display of the Lord's *"great mercy"* toward Elizabeth. Zacharias, well aware of the mercy of God, praised Him for His work *"in the house of David His servant,"* especially in showing His mercy. He had shown that *"mercy"* to *"our fathers"* as part of His covenant heart. Zacharias spoke of his gratitude for all the Lord was doing *"because of the tender mercy of our God"* which would be brought by the Messiah, *"the Sunrise from on high"* (compare with Malachi 4:2). Zacharias prayed from Isaiah 9:2 about how God's light and salvation would "SHINE UPON THOSE WHO SIT IN DARKNESS AND THE SHADOW OF DEATH." Through the Messiah, God would mercifully lead His people in *"the way of peace."*

📖 Note your thoughts and insights about the cry for *"mercy"* from the two blind men in Matthew 9:27–31?

📖 Jesus had a question for these men. What was their reply? What was Jesus' response to them, according to verses 28–29?

📖 What happened to the two men? Summarize what occurred in this situation, according to Matthew 9:30–31.

In or near Capernaum, two blind men cried out to Jesus. They knew they needed the *"mercy"* of God and believed Jesus was indeed the *"Son of David,"* who could show that kind of mercy. Their cry to Him as *"Son of David"* pointed to their belief in Jesus as the promised Messiah, the *"seed"* of David. Jesus specifically asked them if they believed He could act as the *"Son of David"* on their behalf; they believed in Him and His ability. Jesus always looked for faith in Himself, in God's Word and promises; He knew it could be part of a relationship and a trust issue. He immediately *"touched their eyes,"* and they began seeing. Knowing it was not time to reveal Himself openly as the reigning Messiah, Jesus did not want attention brought to His miracles or to Himself; He told them to not let anyone know. Regardless, they *"spread the news."*

IN THEIR SHOES
Prophecies About the Messiah

There are over three hundred prophecies about the first coming of the Messiah. Many never thought of a first *and* a second coming, only of one to set up a political and material kingdom. Many took various prophecies about Messiah's second coming or the Messianic Age and applied them to the first century overthrow of the Roman occupation of Judea. Some popular prophecies included dozens in Isaiah (e.g., 2:1–4; 9:1–7; 11:1–5; 12:2–6; 29:18; 32:3–4; 35:1–10; 42:1–13, 16) as well as many psalms such as Psalm 2. Prophets who spoke of the coming Messiah/Messianic Age, included Micah, Zechariah, and Malachi. He will fulfill all the prophecies and reign forever.

Others longed for the coming of the Messiah, the *"Son of David,"* but were not sure about what He would be like. About the same time as the two blind men were healed in Capernaum (around October, AD 28), some brought a blind and dumb demon-possessed man to Jesus. (We looked at this in Day Two.) Jesus healed him so that he *"spoke and saw."* Based on some of the prophecies, many considered that possibly Jesus could be the *"Son of David"* (Matthew 12:22–23).

One of the many prophecies that spoke of the coming Messiah and the Messianic age was Isaiah 35:5–6. What do you discover about what the Lord would do? What conclusion might the people have drawn?

When the multitudes saw the evident power of Jesus to heal the blind and dumb man, they were *"amazed."* This certainly matched parts of the prophecies they had heard for years. As they heard the healed man speak and saw him with evident sight, they began to talk about this incident and this rabbi. Even with the stern Pharisees present, they asked plainly, *"This man cannot be the Son of David, can he?"*

IN THEIR SHOES
Tyre and Sidon

Known for their sea trade, the cities of Tyre (Southern Phoenicia) and Sidon (Northern Phoenicia) lay on the Mediterranean Coast about twenty miles apart. Sidon lay about fifty miles from the Galilee city of Nazareth. In the time of David and Solomon, Tyre provided cedar timber and workmen for construction of David's Palace, the Temple, and Solomon's Palace. Ahab's wife Jezebel was the daughter of Ethbaal, king of the Sidonians. In the time of Christ, Tyre and Sidon still existed, but were less noteworthy, though both cities still sought to prosper through sea trade.

We find another reference to the *"Son of David"* about a year later (Summer of AD 29). Read Matthew 15:21–28. To where did Jesus go? According to Matthew 15:22–23, what did the Canaanite (Syrophoenician) woman say to Jesus? How did His disciples respond?

📖 Read Matthew 15:24–25. How did Jesus respond to the woman? What did the woman do?

📖 Summarize the interaction between Jesus and the woman in Matthew 15:26–28.

DID YOU KNOW
The Dogs

When Jesus spoke of *"the dogs"* eating *"bread"* and the Syrophoenician woman spoke of them eating *"crumbs"* from the table, they used the Greek word *kunarion* (Strong's #2952), referring to a puppy or puppies (Matthew 15:26, 27; Mark 7:27, 28). Another Greek word *kuon* translated *"dog"* (Strong's #2965) refers to a full-grown dog and sometimes referred to wild, scavenging dogs rather than household dogs.

As Jesus and His disciples traveled in Phoenicia, a Syrophoenician woman cried out to Him as the *"Son of David,"* asking Him to *"have mercy"* on her and heal her demon-possessed daughter. As she continued *"shouting out"* after them, the disciples *"kept asking Him"* to send her away. Instead, Jesus said His work was for *"the house of Israel"* (*"the children"*), not Gentiles (*"the dogs"*). Humbly revealing her faith in Jesus, she quickly responded that even the household dogs fed on whatever *"crumbs"* might fall to the floor. In her response, Jesus recognized her *"faith"* and showed His mercy, healing her daughter *"at once."*

Over six months later (early Spring of AD 30), Jesus traveled toward Jerusalem to encounter the Cross. Near Jericho, two blind men heard that Jesus was coming near. According to Matthew 20:30, what did they cry out? Based on Matthew 20:31, how did the people react? What response came from the blind men?

📖 Read Matthew 20:32–33. What did Jesus say to the men, and how did they respond to Him?

📖 In His mercy, what did Jesus do, according to Matthew 20:34? What did the two men do?

📖 Recording the same incident, Luke noted some further details. What added response does Luke present in Luke 18:43?

DID YOU KNOW?
Two Blind Men or One?

Matthew 20:29–34 notes Jesus' encounter with two blind men whom He healed. Mark 10:46–52 records the same incident but notes only one blind man, as does Luke in Luke 18:35–43, also giving the name of the one as Bartimaeus. Did Jesus heal two blind men or one? Based on Matthew's account, Jesus encountered and healed two men, with Mark and Luke each highlighting only one of the men.

When the two blind men heard Jesus was coming near, they cried out *"have mercy on us, Son of David."* Immediately, the people *"sternly told them to be quiet"* but they cried out even more. Jesus responded to the two men by asking what they wanted Him to do for them. They wanted to be healed of their blindness. In mercy and *"compassion,"* Jesus healed them, and they began following Him. Luke adds that one of them named Bartimaeus was *"glorifying God,"* and the crowd *"gave praise to God."*

STOP AND APPLY—In Need of Mercy— As Jesus ministered in and around Israel, many expressed their need by crying out to Him, *"have mercy, Son of David."* Sometimes when we cry for mercy, we are acknowledging our great need, perhaps even admitting we are undeserving of mercy or worse still, deserving of just punishment. The need of mercy was great in Jesus' day; it is indeed a great need today. Hebrews 4:16 encourages every believer, *"Let us therefore draw near to the throne of grace, that we may receive mercy and may find grace to help in time of need."* Whether unbeliever or believer in Jesus, everyone needs mercy. While you have the opportunity, cry out to Jesus, the *"Son of David,"* for His mercy, whatever the need.

Day Four

The Triumphant Son of David

For centuries, people longed for the Messiah to come. In Jesus' day, they longed for His arrival to conquer Rome and establish His kingdom greater than that which God had established through David. During Jesus' ministry, many spoke of Him as the *"Son of David"* and considered Him the likely candidate for eternal King and Messiah. Many hoped He was the long-awaited Messiah and King; some were sure, even wanting a zealous overthrow of Rome. What should Jesus do? What could He do?

The Old Testament Scriptures painted a picture of a majestic, powerful Messiah, even one who could heal all kinds of diseases and infirmities. Jesus certainly revealed that kind of power. The Lord had spoken to David about his *"seed"* reigning as king over an eternal kingdom, even twice mentioning a *"throne"* (2 Samuel 7:13, 16). People expected a king to come. The Angel Gabriel told Mary that she would bear a Son who would be given *"the throne of His father David"* (Luke 1:32).

DID YOU KNOW

Riding a Donkey

A person riding a donkey would not have been unusual; at times in Israel this pointed to royalty. David gave instructions for his son Solomon to ride on his *"mule"* to the place of Solomon's anointing and declaration as the new king (see 1 Kings 1:33–37, 38, 44). Zechariah 9:9 presents a prophecy of the coming Messiah riding on the colt of a donkey; Matthew quoted this in reference to Jesus riding a colt of a donkey into Jerusalem (the triumphal entry, Matthew 21:5). The people recognized this and honored Him as their king, at least temporarily. A few days later, many cried out, *"we do not want this man to reign over us"* (Luke 19:14) or *"we have no king but Caesar"* (John 19:15). However, Jesus was and is *"the ruler of the kings of the earth"* (Revelation 1:5).

This matter of Jesus' kingship became more prominent as He ministered throughout Israel. When He fed the multitude (five thousand men plus women and children), many considered Him the promised *"Prophet"* and wanted to make Him king then and there, but He escaped from them and their plans (John 6:14–15). Jesus often spoke of the *"Kingdom"* and at times of Himself as a *"King,"* but timing and preparation were crucial and always pointed to the future. Even in His interaction with Governor Pilate, Jesus noted this matter of His kingship and kingdom (John 18:33–39). Jesus was crucified under the charge of being *"King of the Jews"* (John 19:19–22). After Jesus' resurrection and return to heaven, the New Testament writings call Him *"King of kings"* (1 Timothy 6:15; Revelation 17:14; 19:16). What can we learn and apply concerning Jesus as the kingly *"Son of David"* during His earthly days, for today, and for the days to come?

During His ministry years, Jesus made Himself very clear. He stated, *"I do nothing on My own initiative;"* He sought to do and say what the Father told Him to do (John 8:28, 29) and say (John 12:47–50). When the time came for Him to complete His mission, the triumphal entry was part of the Father's plans.

📖 Read Matthew 21:1–7. Summarize the events that occurred. What was significant about Jesus' riding on a donkey?

WORD STUDY
"Hosanna"

The exclamation *"Hosanna!"* is used six times in the New Testament (in Jesus' "Triumphal Entry" and as He ministered in the Temple in Jerusalem). *"Hosanna,"* a transliteration of the Greek word *hosanna* (Strong's #5614) made of two Hebrew words, *yasha* (Strong's #3467), "to be open, wide, or free," thus "safe" or saved and *na'* (Strong's #4994), meaning "now" or "I pray." Together they mean "Oh Save!" or "Save now!" Jesus came to save, but the crowds thought this "salvation" was only from the tyranny and idolatry of Rome rather than from the personal slavery of sin and idolatry in the heart.

📖 According to Matthew 21:8–11, what response came from the crowds in Jerusalem when Jesus came riding on a donkey? John's testimony adds to what Matthew recorded. What do you discover in John 12:12–13? What additional insights do you glean from Mark 11:10?

📖 What response came from the Pharisees? Read John 12:19 and Luke 19:39 and note what you discover?

📖 What response came from Jesus, according to Luke 19:40 and then 19:41–44?

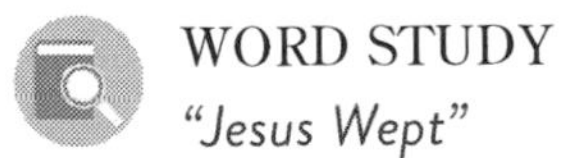

WORD STUDY

"Jesus Wept"

When Jesus stood at Lazarus' tomb, John records *"Jesus wept"* (John 11:35) using the Greek word *dakruo* (Strong's # 1145) meaning to shed tears implying crying quietly, even with few tears. Luke 19:41 presents a contrast with Jesus weeping loudly over Jerusalem's rejection of His message and the *"peace"* He could have brought to each heart. Luke used the Greek word *klaio* (Strong's # 2799) meaning to "wail" aloud or "weep."

On Sunday before Passover, Jesus ordered some of His disciples to retrieve a colt of a donkey for Him to ride into the city of Jerusalem. Matthew carefully notes the fulfillment of the messianic prophecy of Zechariah 9:9 about *"your King"* coming mounted on the colt of a donkey. When the crowds saw Him coming on the donkey, immediately they began spreading their garments and tree branches, including palm branches, on the road for Him to ride over like a carpet for royalty.

Multitudes began to cry out *"Hosanna to the Son of David."* Some shouted, quoting from Psalm 118:26, "BLESSED IS HE WHO COMES IN THE NAME OF THE LORD," adding *"even the king of Israel."* Others shouted, "BLESSED IS THE KING WHO COMES IN THE NAME OF THE LORD," while still others added, *"blessed is the coming kingdom of our father David."* They also spoke of Jesus as *"the prophet Jesus, from Nazareth in Galilee"*—king and prophet; certainly significant! John also notes the Pharisees' agitated response, *"the world has gone after Him"* (John 12:19b). The people wanted a new king and His kingdom.

As the Pharisees listened, they demanded Jesus, *"rebuke Your disciples,"* but Jesus stated that if all became silent, *"the stones will cry out!"* This was much bigger than any ordinary man or any man's plan. The procession continued. As Jesus observed the crowds and heard their cries, He also recognized their shallow understanding and failure to hear Him clearly or respond in repentance and faith in Him. They wanted a military overthrow of Rome with Him as king and Israel as the location of His new kingdom. Instead, Jerusalem would face a siege and destruction. He began to weep aloud.

📖 After entering Jerusalem, Mark 11:11–12a and 11:15 report that late on Sunday Jesus carefully observed the actions and ways of those at the Temple and then left the Temple to spend the night in nearby Bethany. The next morning, He came back to the Temple. Read Matthew 21:12–14. What two significant things did Jesus do in the Temple?

📖 After Jesus healed several blind and lame people in the Temple, what did the children shout, according to Matthew 21:15?

The *"chief priests and scribes"* became *"indignant"* over what Jesus had done and what the children were shouting. How did Jesus respond to their complaints, according to Matthew 21:16?

DID YOU KNOW
A House of Prayer

Quoting portions of Isaiah 56:7 and Jeremiah 7:11, Jesus came into the Temple and dealt with the merchants selling sacrificial animals and exchanging money. In Isaiah, God spoke of gathering people to *"My holy mountain,"* making them *"joyful"* in His *"house of prayer."* God meant the Temple to always be *"a house of prayer for all the peoples."* Jesus sought to stop the actions of the merchants crowding the Court of the Gentiles with their sacrifices and Temple money exchange tables. He wanted to give room for Gentiles (*"the peoples"*) to freely worship, too (Matthew 21:12–13; Mark 11:15–17).

Monday morning, Jesus returned to the Temple where He then *"cast out"* those *"buying and selling in the temple"* and *"overturned the tables of the money-changers"* stationed there. Then, noting what was clearly *"written,"* He quoted portions of Isaiah 56:7 and Jeremiah 7:11, rebuking the merchandisers for making the Temple a "ROBBERS' DEN" instead of doing all that was needful to keep it a "HOUSE OF PRAYER." Jesus included God's words as His own, noting the Temple as "MY HOUSE." In this instance, Jesus made clear His close connection to the Father. He would reveal even more.

When Jesus had finished dealing with the Temple violations, several blind and lame people came to Him, and He *"healed them."* Several children who were gathered in the Temple courts, likely with their families, began shouting as their parents, relatives, and neighbors had done the day before, *"Hosanna to the Son of David."* Jesus was certainly speaking and acting as David would have. When several priests and scribes complained to Jesus, He quoted from Psalm 8 about "INFANTS AND NURSING BABES" giving praise to God. In this, He was making a clear claim to being God, ready to receive the praise of children.

During that week, Jesus faced many challenges from Sadducees, Pharisees, scribes, and other unbelievers. During one of those interactions, Jesus posed the question about David calling the Messiah "MY LORD" though He would obviously be David's *"son"* or descendant. How could this be? They had no answer and stopped challenging Him. [For further information and discussion, see above, the questions at the end of Day Two: Whose Son Is He?]

Much of the discussions and interactions of Passover Week centered around Israel's king and another kingdom. The people wanted the Messiah to come, rid them of Roman domination, and establish a greater kingdom, even better than David's kingdom of long ago. Many looked to Jesus to do that. Much occurred in the next few days. Eventually, Jesus stood before Pilate, accused of claiming to be the *"King of the Jews."* What would Pilate do? Read John 18:33–40 and 19:1–15 and summarize what you find.

What connections to being a *"king"* do you find in this interaction?

Pilate went back and forth between the people and Jesus over the issue of Him possibly being the *"King of the Jews."* Jesus had talked with Pilate about *"My kingdom"* and being *"born"* to be *"king."* Eventually, Pilate chose to have Jesus scourged. The Roman soldiers added their scorn, mocking Jesus as a king, first weaving and placing a *"crown of thorns"* on His head, then placing a kingly *"purple robe"* on Him, even giving Him mock worship, stating, *"Hail, King of the Jews!"* Mathew 27:29 adds a note about *"a reed in His right hand,"* a mock scepter.

After this, Pilate again declared, *"I find no guilt in Him,"* but the crowds continued to clamor for Jesus' crucifixion. Agitated, Pilate told Jesus that he had the power to release or crucify Him. Jesus spoke of His confidence in all authority coming *"from above."* Pilate switched, seeking to release Jesus, but several cried out praising Caesar as their friend and king. Finally, Pilate issued the crucifixion order and stated *"Behold, your King!"* Jesus faced crucifixion and died on a Roman cross.

First Timothy 1:17 speaks of Jesus as *"the King Eternal."* An *Eternal King* cannot remain dead. Jesus arose from the grave the Third Day and appeared to over five hundred believers (1 Corinthians 15:6). He ascended to heaven on Day Forty after His resurrection (Luke 24:50–51; Acts 1:2, 9–11, 22; 1 Timothy 3:16). The early church was born on Pentecost Sunday with around 3000 new believers added to the 120 who had been praying and waiting since Jesus ascended. What did the young church think about Jesus, *"the Eternal King,"* the *"Son of David"*?

📖 In writing to the Roman believers (about AD 57), Paul carefully revealed Jesus the Messiah, His salvation, and His eternal promises. Read Romans 1:1–7. What connection did Paul make between Jesus and David?

📖 Years later (about AD 68), Paul penned his final letter. He wrote to pastor Timothy the letter we know as 2 Timothy. Read 2 Timothy 2:1–9. What connection between Jesus Christ and David did Paul note?

In writing to the Roman believers, Paul made clear the gospel he proclaimed, taught, and wrote about. That gospel centered around Jesus the promised Messiah who was *"a descendant/seed of David"* in terms of His humanity. He revealed His power as the *"Son of God"* through His *"resurrection from the dead,"* thus making clear who He was and is as Lord. He gave His grace, called His apostles like Paul and others to speak, write about, and teach to others so that many Jews and Gentiles came to the *"obedience of faith"* in Jesus. The Roman believers were part of those knowing that *"obedience of faith;"* Paul desired and prayed for them to know and experience the *"grace"* and *"peace"* that comes *"from God our Father and the Lord Jesus Christ,"* the ever-living *"Son of David."*

About eleven years later, Paul penned his last letter known as *2 Timothy*; he exhorted Timothy to keep the message clear to all kinds of people. It would mean living with the discipline, endurance, and tireless effort of a soldier, an athlete, and a farmer. As always, Paul made clear that this message centered around the resurrected Jesus who revealed Himself as the Messiah and *"descendant of David."* Like David, Jesus had a "heart for God," being the Greater David, proving Himself the Greatest Shepherd, Warrior, and King.

📖 Sometime around AD 95, the Roman government exiled the apostle John to the Island of Patmos. On that island, the Lord revealed Himself and His reign to John in what is called the *"Revelation of Jesus Christ."* What do you discover in Revelation 5:1–7? What connection to David is noted in Revelation 5:5?

📖 In the final chapter of the *Revelation* and the final recorded utterance from the Lord Jesus, He made clear to John who He was in time and eternity. Read Revelation 22:16. Who is Jesus?

John carefully recorded the *"Revelation"* from Jesus Christ (Revelation 1:1). In Revelation 4–5, he recorded a throne-room scene: when he heard that no one was found worthy to open the Seven-Sealed Scroll, a sort of 'Title-Deed' to Earth and to the fulfillment of all God's promises, he began to weep. One of *"the elders"* told him, *"Stop weeping."* Why? Because there was One who could open the seals: *"the Lion that is from the tribe of Judah, the Root of David."* One who was both *Before* David and a *Descendant* of both Judah and David had proven Himself as the sacrificial and risen Lamb as well as the victorious and reigning Lion.

The Lord Jesus made clear who He was and is in His last statement recorded in Scripture. He confirmed what *"one of the elders"* had revealed to John: *"I am the root and the offspring of David."* Not only that, but He revealed Himself as *"the bright morning star,"* the symbol of hope and signal of a new day. As Lord and Savior, He would carry out all He had revealed in His *"Revelation"* to John and usher in His New Day, *"the Day of God"* about which Peter wrote (2 Peter 3:12). This matched the *"new heavens and a new earth"* about which Isaiah prophesied hundreds of years before (Isaiah 65:17; 2 Peter 3:13).

DID YOU KNOW
What Day Is It?

Scripture speaks about many specific *"Days"* or eras. Some refer to the present time as "The Day of Man" since the Gentile nations appear to be ruling. The *"Day of the Lord"* is a coming era of judgment mentioned several times in Scripture (Joel 1:15; 1 Thessalonians 5:2). *"The Day of Christ"* (Philippians 1:10) is also noted as *"My day"* (John 8:56), *"the day of Christ Jesus"* (Philippians 1:6), and other designations (see 1 Corinthians 3:13; 2 Timothy 4:8; Hebrews 10:25). Some see these referring to the Rapture and the period immediately following. The *"days of the Son of Man"* noted in Luke 17:22–24 may refer to the Millennial Kingdom. The *"day of God"* noted in 2 Peter 3:12, refers to the time of *"new heavens and a new earth"* or *"the day of eternity"* (2 Peter 3:13, 18; Isaiah 65:17).

STOP AND APPLY—Which King is *Your* King?—Throughout history, hundreds of kings have ruled. No one has claimed or shown himself to be *The* King. Scripture describes Messiah Jesus as *"King of kings"* and *"Lord of lords."* None other is worthy, capable, or able to be king over all. Everyone honors and follows someone as king, even if it is oneself—not a really good choice. The Lord-King Jesus is worthy and capable. Is Jesus *your* King, *your* Lord and Savior? If not, change allegiance today, even *now*!

Day Five

Following My Shepherd

The New Testament could not be clearer; Jesus called any to come to Him, believe Him, follow, love, and obey Him. He is God, the God-Man who deserves worship, adoration, trust, obedience, and love. As the *"Son of David,"* Jesus is the most capable Shepherd. We can find comfort from Him, leadership by Him, and full provision now and forever. As He leads, we follow; as He feeds, we feast. What does He want to do in *your* life in *this* season? Consider these Scriptures that speak of our *Savior*, our *Shepherd*, and our *Sovereign*. Record your thoughts, insights, and prayers.

📖 Jesus is *"the Good Shepherd."* In John 10:11, Jesus says, *"the Good Shepherd lays down His life for the sheep."* Psalm 22 pictures this *Savior* Shepherd. Read these Scriptures and note your insights and applications.

📖 Note about *Psalm 22*: Jesus quotes Psalm 22:1 on the Cross. There is much more in Psalm 22 about Him giving His life. Note verses 1–21 and the pictures pertaining to His death. Note verses 22–31 and the pictures pertaining to His resurrection. Read Psalm 22:1–31 and note your added insights.

📖 *John 10:1–18*. Note what Jesus said about Himself as *"the Good Shepherd"* along with other insights you might discover.

📖 Jesus is *"the Great Shepherd."* Hebrews 13:20 speaks of *"the Great Shepherd"* coming *"up from the dead."* Psalm 23 speaks of the Lord as *"My Shepherd"*—He is indeed the *"Great Shepherd."* Read these Scriptures and note your insights and applications.

Psalm 23

Hebrews 13:20–21

📖 Jesus is *"the Chief Shepherd."* In 1 Peter 5:4, He is mentioned as *"the Chief Shepherd"* who will return with rewards for faithful service in the *"flock."* Psalm 24 shows us this *Sovereign* Shepherd. Read these Scriptures and note your insights and applications.

Psalm 24

1 Peter 5:1–5

📖 Someone has said a shepherd 'guides, grazes, and guards.' Look at these Scriptures and note how our Lord Jesus fulfills these areas.

Matthew 2:6 (quoting Micah 5:2, 4 and 2 Samuel 5:2 and/or 1 Chronicles 11:2 (about David))

Matthew 4:18–22

Matthew 9:9–13

Matthew 16:24–27 and Luke 9:23–26

John 6:63, 66–69

John 16:7–15

John 17:6–8, 11–12, 14–21

The Lord is ever a Shepherd; he does not change from eternity past, through time, and into eternity future. What do you discover about *"the Lamb,"* another descriptive name of Jesus, in Revelation 7:16–17?

TAKEAWAYS

Jesus, the "Son of David"

There are five takeaways from *Jesus, the "Son of David."* 1) God Keeps His Word. He promised the *"seed"* of the woman and sent His only Son Jesus, the ultimate *"Seed"* and *"Son of David."* 2) As the *"Son of David,"* Jesus revealed the heart of God as the Perfect David. 3) Jesus revealed the *"Mercy"* of God in ways David never could. 4) Jesus is the ideal Shepherd King, guiding His sheep to *"springs of the water of life."* 5) Jesus is the best *"Son of David"* and the Great *"King of kings,"* forever reigning with justice, lovingkindness, holiness, and love.

Lord, You are indeed the best *"Son of David,"* revealing Yourself as the King of kings, the Lord of lords, the Good Shepherd, and certainly a *"man after"* the heart of God; You followed Your Father every day in all Your choices, words, and ways. I praise You as the greatest Shepherd King, the *"Son of the Most High,"* whose kingdom will never end. I honor You for possessing all the good qualities of the many leaders throughout history, but none of the bad characteristics. You are the sinless *"Son of David,"* the Lord, Messiah, and Savior, the Last Adam, the greater Enoch and better Noah, the greater Melchizedek, Abraham, Moses, David, and Solomon in every way. Thank You that You were and are full of *"mercy"* as many attested during Your earthly walk; You healed, forgave, and showed the love of the Father. Thank You for showing mercy to me, for loving and forgiving me and giving me Your eternal life! In the name of Jesus, our faithful *"Son of David"* and Savior, Amen.

A Chronology of the Life and Ministry of the Lord Jesus Christ

This Chronology is an attempt at an overview of what the Scriptures present about the sequence of events in the life and ministry of the Lord Jesus Christ. All of Scripture is One Story, His Story, for History is really His-Story. We see this from Genesis 1:1, when Christ the Creator of all made all (John 1:1–3). He created time. He spoke the first "Gospel" Promise (Genesis 3:15—Jesus is the *"Seed"* of the Woman) to Adam and the Woman after sin entered by Adam's self-willed choice. Ultimately, the many people, prophecies, and pictures in Scripture relay something about this Coming Messiah Savior. In Scripture, we see Him, our only Savior and how only He could take care of our sin—our rebellion and refusal to worship and obey Him. By faith in Him, Jesus gives us His righteousness forever—first positionally, then forever experientially. At the heart of His righteousness, is His perfect worship and obedience to the Father fully carried out, forever past, present, and future.

Every leader in Scripture is a picture of the Coming One, either in *contrast* like Cain or Nimrod—He is not like them—or in *comparison* like Abel or Noah—He is like them in some ways. Abel is not the Messiah, the *"Seed"* of the Woman, but he is something like the Coming Messiah, just not fully Him. The Messiah would be the *"Seed"* of the Woman and the fuller revelation of the Angel of the LORD (Christ manifested in the Old Testament, a 'Christophany'). He is One Greater than Abel, Enoch, Noah, Abraham, Isaac, Israel, Judah, Moses, Joshua, Gideon, David, Solomon, and any number of other men and women of faith.

The Scriptures, especially the four Gospel accounts and the other New Testament writings present the Lord Jesus in His Eternity as God (John 1), His Birth as the God-Man, His Childhood, and Youth (Luke 1–2), and His Manhood, His Life, Ministry, Death, Resurrection, Ascension, Enthronement, High Priesthood, and His Victorious Return as King of kings and Lord of lords (Luke-Acts, Hebrews). This chronology does not explain all those factors, but simply seeks to trace His steps especially in those thirty-three years of His Earth Walk.

As with any human attempt, it is incomplete, doubtless has some faults, failures, shortcomings—none intended. My recommendation? Be a Berean, searching the Scriptures to see if these things are so (Acts 17:11). Follow the advice I received one day about any book (except Scripture): treat it like fish. Eat the meat and throw away the bones. That is true of any human-authored word. The Word of God, the Scriptures, which have touches of human authoring are fully God-breathed, no error or "bones" to throw away. And God never put 'filler' in to make a verse or passage a little longer.

His Scriptures are enough, but He has also given us His Spirit to guide us in truth as we read, imbibe, and obey His Word. Therefore, I have put together this chronology with the help of several others and their tools. Let me mention a few that have been of particular help—A. T. Robertson's *A Harmony of the Gospels for Students of the Life of Christ, The NIV/NASB Harmony of the Gospels* by Robert L. Thomas and Stanley N.

Gundry, *The MacArthur Study Bible* and John MacArthur's compilation of Jesus' life entitled *One Perfect Life: The Complete Story of the Lord Jesus.* I do not agree with every detail presented by these authors; that's why I have put together this chronology. I trust it will be a help in knowing and walking with the Lord Jesus moment by moment, for if what we read and learn does not help in knowing God and growing in His grace, it is not doing what God intended it to do (That's clear from passages such as Psalm 1:1–6, Psalm 2:1–12, and 2 Timothy 3:14–17).

I pray this chronology will make the Eternal Person, the Earthly Life, Words, and Deeds, and even the Attitude of the Lord Jesus come more alive. More than that, I pray this will be a *meeting place* with the Lord *Himself* as He shows Himself and speaks in the Gospels and other Scriptures. Paul said it well and I repeat his words, *"I beseech you therefore, brethren, by the mercies of God, that you present your bodies a living sacrifice, holy, acceptable to God, which is your reasonable service* [*of worship*]. *And do not be conformed to this world, but be transformed by the renewing of your mind, that you may prove what is that good and acceptable and perfect will of God"* (Romans 12:1–2—NKJV).

A Chronology of The Life and Ministry of the Lord Jesus Christ

Date / Age	Event	Scripture
The Eternal Son of God, One with God the Father and One with God the Holy Spirit		
Eternity	Jesus Christ is the Eternal Son of God, the *"I AM,"* One with the Father and the Holy Spirit. He has *always* been, is eternal, with no beginning and no ending. He is before Abraham and before John the Baptist (John 1:30; 8:58).	Micah 5:2; Psalm 102:25–27; John 1:1–2, 30; 8:58; 17:5, 24; 2 Cor. 4:4–6; Hebrews 1:3–4, 5–13; 13:8; Revelation 1:8, 11; 22:13, 16
Eternity and Time	Jesus Christ is the Creator of all. He is eternal, ever living. He is the Living Lord of Creation, the Creator of Adam in Genesis 2:7, breathing *"into his nostrils the breath of life; and man became a living being."* He is the resurrected Lord of the New Creation, breathing on His disciples, promising the Holy Spirit, forgiveness, and Eternal Life in John 20:19–23.	Genesis 1:1; 2:7, 22; John 1:1–3,30; 8:58; 20:19–23; 1 Corinthians 8:6; Colossians 1:15–18; Hebrews 1:1, 10–12; 11:3
Eternal Lord	Christ is the Angel of the LORD, the pre-incarnate Christ, who appeared (a "Christophany" in the Old Testament) or spoke many times (about 35 times) in the Old Testament for His purposes among His people.	Genesis 18:1–14; 22:11–18; 32:24–30; Exodus 3:2; Joshua 5:13–15; Judges 6:11–24; 13:1–23; Isaiah 37:35–36

The Scriptures Give Many Promises, Prophecies, and Pictures of the Coming of the Messiah/Christ		
Creation to Malachi ca. 400 BC	The *"Messiah"* / *"Christ"* was *promised* and *prophesied* through many prophets throughout the years of the Old Testament. There are over 300 Old Testament prophecies fulfilled in the birth, life, ministry, death, resurrection, enthronement, and return of Jesus Christ. Isaiah 9:6–7 speaks of the *"Mighty God"* coming as a *"Child"* and a *"Son"*—the God-Man.	Genesis 3:15 (*"her Seed"*); 22:17–18; 49:10; Isaiah 9:6–7
Creation to Malachi ca. 400 BC	Jesus fulfills all the Types, Signs, and Symbols of the Old Testament—as King, Prophet, and High Priest, in the symbols and signs of the Sun, Moon, and Stars, in the Patriarchs and Men and Women of Faith, in the pictures in the Tabernacle / Temple (e.g., John 1:14—*"the Word* [Jesus] *dwelt / "tented" or "tabernacled" "among us"*), and in the pictures in the Priesthood, the Sacrifices / Offerings, the Laws, the Feast Days / Weeks, as well as in various accounts throughout the Word of God.	Genesis 14:18–20; Exodus 25–40; Deuteronomy 18:15–18; Psalm 2; 110; 118; Isaiah 6:1; 7:14; 9:6–7; Malachi 4:2; John 1:1, 14, 18; 3:14; Colossians 2:16–17; Hebrews 2:17–18; 3:1; 4:14; 5:5–10; 6:20; 7:1–28; 8:1–3, 6; 9:11–28; 10:19–22
The Birth and Early Years of Jesus the Messiah / Christ		
5 / 4 BC Possibly in May/June	Isaiah and Malachi prophesied about the coming of the one to prepare the way for the Messiah. In His time, the Lord sent the angel Gabriel to Zacharias, a priest *"of the division of Abijah."* As he offered the daily incense in the Temple, the angel told of the coming birth of his son John to him and Elizabeth. John would be the prophet to prepare the way for the Messiah.	Malachi 3:1; 4:5–6 Isaiah 40:3 Matthew 11:10 Mark 1:2; Luke 1:5–25, 76; 7:27
5/4 BC Possibly in Dec	When Elizabeth was in her sixth month of pregnancy, the angel Gabriel went to Mary in Nazareth and told her she would bear the Messiah Jesus by the work of the Holy Spirit. He would come as King and Son of the Most High.	Matthew 1:18 Luke 1:26–38
5/4 BC Possibly in Dec	Mary traveled to the home of Zacharias and Elizabeth and stayed for three months. John's birth occurred soon after (about six months before Jesus' birth). John grew up. Around age 30, John began his ministry in the deserts.	Luke 1:39–56, 57–80
Possibly in Dec	Mary returned to Nazareth. In or near the ninth month of her pregnancy, Mary and Joseph traveled to Bethlehem as part of the Roman government's required census. This travel could have occurred in August or September.	Matthew 1:19–25 Luke 2:1–5
5/4 BC Possibly in Dec and Birth	Isaiah prophesied the Messiah/Christ would be born of a virgin. In the virgin Mary's womb, Jesus was conceived *"of the Holy Spirit"* and Mary gave birth to Jesus our Savior, "'IMMANUEL,' *which translated means,* 'GOD WITH US'."	Isaiah 7:14 Matthew 1:20–25 Luke 1:26–55

5/4 BC Possibly mid to late June	While in Bethlehem, Mary gave birth to the infant Jesus. Micah prophesied that the Messiah / Christ would be born in Bethlehem, while at the same time forever being *"from the days of eternity"* (5:2). Jesus was born in Bethlehem of Judea. It is possible that Jesus was born on Tishri 15, the first day of the Feast of Tabernacles (late September). Many expected Him to be born at this Feast because of the many prophetic promises of God's Presence with His people, as He had been with them in the Wilderness.	Micah 5:2 Matthew 2:1, 5–6 Luke 2:6–7
	In the fields near Bethlehem, a host of angels announced the birth of baby Jesus to local shepherds watching the Temple flocks. They ran to Bethlehem, saw the infant, rejoiced, and began telling the story.	Luke 2:8–20
	Jesus was born in the Royal/Legal lineage (genealogy) of Joseph (Matthew 1:1–17) giving Him legal status as Messiah and in the Physical blood-line lineage (genealogy) of Mary giving Him physical status as Messiah, the *"Son of David"* (Luke 3:23–38).	Matthew 1:1–17 Luke 3:23–38
8 Days	At 8 days of age, possibly in the city of Bethlehem or at the Temple in Jerusalem, Mary and Joseph circumcised the baby Jesus and gave Him the name *"JESUS."* It is possible Jesus was circumcised on Tishri 22, the eighth day of the Feast of Tabernacles (possibly in 5/4 BC).	Leviticus 12:3; 23:33–36 Luke 2:21
40 Days	When Jesus was 40 days of age, Mary and Joseph traveled about five miles from Bethlehem to the Temple in Jerusalem to offer the required sacrifices for the purification rites of a mother who bore a son. Forty days after Tishri 15 was the date Cheshvan or Bul 24 (around early November).	Luke 2:22–24 Leviticus 5:11; 12:2–8; Numbers 3:13; 8:17
40 Days	At the Temple in Jerusalem, Simeon gave praise to God in a song of praise. Anna, a prophetess, gave thanks to God for the birth and appearance of the Messiah and *"the redemption in / of Jerusalem."*	Luke 2:25–38
3/2 BC? A *"Child"* Possibly 15 to 24 months of age	*"Wise Men / Magi"* came from the East to Jerusalem to see the newly born *"King of the Jews."* They found the toddler *"Child"* with Mary His mother in a *"house"* in Bethlehem. They worshiped Him and gave Him gifts. The designation *"Child"* (Greek—*paidion*—a *little* child—Matthew 2:11) refers to a little child with some ability to speak. He could have been 15 to 24 months of age.	Matthew 2:1b–12
3/2 BC? A *"Child"* (15-24 months)	God warned Joseph in a dream that king Herod would try to destroy the Child. He instructed him to flee to Egypt. Joseph, Mary, and the Child Jesus fled at night to Egypt and stayed until after the death of Herod (ca., between January and April, 1 BC).	Matthew 2:13–15
3/2 BC?	In anger and jealousy, Herod ordered all boys aged two and younger in and around Bethlehem to be killed. This fulfilled the prophecy of Jeremiah 31:15.	Jeremiah 31:15 Matthew 2:16–18

January (or soon after), 1 BC	According to the historical account of Josephus, *"Herod the king"* died in Jericho possibly in January of 1 BC, sometime between the events of a lunar eclipse and the Passover (March/April). Others give a possible date of March, 4 BC. Herod died at the age of 70. He was buried in the Herodian Palace in Bethlehem, within about two miles of where Jesus was born.	Josephus, *Jewish Antiquities*, 17.6.4 (166-167); 17.9.3 (213-215); *The Jewish War* 2.1.1, 3.
From 4 BC to AD 6	Herod Archelaus reigned over Judea after his father's death. (Herod the Great expressed his wish in 4 BC, giving Archelaus his son legal claim from 4 BC (possibly ruling as co-ruler). He officially reigned beginning in 1 BC and was deposed in AD 6.)	Matthew 2:21–22; Josephus, *Jewish Antiquities*, 17.8.1-2 (188-195).
1 BC/ AD 1? A Child, over age 2, possibly 3-4	When Joseph brought Mary and Jesus from Egypt back to Judea, he discovered that Herod's son Herod Archelaus was reigning over Judea as king. God warned Joseph in a dream not to go back to Judea. He went to Nazareth of Galilee where they settled. Jesus was likely over two years of age, possibly three or four.	Matthew 2:19–23 Luke 2:39
Childhood, Ages 2-12	Jesus *"grew and became strong in spirit, filled with wisdom; and the grace of God was upon Him"* (Luke 2:40).	Luke 2:40
Age __?—Adulthood	Using four "Servant Songs," Isaiah prophesied of the coming Messiah, the *"Servant"* of the LORD. The third one (Isaiah 50:4–9) begins with a prophecy about the Messiah's morning time—*"The Lord GOD has given Me the tongue of disciples, that I may know how to sustain the weary one with a word. He awakens Me morning by morning, He awakens My ear to listen as a disciple"* (Isaiah 50:4—NASB). This speaks of Jesus' regular time with His Father every morning and His being discipled daily by His Father and His Word.	Isaiah 50:4 Mark 1:35 John 8:26–29; 12:44–50
AD 8/9? Age 12	At the age of 12, Mary, Joseph, Jesus and His half-brothers (James, Joseph, Simon, Jude) and half-sisters (at least two) traveled from Nazareth to Jerusalem for Passover Feast Week (Nisan, AD 8/9).	Luke 2:41–43a Matthew 13:55–56
	Jesus stayed in the Temple area at the end of Passover Week, at least three days, *"sitting in the midst of the teachers, both listening to them and asking them questions"* (Luke 2:46).	Luke 2:43b–47
	After three days, Joseph and Mary found Jesus in the Temple area and were *"amazed,"* wondering why He had done this. He stated, *"Did you not know that I must be about My Father's business?"* / [literally, *"in the things of My Father"*]?" (Luke 2:49) They did not understand His statement.	Luke 2:48–50
	The "Silent" Years of Jesus in Nazareth, Age 12-30	
Age 12-30	Jesus traveled with Joseph and Mary back to Nazareth, continued in subjection to them, *"and Jesus increased in wisdom and stature, and in favor with God and men"* (Luke 2:52).	Luke 2:51–52

Age 12-30	In Nazareth, Jesus worked six days a week with Joseph and His half-brothers in the family business as a *"carpenter"* / craftsman / stone mason (Greek, *tekton*).	Matthew 13:55 Mark 6:3 Luke 4:22
Age 2-30	*"As was His custom,"* Jesus attended the weekly Synagogue service with His family every Sabbath (Saturday) in Nazareth.	Luke 4:16
April-September AD 26 John was age 30	John the Baptist began his ministry in the *"Wilderness of Judea,"* in *"Bethabara beyond the Jordan."* He proclaimed and presented himself as a *"Voice of one crying in the wilderness: Prepare the way of the LORD..."* He preached *"a baptism of repentance for the forgiveness of sins."* Jesus was still in Nazareth. About six months later, He came to John the Baptist to be baptized by him (September or October).	Isaiah 40:3–5; 52:10; Malachi 3:1–2a; Matthew 3:1–12; Mark 1:2–8; Luke 3:1–18; John 1:19–28
	The Early Years of Jesus' Ministry	
September Early October AD 26 Age 30	Jesus came to John the Baptist to be baptized by him in the Jordan River, in the area of Bethabara, in the Wilderness of Judea. He said this was *"to fulfill all righteousness,"* to identify with sinners, to prepare to die for sinners, and impute His perfect righteousness to each believer, thus doing the Father's will and carrying out all His good purposes (2 Corinthians 5:21).	Matthew 3:13–15 Mark 1:9–11 Luke 3:3, 21–22 John 1:29–34
September Early October AD 26 Age 30	<u>Jesus</u> was *praying* as He was being baptized in the Jordan River. The heavens opened and *"the <u>Holy Spirit</u> descended in bodily form like a dove"* and rested on Jesus, anointing Him for His ministry. The <u>Father's</u> Voice came from heaven saying, *"You are My Beloved <u>Son</u>; in You I am well pleased"* (Luke 3:21–22). The Triune God revealed Himself in Three Persons.	Matthew 3:16–17; Mark 1:10–11; Luke 3:21–22; John 1:32–34
October and part of November AD 26 Age 30	The Spirit of God led Jesus into the Wilderness for a time of testing by the devil. He fasted and prayed 40 days and 40 nights, facing every kind of temptation, but He never yielded to temptation or sinned in any way.	Matthew 4:1–11 Luke 4:1–13 Hebrews 2:18; 4:15
	Year One of Jesus' Ministry—Late AD 26 and AD 27—Age 30	
December AD 26 Age 30	Jesus returned from the Wilderness temptations *"in the power of the Spirit."* He began teaching in the synagogues throughout the region of Galilee.	Luke 4:14–15
January AD 27 Age 30	Jesus ministered in the region where John the Baptist was baptizing. There, John identified Jesus as *"the Lamb of God that takes away the sin of the world"* (John 1:29, 36).	John 1:19–36
January AD 27 Age 30	*"Come and See"*—Over a two-day period, Jesus met and called several disciples to *"come and see"* and follow Him (John 1:39). Those who met Jesus included John, Andrew, Andrew's brother Simon Peter, Philip, and Nathanael.	John 1:37–51

February/ March AD 27 Age 30	Along with His mother Mary, Jesus and at least the five men attended a wedding at Cana in Galilee. Jesus performed His *first miracle* and those disciples with Him there *"believed in Him"* (John 2:11).	John 2:1–11
March AD 27	Jesus went to Capernaum and stayed a few days along with His mother, brothers, and disciples.	John 2:12
March AD 27 Age 30	Jesus and several disciples went to the Passover celebration in Jerusalem (the first of four Passover Feasts in His ministry years). There Jesus cleansed the Temple of the crooked merchants and their merchandising, rebuking the sellers there. He spoke of His body as the *"temple"* being destroyed and raised in three days.	John 2:13–25
March AD 27 Age 30	During Passover week in Jerusalem at the Temple, Jesus spoke of His body as the *"temple"* being destroyed and raised in three days. This was His *first* mention of His resurrection, though veiled in the language about the *"temple."* Several mentioned this incident and His words in His trial.	John 2:19, 21–22 See also Matthew 26:59–62; Mark 14:57–59
	While at the Passover Feast week in Jerusalem, Jesus caught the attention of several there from Galilee. Later they welcomed Him in Galilee.	John 4:45
March/ April AD 27 Age 30	Perhaps in Galilee or in Jerusalem, Nicodemus, a Jewish Teacher came to Jesus at night to ask Him about His teachings and His ministry. Jesus emphasized the necessity of a person being *"born again"* or born *"from Above"* by the working of the Holy Spirit to see and enter the Kingdom of God. Jesus revealed Himself as the Son to be lifted on a cross for anyone to believe in and receive eternal life. He also drew a distinction between those who believe in Him for eternal life and those who do not believe one day facing the condemnation under which each already stands.	John 3:1–21
April/May AD 27 Age 30	Jesus and His disciples came into Judea (John 3:22), ministered, and baptized there for a time. More people began coming to Jesus than to John the Baptist who continued to minister during this time, having not yet *"been thrown into prison"* (John 4:24). John rejoiced as a Friend of the Bridegroom Jesus, seeing this as his and Jesus' ministry given from heaven: *"a man can receive nothing unless it has been given him from heaven"* (John 3:27).	John 3:22–36
Spring AD 27	Herod Antipas imprisoned John the Baptist in his palace-fortress in Machaerus, east of the Dead Sea. Herod did this for John's Biblical and moral opposition to Herod's marriage to Herodias, the wife of his brother Philip (also Herod's niece). This occurred possibly in the late Spring of AD 27.	Matthew 14:3–5 Mark 6:17–20 Luke 3:19–20

May/June AD 27 Age 30	Because of the opposition and uproar of the Pharisees in Judea, Jesus and His disciples left Judea to go into Galilee. They passed through Samaria and stopped outside the village of Sychar for a meal.	Matthew 4:12 Mark 1:14 Luke 4:14a John 4:1–5
	Jesus stayed by the well of Jacob outside Sychar where He met and conversed with an immoral woman from the village. Jesus revealed Himself as the Messiah and challenged her to admit her sin and believe in Him to receive *"living water."* She did and told the village about this Jesus being the Messiah.	John 4:6–30
May/June AD 27 Age 30	At Jacob's well outside Sychar, Jesus taught His disciples about the eternal *"food"* of *"the will of Him who sent Me."* Then, that day and the next two days, many from that village heard Him gladly, and believed on Him as *"the Savior of the world."* Jesus' reference to *"the harvest"* (in 4 months) may refer to the Autumn harvests.	John 4:31–42
Summer AD 27 Age 30	Jesus and these disciples left Sychar and went into Galilee where many believed in Him based on the miracles they had seen at the Passover Feast in Jerusalem. News about Jesus began to spread.	Mark 1:14c–15 Luke 4:14–15 John 4:43–45
Early Summer AD 27 Age 30	At Cana, a city in the Galilee region, a royal official came to Jesus from Capernaum asking Him to come and heal his son. Jesus spoke a word of healing—*"your son lives."* The man believed Him and, though about 16 miles away, his son was healed at that precise moment.	John 4:46–54
Late Summer AD 27 Age 30	Jesus traveled to Nazareth where He had grown up. In the synagogue, He read from Isaiah 61:1–2a, proclaiming Himself as the fulfillment of the Messianic prophecy. When He mentioned "THE FAVORABLE YEAR OF THE LORD," it may refer to His ministry as a time of Jubilee. It is possible this was also a reference to that year as a Jubilee Year.	Luke 4:16–22 Isaiah 61:1–2a Leviticus 25:10
Late Summer AD 27 Age 30	When Jesus spoke of the Lord working in the lives of non-Jews, this filled the people of Nazareth *"with rage"* and they rejected Him as Messiah. They attempted to execute Him by throwing Him off the cliff on the edge of town. Jesus escaped and traveled to Capernaum.	Luke 4:23–30
	Jesus traveled to Capernaum and began teaching there. He settled there for a time. Matthew 9:1 speaks of Capernaum as Jesus' *"own city."*	Matthew 4:13–16; 9:1b; Luke 4:31
Autumn AD 27 Age 30/31	*"Fishers of Men"*—Jesus called four of His disciples as they were fishing near the shore—Simon Peter and his brother Andrew, James and his brother John—to *"follow Me, and I will make you fishers of men"* (Matthew 4:19). At least some of these had met and heard Him a few months earlier.	Matthew 4:18–22 Mark 1:16–20 Luke 4:31a
"Sabbath"	Jesus taught in the synagogue in Capernaum and healed a demon-possessed man there on the Sabbath.	Mark 1:21–28 Luke 4:31b–36

Same "*Sabbath*" Autumn AD 27 Age 30/31	In Capernaum, on the Sabbath, Jesus left the synagogue and went to the house of Simon Peter and Andrew. Jesus healed Simon Peter's mother-in-law and she began serving them. That Saturday evening, many others came to the house. Jesus healed them.	Matthew 8:14–17 Mark 1:29–34 Luke 4:38–41
Autumn AD 27 Age 30/31	Sunday morning, after the evening and late night of ministry in Capernaum, Jesus awoke "*a long while before daylight,*" went out to "*a solitary place*" and there "*He prayed.*"	Mark 1:35 Luke 4:42a
	Simon Peter and others searched for Jesus and found him in that "*solitary place,*" urging Him to come back into town where many awaited Him. Jesus said He and His disciples needed to go to other towns.	Mark 1:35, 36–38 Luke 4:42b–43
	Jesus and His disciples traveled to several towns, "*preaching in their synagogues throughout all Galilee, and casting out demons*" (Mark 1:39). The report of Jesus' teaching and miracles began to spread further throughout Galilee and beyond.	Matthew 4:23–24 Mark 1:39 Luke 4:37, 44
	Year Two of Jesus' Ministry—Late AD 27 and AD 28—Age 31	
Winter AD 27 Age 31	Jesus returned to Capernaum where He issued a second call to Simon Peter and others. They would "*be catching men.*" Luke 5:10 uses the word *zogron/zogreo*, "*taking alive,*" meaning to catch and keep people alive, a reference to eternal life (*zoe*).	Luke 5:1–11
	In one of the cities of Galilee, Jesus healed a leprous man. The news spread about Jesus' healing the man. Many came to Him, and He healed them, even though He stayed away from towns.	Matthew 8:2–4 Mark 1:40–45 Luke 5:12–15
Winter AD 27+ Age 31+	Jesus often withdrew to deserted places to pray. This statement covers Jesus' entire ministry.	Luke 5:16
Winter AD 28 Age 31	Jesus came home to Capernaum where a great crowd gathered at a home. Jesus preached the Word. While there, four men brought a paralyzed man on a stretcher (lowering him through the roof). Jesus told the paralyzed man, "*your sins are forgiven.*" The Pharisees and teachers of the Mosaic Law opposed Jesus for this statement about forgiving sins. To the amazement of the crowd, Jesus then healed the paralyzed man who then walked home.	Matthew 9:1–8 Mark 2:1–12 Luke 5:17–26
Winter AD 28 Age 31	In the city of Capernaum, Jesus called Matthew (Levi, son of Alphaeus), a Jewish man and a tax collector for the Roman government, to come and follow Him. Matthew left his tax-collector's booth and "*everything*" to follow Jesus.	Matthew 9:9 Mark 2:13–14 Luke 5:27–28

	In Capernaum, Matthew invited several of his tax-collector associates and other *"sinners"* to dinner at his house along with Jesus and His disciples. Jesus responded to the objections of the Pharisees, noting that He came in mercy to call *"sinners"* or *"the sick"* to *"repentance"* and healing, not to call the righteous.	Matthew 9:10–13 Mark 2:15–17 Luke 5:29–32
	In Capernaum, certain disciples of John the Baptist and the Pharisees practiced regular fasting. They asked Jesus' disciples why they did not. Jesus responded with three parables (1. Bridegroom's guests celebrate, 2. No one sews new cloth on an old garment, 3. New wine is poured into new wineskins). Jesus is bringing in a New Day, a New Way, a New Life.	Matthew 9:14–17 Mark 2:18–22 Luke 5:33–39
Early Spring AD 28 Age 31	*"Some time later"* Jesus traveled to Jerusalem for a Feast (This was perhaps Passover, the First Feast of Spring. Some suggest one of the Fall/Autumn Feasts: Trumpets, Day of Atonement, or the Feast of Tabernacles).	John 5:1
	At the Pool of Bethesda in Jerusalem, Jesus healed a man who had been sick for 38 years. It was a Sabbath. .	John 5:2–9
	Some began to chasten the healed man for carrying his pallet on the Sabbath. He testified that Jesus had healed him.	John 5:10–15
	Because Jesus healed the sick man at Bethesda on a Sabbath, the Jewish leaders began *"persecuting Jesus."*	John 5:16
	At this time in Jerusalem, Jesus focused everyone's attention on God as His Father and the fact that He was working with His Father. Some of the Jewish leaders wanted to kill Jesus for breaking the Sabbath and for *"making Himself equal with God."* They considered Jesus' words about being one with the Father to be a claim to Jesus' deity.	John 5:17–18
	During this time in Jerusalem, Jesus began explaining Himself and His working, pointing to how He was like the Father in what He did. He spoke about His relationship with the Father. He focused on the future resurrections and the role of the Father and of Him, the Son. (If this occurred during Passover Season, it matches the events of that week. The Feast of First Fruits occurs during Passover week and points to Resurrection.)	John 5:19–29
	Using the pattern of a trial procedure, Jesus spoke of at least four witnesses to His claims (the witness of John the Baptist, of Jesus' works, of the Father, and of Scripture, especially the writings of *"Moses"* (notably *Genesis, Exodus, Leviticus, Numbers, Deuteronomy*).	John 5:30–47

Late Spring AD 28 Age 31	On a Sabbath, Jesus and His disciples went through a grain field near Capernaum; the disciples picked some grain and ate it. The Pharisees claimed this was law-breaking (it was not—Deuteronomy 23:25), but Jesus defended the disciples pointing to David and his men eating *"showbread"* from the Tabernacle (1 Samuel 21:1–6), and priests working on the Sabbath in the Temple. He also quoted from Hosea 6:6 about showing *"mercy"* as greater than *"sacrifice"* (or any Sabbath rule or Temple regulation). Jesus claimed Himself as Lord of the Sabbath. Matthew placed this incident with Jesus' call to come to Him, be given rest, and find rest (Matthew 11:28–30). He is indeed *"Lord of the Sabbath"* and Lord of Rest (Matthew 12:8).	Matthew 12:1–8 Mark 2:23–28 Luke 6:1–5
Late Spring AD 28 Age 31	*"On another Sabbath"* (Luke 6:6), Jesus attended the synagogue in Capernaum and there healed a man with a withered hand. The Pharisees considered this law-breaking, but Jesus countered with questions about doing good versus evil on the Sabbath. He gave an example of good—taking care of a sheep on the Sabbath. Being righteously angry at their evil ways, Jesus revealed His righteous heart and deeds, healing the man. They wanted to accuse Him of wrong. When He healed the man, they were filled with anger and began thinking of ways to kill Him.	Matthew 12:9–14 Mark 3:1–6 Luke 6:6–11
Late Spring/ Summer AD 28 Age 31	Aware of the opposition of the Pharisees, Jesus and His disciples withdrew from Capernaum to another area around the Lake of Galilee. Many sick, diseased people from Judea, Jerusalem, Idumea, the regions across the Jordan, as well as from Tyre and Sidon followed Him and *"He healed them all."* Jesus fulfilled the prophecies of Isaiah 42:1–3 and 11:10 [quoted from the Septuagint (LXX), the Greek language Old Testament].	Matthew 12:15–21; Mark 3:7–12 Isaiah 42:1–3; 11:10-LXX [cf. Romans 15:12]
Summer AD 28 Age 31	On a nearby mountain, Jesus spent the night in prayer, after which He called His disciples to Himself. He chose The Twelve as His *"apostles"* to be *"with Him,"* to be sent out by Him. The Twelve: Simon Peter, Andrew, James and John of Zebedee (*"Sons of Thunder"*), Phillip, Bartholomew, Matthew the tax-gatherer, Thomas, James of Alphaeus, Simon the Zealot, Judas (Lebbaeus or Thaddeus) of James, Judas Iscariot (of Kerioth) in Idumea (place of several with Edomite heritage/descendants).	Matthew 10:3—Thaddeus or Lebbaeus (KJV) Mark 3:13–19 Luke 6:12–19
Summer AD 28 Age 31	Because of the crowds coming to Him, Jesus went up on a mountainside (likely a hillside) north of the Sea of Galilee and He taught them what is known as *The Sermon on the Mount*.	Matthew 5:1–7:29 Luke 6:20–49
	Jesus came down from the mountainside to Capernaum. There, a Roman Centurion sent some Jewish elders to ask Jesus to come and heal his ailing servant. Jesus went, but before He could get to the house, the Centurion (or the Centurion with certain Jewish men) stopped Him and said to simply heal the servant from where He was (not enter a Gentile's house). Jesus, amazed at the Centurion and his faith, healed the servant.	Matthew 8:1, 5–13 Luke 7:1–10

	Jesus and His disciples traveled to nearby Nain and when approaching the town, stopped a funeral procession. Jesus touched the coffin and told the dead son of the widow (only son) to *"arise."* He arose from the dead to the amazement of all. The report about Jesus spread *"throughout all Judea and all the surrounding region."*	Luke 7:11–17
	A deputation from the imprisoned John the Baptist came to Jesus asking if He was the Christ / the Messiah or should they expect another. In Matthew 11:3, the two men asked if Jesus were *"the Expected One"* or should they look for someone else—using the Greek word *heteros*, "another of a *different* kind," while in Luke 7:20 the two men used the Greek word *allos*, "another of the *same* kind." Which is it? Likely, the men used both words—*"Are You the Expected One* (the Messiah), or do we look for someone *different* from You or for someone *like* You?" Jesus did not leave them without an answer as He healed many there and had a message for John.	Matthew 11:2–3 Luke 7:18–20
	At that time, Jesus healed many. In answer to the disciples of John the Baptist, Jesus quoted from Isaiah 35:5 and 61:1, prophecies about the Messiah. Everything was on track. God was working through Jesus as the Messiah just as He said.	Matthew 11:4–5 Luke 7:21–22 Isaiah 35:5; 61:1
	Jesus sent a further word to John the Baptist. It serves as The Hidden Beatitude—*"And blessed is he who keeps from stumbling over Me"*—recorded in the subjunctive mood meaning one *may stumble* over Me and My ways, but he or she *does not have to stumble*. He or she will be *"blessed"* in trusting Jesus rather than stumbling in doubt about Him.	Matthew 11:6 Luke 7:23
Summer AD 28 Age 31	Jesus gave praise about John the Baptist quoting Malachi 3:1 as fulfilled in him and saying, *"among those born of women, there is no one greater than John."* He also noted the response of people: each could either receive John as sent from God along with receiving God's purpose for each in receiving Jesus as Messiah <u>or</u> each could reject God's prophet and reject God's purpose by rejecting Jesus as Messiah.	Matthew 11:7–19 Luke 7:24–35 Malachi 3:1
Summer AD 28 Age 31	In referring to John the Baptist and his ministry, Jesus spoke of the Kingdom suffering *"violence"* or pressing on persistently and those entering it being persistent in coming. Later, Jesus, in rebuking the Pharisees' unbelief, referred to John the Baptist and those who believed his message as persistently pressing in to the Kingdom (noted in Luke 16:16).	Matthew 11:12 Luke 16:14–<u>16</u>
Likely, sometime in AD 28, John the Baptist and Jesus, both Age 31	Herod Antipas had a birthday celebration, (possibly) in Tiberius or at his palace/fortress at Machaerus, east of the Dead Sea. After Herodias' daughter (Salome) *"danced"* before Herod Antipas (tetrarch of Galilee) and his guests, he promised her any request. At her mother Herodias' insistence, she asked for *"the head of John the Baptist on a platter."* Somewhat reticent, but still proud, Herod ordered John beheaded; they brought his head on a platter. Mourning, the disciples of John the Baptist buried his body in a tomb.	Matthew 14:3–12 Mark 6:17–29 Acts 13:25

Year Three of Jesus' Ministry—Late AD 28 and AD 29—Age 32		
Late Fall AD 28 Age 32	Jesus reproached the cities of Chorazin, Bethsaida, and Capernaum for their unbelief in Jesus as the Messiah. He noted their unbelief as worse than that of the Gentile cities of Tyre, Sidon, and Sodom.	Matthew 11:20–24 Luke 10:13–15
	In reproaching the cities of Chorazin, Bethsaida, and Capernaum, Jesus focused Himself on His Father and prayed to Him who hides things from the proudly wise and intelligent and reveals truth to the those who are humble like a baby, willingly dependent on others, especially God. In this context, Matthew noted Jesus' Invitation to come to Him for *"rest"* for their *"souls"* as well as finding *"rest"* in learning from Him. Matthew also placed this with the Sabbath incident of the disciples eating from a grain field in which Jesus defended their freedom, focused all on *"mercy,"* and clarified His place as *"Lord of the Sabbath,"* thus Lord of *"rest"* (see Matthew 12:1–8, 9–14).	Matthew 11:25–27 and 11:28–30 Jeremiah 6:16
Fall AD 28 Age 32	Simon the Pharisee invited Jesus to his home for a meal. There, an immoral woman came in and began washing His feet with her tears, then kissed and anointed them with fragrant oil. Simon was incensed, but Jesus honored her in the Parable of the Two Debtors. He then forgave her sins and blessed her with His salvation and peace.	Luke 7:36–50
	Jesus traveled through several towns and villages [in Galilee] preaching the Gospel of the Kingdom of God and healing many. Luke made special note of the women who followed Him and provided monetary support for Rabbi Jesus. [The women included Mary Magdalene (from Magdala), Joanna, wife of Herod's steward Chuza, Susanna, and *"many others."*)	Luke 8:1–3
	Jesus returned to His new home in Capernaum where many gathered to hear Him. During this time, some of *"His own people,"* likely His family, came there and sought to stop or restrain Him. During this day, Jesus made it clear that His true family followed His Father by hearing and obeying His Word and doing His will.	Matthew 12:46–50 Mark 3:19b–21, 31–35 Luke 8:19–21
	In Capernaum, Jesus healed a demon-possessed man. The Pharisees and scribes from that area accused Jesus of being in league with Beelzebub ("lord of flies," used of the devil). Jesus spoke clearly about His Kingdom being no *"kingdom divided"* or no *"house divided"* and the difference between His Kingdom and Satan's kingdom. To blaspheme the obvious work of the Holy Spirit meant eternal doom. The Pharisees' evil words revealed their evil hearts.	Matthew 12:22–37 Mark 3:22–27 Luke 11:17–23
	When the Pharisees requested a miraculous Messianic *"sign"* from Jesus, He instructed them to pay attention to Jonah, to the Queen of the South (Sheba), and to Solomon. He was the *"greater"* sign, and they were a *"wicked generation."*	Matthew 12:38–45 Luke 11:24–26, 29–32

	"On the same day," Jesus spoke from a boat to a great crowd by the Sea of Galilee the Parable of the Soils. His disciples asked Him about this and other parables. He explained what He was doing, how most do not hear or believe, and what the four soils meant.	Matthew 13:1–23 Mark 4:1–20 Luke 8:4–15
Fall AD 28 Age 32	Jesus spoke the Parable of the Lamp which was also part of His Sermon on the Mount (Matthew 5:15–16).	Mark 4:21–25 Luke 8:16–18
Fall AD 28 Age 32	Jesus told the multitudes other Parables, each about the Kingdom—the Sprouting Seed, the Wheat and Tares, the Mustard Seed, the Leaven. Afterward, Jesus explained these to His disciples.	Matthew 13:24–35; Mark 4:26–34; Luke 13:18–21
Fall AD 28 Age 32	After speaking to the multitudes through several Parables, Jesus explained about the Tares in the Parable of the Wheat and Tares and told His disciples the Parables of the Treasure Hidden in a Field, the Pearl of Great Price, the Dragnet, and the Householder.	Matthew 13:36–53a
	"On the same day," in the evening, Jesus and His disciples got in a boat to cross the Sea of Galilee. A storm arose and, in fear, they awoke Jesus from a deep sleep. To their amazement, He stilled the storm, and questioned their lack of faith.	Matthew 8:23–27; 13:53b Mark 4:35–41 Luke 8:22–25
	In the country of the Gadarenes on the East side of the Sea of Galilee, two demon-possessed men met Jesus. One of them ran to Jesus and the demons cried out to Jesus. He discovered the name of the demon to be *"Legion,"* one of many, and Jesus commanded them to go into a herd of swine which then rushed off the cliffside into the Sea. The man now made whole, wanted to go with Jesus. He told him instead to go to his friends and *"tell them what great things the Lord has done for you, and how He had compassion on you."* The newly delivered man told his testimony about Jesus throughout the Decapolis (east side of the Sea of Galilee).	Matthew 8:28–34 Mark 5:1–20 Luke 8:26–39
	Jesus and His disciples crossed back over the Sea of Galilee to Capernaum where Jairus, a ruler of the synagogue, pleaded with Jesus to come heal his daughter who was near death. Jesus followed and on the way a woman with a twelve-year issue of blood touched His outer cloak (likely one of the corner tassels—*tzitzits*—Numbers 15:38–40; Deuteronomy 22:12). This revealed her testimony of faith in Jesus as the Messiah (*"sun of righteousness"*) who would have *"healing in its wings,"* His outer cloak (Malachi 4:2). Jesus spoke of her being *"healed"* (Greek word *hugies*—physically whole) and made *"well"* (Greek word *sozo*—saved spiritually). Thus, she could *"go in peace."*	Matthew 9:18–22 Mark 5:21–34 Luke 8:40–48
	In Capernaum, Jesus then went to Jairus' house where everyone said the age-twelve daughter had died. Jesus went in with Jairus, his wife, Peter, James, and John. He said *"Talitha cumi," "Little girl, I say arise,"* She came to life for all to see. *"Talitha"* can also be translated "little lamb."	Matthew 9:23–26 Mark 5:35–43 Luke 8:49–56

	In Capernaum, two blind men sought Jesus to heal them. He touched their eyes and healed them. After that, Jesus healed a demon-possessed mute man. The Pharisees continued to accuse Jesus of working by Satan's power.	Matthew 9:27–34
	Jesus traveled to Nazareth where, again, they revealed their unbelief in Jesus. He healed a few people there. Jesus *"marveled"* at their unbelief (Mark 6:6a).	Matthew 13:54–58 Mark 6:1–6a
	Jesus traveled to several villages in Galilee, preaching the Kingdom of God and healing many. He revealed His compassion for the multitudes and called His disciples to *"pray the Lord of the Harvest to send out laborers."*	Matthew 9:35–38 Mark 6:6b Luke 9:1–2
	In Galilee, Jesus *"summoned His twelve disciples"* and *"gave them authority,"* preparing to send them out *"two by two"* to deliver the demonized, heal the sick, and preach the Kingdom of God. The Twelve: Simon Peter, Andrew, James and John, sons of Zebedee, Phillip, Bartholomew, Thomas, Matthew the tax collector, James, the son of Alphaeus, Lebbaeus Thaddaeus, Simon the Canaanite (or Canaanean (Zealot)), and Judas Iscariot.	Matthew 10:1–4 Mark 6:7–9 Luke 9:1–2
Fall AD 28 Age 32	Jesus gave clear instructions to the Twelve about their ministry in various towns and villages in Galilee. He told them not to take any supplies, but to depend on people to provide as needed (possibly alluding to the principle found in Deuteronomy 25:4—See 1 Corinthians 9:3–12; 1 Timothy 5:17–18).	Matthew 10:5–42 Mark 6:10–11 Luke 9:2–5; 12:2–10
Fall/Winter AD 28 Age 32	Jesus sent the Twelve out *"two by two"* to the various towns and villages. They went out *"preaching the gospel,"* seeing many delivered, and many sick being healed. Jesus also went into various cities preaching and teaching.	Matthew 11:1 Mark 6:12–13 Luke 9:6
Winter AD 29 Age 32	During this time period, Herod the Tetrarch (Herod Antipas) heard about the things Jesus and His disciples were doing. He thought Jesus was John the Baptist raised from the dead.	Matthew 14:1–2 Mark 6:14–16 Luke 9:7–9
March AD 29 Age 32	Sometime in the Spring of AD 29, the twelve *"apostles"* returned from their preaching tour of the Galilee region and reported *"what they had done and what they had taught."* Jesus took them to retreat with Himself.	Mark 6:30 Luke 9:10
Unsure of when Jesus heard of the beheading of John	The disciples of John the Baptist who buried his body, later came to Jesus and told him of John's execution. There is no indication of *when* this occurred. Sometime after Jesus heard of the beheading of John the Baptist, He took the twelve disciples and retreated to *"a deserted place"* near the city of Bethsaida on the northeast shore of the Sea of Galilee. The multitudes followed Him, seeking His healing ministry.	Matthew 14:12 Mark 6:29, 31–33 Luke 9:10 John 6:1–3

March AD 29 Age 32	After the disciples (named *"apostles"*) returned from their mission and told Him what they had done and taught, Jesus led them by boat across the Sea of Galilee to a location likely on the northeast side of the Sea of Galilee (in the area near Bethsaida, northeast shore of the Sea) for a retreat and *"rest."* Great multitudes from various cities came to where Jesus was.	Matthew 14:13–14; Mark 6:30–33 Luke 9:10–11 John 6:1–2
	This was the Passover Season. Seeing the needy multitude, Jesus taught and healed many. As evening came, recognizing their weariness and the remoteness of the place, Jesus miraculously turned five barley loaves and two dried fish into enough to feed 5,000 men, plus women and children.	Matthew 14:14–21; Mark 6:34–44 Luke 9:12–17 John 6:3–14
	Jesus perceived that the people wanted to make Him king, so He withdrew to a mountain to pray. He sent the disciples in a boat from the area of Bethsaida (Northeast shore) of the Sea of Galilee to Gennesaret near Capernaum (Northwest shore).	Matthew 14:22–23, 34; Mark 6:45–46, 53 John 6:14–15
	From His hillside place of prayer, Jesus saw the disciples struggling with the wind and waves on the Sea of Galilee. Jesus came to them walking on the water, declaring literally, "I AM, do not fear." Peter also walked on the water at Jesus' approval and command.	Matthew 14:24–33; Mark 6:47–52 John 6:16–21
	Jesus and the disciples landed at Gennesaret (southwest of Capernaum, on the Northwest shore of the Sea of Galilee). People from Gennesaret and nearby places where Jesus went came to Jesus for healing, many simply touching the *"hem of His garment"* (likely a *tzitzit*, one of the four corner tassels (Numbers 15:38–40; Deuteronomy 22:12; Malachi 4:3).	Matthew 14:35–36 Mark 6:54–56
	The day after the Feeding of the 5000, near Capernaum, people wondered how Jesus had gotten there since there was only the boat the disciples came in. Jesus knew they sought Him for more food, and He urged them not to seek temporary food or even *"manna,"* but seek *"the food which endures to everlasting life"* and believe in Him as sent from the Father. He spoke of believing in Him as *"the Bread of Life."*	John 6:22–40
Spring AD 29 Age 32	Many Jews in the synagogue in Capernaum reacted with unbelief toward Jesus, angry that He claimed to be *"the bread which came down from heaven"* and that He declared that the Father had sent Him.	John 6:41–59
	In Capernaum, many disciples complained about these words of Jesus as *"a hard saying."* Jesus made it clear that His words *"are spirit and are life,"* and were meant to be believed. Many disciples abandoned Him, but Peter said, *"Lord, to whom shall we go? You have words of eternal life."* Peter also professed his faith in Jesus as *"the Christ, the Son of the living God."*	John 6:60–71

Summer AD 29 Age 32	Jesus remained in Galilee, avoiding Judea where many Jewish leaders wanted to kill Him. Certain Pharisees came from Jerusalem to Galilee and complained about Jesus' disciples eating with *"unclean hands"* (without *traditional* ceremonial washings). Quoting Isaiah 29:13, Jesus confronted the Pharisees for not obeying the clear commands of Scripture, especially *"Honor you father and mother."* Jesus focused the people and His disciples on the heart and obedience rather than ceremonies and foods.	Matthew 15:1–20 Mark 7:1–23 John 7:1 Exodus 20:12; 21:17; Leviticus 19:3; 20:9 Isaiah 29:13
Summer AD 29 Age 32	Jesus and His disciples traveled north out of Israel to the Gentile region of Tyre and Sidon.	Matthew 15:21 Mark 7:24a
Summer AD 29 Age 32	In the area of Tyre and Sidon, though Jesus tried to stay hidden, a Syro-Phoenician /Canaanite (Gentile) woman sought Him as the *"Son of David"* / Messiah to heal her daughter of demonic possession. His response tested her faith and seeing her faith, Jesus healed the daughter.	Matthew 15:22–28 Mark 7:24b–30
	Jesus traveled with His disciples east of Tyre and Sidon, north and then east of the Sea of Galilee to the Gentile-dominated area of the Decapolis. There, He healed a deaf man. Many came to Him and for *"three days"* He taught and healed many there. They *"marveled"* and *"glorified the God of Israel."*	Matthew 15:29–31, 32 Mark 7:31–37
	After *"three days"* in a remote region east of the Sea of Galilee, Jesus knew the multitudes (4000 men plus women and children) needed food. He took seven loaves and a few fish, multiplied them, and fed everyone with seven baskets leftover.	Matthew 15:32–38 Mark 8:1–9
	After sending away the crowds, Jesus and His disciples traveled by boat from the Eastern/Northeastern shore of the Sea of Galilee to the region of Dalmanutha near Magdala / Magadan on the Northwestern shore.	Matthew 15:39 Mark 8:10
	In the Magdala region, several Pharisees and Sadducees began to seek a sign from Jesus, but He only pointed to their knowledge of the weather and then to *"the sign of the prophet Jonah."*	Matthew 16:1–4 Mark 8:11–12
	Now on the northwestern corner of the Sea of Galilee area, Jesus warned His disciples of the *"the leaven of the Pharisees and Sadducees,"* referring to their invasive corrupt teachings.	Matthew 16:5–12 Mark 8:14–21
	Jesus and His disciples left the Capernaum area and traveled east to Bethsaida. Some people brought a blind man to Him. Jesus took him out of town, then spit in his eyes, touched him twice, and he could see clearly.	Mark 8:22–26
Late Summer AD 29	Jesus led His disciples away from the Bethsaida area north to several towns in the region of Caesarea Philippi.	Matthew 16:13a Mark 8:27a

	While on the road in the area of Caesarea Philippi, Jesus was praying alone, and His disciples joined Him. Jesus asked them, *"Who do men say that I, the Son of Man, am?"* They responded with *"John the Baptist... Elijah ... Jeremiah, or one of the prophets."* Jesus asked, *"But who do you say that I am?"* Peter responded, *"You are the Christ, the Son of the Living God."*.	Matthew 16:13b–20 Mark 8:27b–30 Luke 9:18–21
	At Caesarea Philippi, after the declaration that Jesus was the Christ, Jesus revealed for the *second* time His coming Crucifixion and Resurrection. He would be rejected, killed, but would rise again after three days. At the tomb, an angel quoted Jesus about *"the Son of Man"* being crucified and risen. That could have been said here or at another place and time.	Matthew 16:21–23 Mark 8:31–33 Luke 9:22; 24:6–7
	At *this time*, Peter rebuked Jesus for His words about His crucifixion. Jesus, in turn, rebuked Peter and his words as from Satan.	Matthew 16:22–23
	In the region of Caesarea Philippi, after the clear revelation of Jesus as the Christ and His prophecy of His coming death and resurrection, Jesus called each disciple to *"take up his cross daily, and follow Me... for what will it profit a man if he gains the whole world, and loses his own soul?"* He spoke of the reward for each and the certainty of His glorious return.	Matthew 16:24–28 Mark 8:34–38 Luke 9:23–26
	Jesus spoke of some of His disciples seeing the kingdom of God. About six to eight days later, He took Peter, James, and John up nearby Mount Hermon where Jesus was transfigured before their eyes—His face and clothing became glistening white. Moses and Elijah appeared talking with Jesus about His coming *"departure"* —Greek, *exodos* [His death by crucifixion, His resurrection, ascension, and enthronement]. The Father spoke from a bright glory cloud and told the three to *"hear"* Jesus.	Matthew 17:1–13 Mark 9:1–13 Luke 9:27–36 2 Peter 1:17–18
	As they were coming down the mountain, Jesus spoke of being *"risen"* from the dead. This was the *third* or *fourth* mention.	Matthew 17:9
Late Summer AD 29 Age 32	The next day, at the foot of the mountain, Jesus and the three encountered disputing scribes, an unbelieving crowd, and a father with his demon-possessed son whom the other disciples could not cure. Jesus commanded the demon to leave, and the son was cured. Jesus showed them their unbelief and the need for sure faith and prayer.	Matthew 17:14–21 Mark 9:14–29 Luke 9:37–43a
Late Summer AD 29 Age 32	Jesus traveled back south through Galilee. He spoke to His disciples again—the *fourth or fifth* time—about His coming Crucifixion and Resurrection after three days. They did not understand Him and were fearful of asking any questions about this matter.	Matthew 17:22–23 Mark 9:30–32 Luke 9:43b–45
Late Summer AD 29 Age 32	Back in Capernaum, certain officials asked Peter about Jesus paying the Temple tax (half shekel, two days' wage, for upkeep of the Temple in Jerusalem). Jesus instructed Peter to go to the Sea of Galilee, catch a fish, take the shekel coin out of its mouth and pay the tax for Jesus and Peter.	Matthew 17:24–27 Mark 9:33a

	On the road to Capernaum, the disciples argued about which of them was the greatest. In Capernaum, Jesus spoke to them about true humility, being last and servant of all. Jesus then took a child and set him in their midst. He spoke to them about having the humility and faith of a child to enter the kingdom of heaven. Whoever receives a child in His name, honors Jesus and the Father.	Matthew 18:1–5 Mark 9:33b–37 Luke 9:46–48
	John told Jesus about someone else casting out demons in Jesus' name. The disciples forbade him, but Jesus said, *"Do not forbid him, for he who is not against us is on our side."* He also spoke of the value and reward of giving even a cup of water in Jesus' name. Each child or each lost sheep is of great value to God. Help others believe in Jesus and never cause any who believes to stumble in sin. Be on guard against any offenses to others.	Matthew 18:6–14 Mark 9:38–50 Luke 9:49–50
	Jesus carefully explained how to win back a sinning brother and how important it is to forgive one another, even *"seventy times seven."* Lack of compassion and unforgiveness toward others will be met by the Father's extreme displeasure, anger, and chastisement.	Matthew 18:15–35
Mid-September AD 29 Age 32	While in Galilee, Jesus' half-brothers did not believe Him to be the Messiah, but mockingly told Him to go to Judea for the Feast of Tabernacles to show *"the works"* He was doing. Jesus said, *"My time has not yet come,"* likely referring to the Father's exact timing for showing Himself as the Messiah.	John 7:2–10a
Last Six Months of Jesus' Ministry—Fall/Winter, AD 29-April, AD 30—Age 33		
Fall AD 29 Age 33	After His half-brothers left Galilee, Jesus journeyed from Capernaum through Samaria on the way to Jerusalem for the Fall Feast of Tabernacles, *"as it were in secret"* because of others' unbelief. He likely turned age 33 around this time. On the journey, Jesus refused the request of James and John to call down fire on a non-receptive Samaritan village. Jesus spoke to some of His followers about the cost of following Him.	Matthew 8:19–22 Luke 9:51–62 John 7:10b
Early Fall AD 29 Age 33	In Jerusalem, during the Feast of Tabernacles, several debated over whether Jesus was the Messiah. In the middle of the Feast week, Jesus taught and spoke about His relationship with the Father; perplexing many.	John 7:11–36
Fall AD 29 Age 33	On the *"Great Day"* of the Feast (the 7th day) during the morning water-pouring ceremony, Jesus called any who thirsted to come to Him for living water. He spoke of the work of the Spirit. John noted this work of the Holy Spirit would happen after Jesus was *"glorified"* (in and after His crucifixion, resurrection, ascension, and enthronement).	John 7:37–39
October AD 29 Age 33	Many in Jerusalem debated about whether Jesus was the Messiah (*"the Prophet," "the Christ"*), but stumbled over the fact that He appeared to come from Galilee, not Bethlehem where David was born.	John 7:40–44

October AD 29 Age 33	The chief priests and Pharisees in Jerusalem sought to arrest Jesus but could not. Even though Nicodemus urged that they first hear Him, they argued that no prophet could come out of Galilee.	John 7:45–52a
	At the end of the seventh day of the Feast of Tabernacles, everyone went to his own home and Jesus went from Jerusalem to the Mount of Olives (probably Bethany) for the night.	John 7:53b
October AD 29 Age 33	On the morning of the eighth day of the Feast of Tabernacles, a special Sabbath, Jesus came to the Temple to teach. The scribes and Pharisees brought a woman caught in adultery, to see if Jesus would call for her death based on Mosaic law. He stopped, stooped, and wrote on the ground. All departed. Jesus did not condemn her but said, *"go and sin no more."*	John 8:1–11 [Leviticus 23:39, *"eighth day,"* the Seventh Sabbath of the Feasts]
October AD 29 Age 33	The Festival of Lights had been celebrated each night of the Feast of Tabernacles, as people called for the Lord to 'tabernacle' with them with His Shekinah Pillar of Fire like He had in the Wilderness in Moses' day. On the eighth day of the Feast, Jesus proclaimed, *"I Am the Light of the world"* and called any to follow Him.	John 8:12
October AD 29 Age 33	The Pharisees debated with Jesus about His claims. Jesus spoke of Himself as *"the Son of Man,"* of His relationship with the Father, of hearing Him and pleasing Him. Most refused to believe Him, but a few did believe.	John 8:13–30
	To those who believed in Jesus, He spoke of abiding in His word, knowing the truth, and being made free. Many unbelievers spoke of themselves as Abraham's children, not slaves, therefore not needing freedom. Jesus showed them the contrast between them as unbelievers who were enslaved to sin as well as being of their *"father the devil"* and Abraham the believer who *"rejoiced to see My day."* Jesus declared *"before Abraham was, I Am,"* thus claiming to be God. In continuing unbelief, they sought to stone Him, but He escaped.	John 8:31–59
	In Jerusalem, on the 8th day of the Feast (a Special Sabbath) (same day Jesus said, *"I Am the Light of the world"* (John 8:12)), He healed a man blind from birth. He stated again, *"I Am the Light of the world"* (John 9:5), made clay from dirt mixed with His saliva, placed it on the man's eyes, and told him to wash in the Pool of Siloam, the same pool the priests went to every morning of the Feast for the Water-drawing Ceremony. The man came back seeing!	John 9:1–7 [Leviticus 23:39]
	Certain people along with the Pharisees debated whether this was the same blind man. He assured them he was. They argued this could not be of God, because Jesus did this on the Sabbath (the 8th Day of the Feast, a Special Sabbath). They questioned the parents who agreed this was their son who had been born blind. He consistently testified, *"One thing I know: that though I was blind, now I see."* They cast him out of the synagogue.	John 9:8–34 [Leviticus 23:39]

	This same day, Jesus came to the man He had healed and talked of belief *"in the Son of God."* He revealed Himself as that *"Son of God;"* the healed man worshiped Jesus. To the Pharisees who refused to believe or worship, Jesus spoke of their blindness, saying, *"your sin remains"*—unforgiven and under judgment.	John 9:35–41
October (or possibly November) AD 29 Age 33	Jesus began talking about Himself as the Good Shepherd and the Door of the sheep and His people as His sheep who believe Him, follow Him, and are protected from the thief who comes *"to steal, and to kill, and to destroy."* Jesus came to give abundant life to His sheep and spoke of willingly laying down His life for the sheep. Many debated about Jesus, some saying no one who opens the eyes of the blind could have a demon.	John 10:1–21
Fall AD 29 Age 33	Jesus sent Seventy disciples out *"two by two"* into the cities and places where He was about to go—likely in Judea and perhaps Perea as well. He gave them clear guidelines on praying first, then told them how to approach each place seeking *"a son of peace,"* receiving whatever food and drink each provided—since *"the laborer is worthy of his wages."* He spoke of staying where the people were receptive and leaving where they were not. He then spoke again His *"woe"* on Chorazin, Bethsaida, and Capernaum for their unbelief and rejection of Jesus.	Luke 10:1–16
Late Fall AD 29 Age 33	The Seventy returned to Jesus *"with joy"* over their ministry, even demons being subject to them in His name. Jesus compared their being cast out on earth with Satan being cast out of heaven, all under His authority. Of greater value is having one's name *"written in heaven."* Jesus rejoiced in His Father's work. He then spoke of the blessedness of the disciples' ministry.	Luke 10:17–24
	Probably in Jerusalem, a scribe/lawyer asked how to *"inherit eternal life."* Jesus asked, *"What is written in the law?"* The man quoted Deuteronomy 6:5 and Leviticus 19:18 about loving God and loving people and asked, *"Who is my neighbor?"* Jesus told the Parable of the Good Samaritan, noting it is one's actions that show one's genuine faith.	Luke 10:25–37
Winter AD 29 Age 33	Likely in late Fall or early Winter, Jesus came to the home of Martha and Mary in Bethany (near Jerusalem). There Mary sat at Jesus' feet listening to His Word; Martha became very distracted with the details of a meal for their guests. Jesus commended Mary and corrected Martha.	Luke 10:38–42
Winter AD 29 Age 33	Having seen Jesus pray many times over the months and after seeing Him in prayer once again, the disciples asked Him, *"Lord, teach us to pray, as John also taught His disciples."* Jesus then gave them the pattern often called "The Lord's Prayer."	Luke 11:1–4
	To further enforce the meaning and importance of prayer, Jesus told His disciples the Parable of the Importunate or Persistent Neighbor. He then urged them to continue to ask, seek, and knock.	Luke 11:5–10
	Jesus urged His disciples to ask the Father for the Holy Spirit (His power and work) like a child asking a father for food—simple bread, or a fish, or an egg. The Heavenly Father will always give what is best.	Luke 11:11–13

	Perhaps in Jerusalem, Jesus healed a demon–possessed mute man and the man began to speak. Some Jewish leaders accused Jesus of being in league with Beelzebub ("lord of flies"—used of the devil) in casting out demons.	Luke 11:14–15
	Some in the crowd around Jesus and the newly healed non-mute man, sought from Jesus a *"sign from heaven,"* perhaps as added proof of His identity. Jesus reasoned with them about His ministry of victory over Satan. A woman spoke of the blessing of being His mother. Jesus countered, *"More than that, blessed are those who hear the word of God and keep it!"*	Luke 11:16–28
	Jesus continued talking and dealt with the request for *"a sign."* He spoke of Himself, *"the Son of Man,"* being a sign to that generation as Jonah was to Nineveh and the Ninevites.	Luke 11:29–32
	Jesus spoke about a Lamp and a Lampstand and how *"the lamp of the body is the eye"*—a *"good"* eye is open, receptive to light, a *"bad"* or 'evil-eye' is closed to light, thus in darkness. Be receptive to the light/words of Jesus, like Nineveh heard Jonah, or face darkness in unbelief and unrepentance.	Luke 11:33–36 (see also Matthew 6:22–23)
	A Pharisee asked Jesus to dine at his house; he marveled that Jesus did not go through the traditional ceremonial washing before the meal. Using the occasion to focus attention on the inner person versus outward traditions or ceremonies, Jesus three times proclaimed a *"woe"* on the Pharisees.	Luke 11:37–44
	A lawyer / scribe took Jesus' words and woes to apply to all scribes as well. Jesus then three times proclaimed a *"woe"* on the scribes. The Pharisees and the scribes began to verbally assail Him, seeking to catch Him in error.	Luke 11:45–54
	When a large crown gathered, Jesus warned His disciples of *"the leaven of the Pharisees, which is hypocrisy."* He then spoke of the time when all motives and words would be uncovered and revealed. He reminded them of their value, more than sparrows, and of their future commendation from Him for speaking of Him before others. He assured them of the Holy Spirit's work in their witness, even at the *"very hour"* needed.	Luke 12:1–12
	Someone in the crowd asked Jesus to be an arbitrator in an inheritance dispute. Jesus warned of *"covetousness"* and then told the Parable of the Foolish Man who had treasure for himself but was *"not rich toward God."*	Luke 12:13–21
	Jesus urged people to seek the kingdom of God, trusting the Father for food, clothing, and life. Be ready to sell or give whatever and focus on eternal treasure in the heavens. Where one's treasure is, there is one's heart.	Luke 12:22–34
	Likely in Judea, Jesus told the Parable of the Prepared Servant ready for his master's return, whenever that might be. Be ready for the return of the Son of Man, even at an unexpected hour. Peter asked how this parable applied to the disciples and the crowds. Jesus answered with the Parable of the Faithful and Wise Servant / Steward versus the unwise steward who is not prepared when His master returns. The master will deal with each one.	Luke 12:35–48

Winter AD 29 Age 33	Jesus knew His coming meant bringing a division on the earth—over Who He is and the Salvation He alone can bring. There were many mysteries about Him and His mission. He knew part of His mission included casting a *"fire"* on earth and He knew He would soon undergo a *"baptism,"* an identification, in fulfilling His mission.	Luke 12:49–53
Winter AD 29 Age 33	Jesus rebuked those who could tell the signs of the weather but failed to see the present time. He urged each one to do what is right and to reconcile oneself with any opponent.	Luke 12:54–59
	Probably in Jerusalem, some in the crowds spoke of Governor Pilate mingling certain Galileans' blood with their sacrifice in Jerusalem. Jesus also noted the eighteen who were killed by the falling Tower in Siloam. Then He stated these were no worse sinners than anyone present. His conclusion: *"Unless you repent, you too will all perish."*	Luke 13:1–9
	Likely in Jerusalem, Jesus taught in one of the synagogues on a Sabbath. Jesus healed a woman afflicted for eighteen years with a demonic infirmity; the synagogue ruler became indignant because it was a Sabbath. Jesus rebuked them for their hypocrisy—any of them would take care of a beast in need on the Sabbath but balked at a woman being released in her need.	Luke 13:10–17
Winter AD 29 Age 33	To the synagogue crowd in Jerusalem, Jesus spoke of the Kingdom of God being like a mustard seed becoming like a tree big enough to receive birds and being like yeast whose influence spreads throughout the dough.	Luke 13:18–21
December AD 29 Age 33	During December and the Feast of Dedication (*Hanukkah—"winter"*) in Jerusalem, many questioned Jesus about whether He was the Messiah, *"the Christ."* Jesus again spoke of His sheep as those who believe Him, hear His voice, and follow Him. He and the Father secure them in His *"Hand."* Jesus also said, *"I and the Father are one"* which caused them to try to stone Him since He claimed to be God. He spoke to them and then escaped.	John 10:22–39
	Ministry in Perea	
January AD 30 Age 33	Jesus and His disciples left Jerusalem and traveled east *"beyond the Jordan,"* likely to the area of Perea where John the Baptist had baptized many. There many came to Jesus and professed their belief in Him.	John 10:40–42
	Traveling in Perea, with Jerusalem as His purposeful destination, Jesus taught in several cities and villages. Jesus urged all to enter the Kingdom for the door was about to be shut by the Master in the face of their unbelief.	Luke 13:22–30
	On the same day, some Pharisees in Perea warned Jesus to leave and escape Herod who wanted to kill Him. Jesus spoke of His unflinching ministry and move toward Jerusalem where many prophets had perished.	Luke 13:31–33

	While in Perea, Jesus lamented over Jerusalem for killing the prophets and stoning those sent to her. He warned of the city being left desolate but assured His listeners that all would see Him again and cry out, *"Blessed is He who comes in the name of the LORD!"*	Luke 13:34–35
	On a Sabbath in Perea, Jesus went to eat in the home of a Pharisee. There Jesus healed a man with dropsy and the legality of healing on the Sabbath came up. Jesus responded, noting how anyone would rescue an animal from a pit even on a Sabbath day. How much more should a man be healed?!	Luke 14:1–6
January AD 30 Age 33	Jesus told a Parable of the Presumptuous Banquet Guest, emphasizing the need to humble oneself, allowing the Lord to exalt rather being humbled by others when one exalts himself or herself.	Luke 14:7–11
	At a Pharisee's home in Perea, Jesus told him who had invited Him to a meal to invite the needy rather than close friends and relatives. God will fully repay this at *"the resurrection of the just."*	Luke 14:12–14
	Someone at the meal said, *"Blessed is he who shall eat bread in the kingdom of God!"* Jesus responded with the Parable of the Great Banquet and the Three Excuses and spoke of inviting all who would be willing to come.	Luke 14:15–24
February AD 30 Age 33	As Jesus traveled about Perea, *"great multitudes"* followed. He spoke of taking up one's cross and forsaking all. Count the cost like a tower builder or a king going to battle. Have no admixture in salt or in one's heart.	Luke 14:25–35
February AD 30 Age 33	Several tax collectors and sinners *"drew near ... to hear Him."* The Pharisees and scribes objected. To counter their objections, Jesus spoke the Parables of the Lost Sheep (99 and 1), the Lost Coin, and the Lost Sons (Prodigal).	Luke 15:1–32
February AD 30 Age 33	At this time, Jesus told His disciples the Parable of the Unjust Steward and spoke about being faithful and just to gain true riches from God. *"No servant can serve two masters"* or serve *"God and mammon."*	Luke 16:1–13
	The Pharisees who heard Jesus telling these truths were *"lovers of money"* and looked down on Him. Jesus rebuked them for loving what men loved rather than loving God and His Word.	Luke 16:14–17
	Jesus stated any man who divorces his wife and marries another commits adultery and whoever marries the divorced wife also commits adultery. In other passages, this refers to divorce apart from unfaithfulness by a spouse.	Luke 16:18
	Jesus told the story about a greedy, unbelieving rich man and Lazarus, a believing beggar man. Both died, the rich man going to Hades and torment and Lazarus carried *"by the angels"* to the comfort and reward of Abraham's bosom and God's presence. The key to belief is hearing and obeying the Word of God, not miracles, or money, or any other physical evidence.	Luke 16:19–30

	Jesus spoke to His disciples about offenses and forgiving others. Live by faith and do what is commanded by the Lord. In being faithful in what God wants, one is simply a servant, even *"unprofitable,"* and nothing more.	Luke 17:1–10
	While in the area beyond the Jordan, Jesus received word that His friend Lazarus was sick. Jesus waited two days and then traveled to Bethany (near Jerusalem), knowing that Lazarus had died three or four days earlier. He came, comforted Mary and Martha, and spoke of Himself as *"the Resurrection and the Life."* He went to Lazarus' tomb and called him to life from the dead. Many believed in Jesus as a result. Others reported all these events to the Pharisees.	John 11:1–46
	In Jerusalem, the chief priests and Pharisees seeking to protect their positions, met together and discussed killing Jesus. The High Priest Caiaphas said, *"it is expedient for us that one man should die for the people, and not that the whole nation should perish."* They plotted to put Jesus to death.	John 11:47–53
	Jesus no longer walked openly in Jerusalem. He went for a time to the city of Ephraim (or Ephron) about twelve miles from Jerusalem. It is possible that Jesus left there to go back into Perea and Galilee, before coming back to Jerusalem for Passover at the first part of April.	John 11:54
The Journey to Jerusalem—February, March, AD 30—Age 33		
February AD 30 Age 33	Jesus passed through Perea into Galilee and Samaria. In the area of Galilee and Samaria, in a certain village ten lepers cried out to Him for healing. One, a *"foreigner,"* likely a Samaritan, returned to Jesus and thanked Him.	Luke 17:11–19
	As Jesus traveled, a Pharisee asked Him when the kingdom of God would come. Jesus focused on the inner nature of the kingdom. He spoke about the future *"days of the Son of Man"* (possibly the Millennium) and how suddenly or surprisingly it would come for all to see clearly.	Luke 17:20–37
	To emphasize prayer, Jesus told the Parable of the Unjust Judge and the Widow. Do not give in to the evil of the world, the flesh, or the devil, but continue to pray trusting the Father until the Son of Man comes.	Luke 18:1–8
	To those who trusted in themselves as being righteous, Jesus told the Parable of the Pharisee and the Tax Collector, who went from the Temple to his home a justified man, whereas the proud Pharisee remained unrighteous and unjustified.	Luke 18:9–14
	Jesus had traveled from Galilee through Samaria and came to *"the region of Judea beyond the Jordan."* Here He healed many as great multitudes continued to follow Him.	Matthew 19:1 Mark 10:1
	With their questions, the Pharisees tested Jesus about divorce. He focused their attention on God's intention in His Word. A husband and wife are to stay together, not divorce. Jesus permitted divorce in cases of sexual immorality.	Matthew 19:2–12 Mark 10:2–12

February AD 30 Age 33	Some brought their infants and little children to Jesus for Him to touch and bless. The disciples rebuked them, but Jesus said to allow the children to come to Him. The kingdom is made of people who are childlike.	Matthew 19:13–15; Mark 10:13–16; Luke 18:15–17
February AD 30 Age 33	A rich young ruler asked Jesus how he could *"inherit eternal life."* Jesus focused him on the good God and the commands, which he claimed to have kept. Jesus told him to sell all, distribute to the poor, trust the Father for riches, and follow Jesus. He went away sad, since he loved his riches and did not want to sell all. Jesus said riches often get in the way of following God, but God is able to save anyone.	Matthew 19:16–26 Mark 10:17–27 Luke 18:18–27
	Peter spoke up about how they had forsaken all to follow Jesus. Jesus said every faith step one makes in forsaking all and following Jesus will be met with God's reward and His promise of eternal life for all who believe in Him. Each believer will be part of *"the regeneration"* (the Millennial Kingdom) ruled by *"the Son of Man"* (see Acts 3:21; 1 Corinthians 6:2–3; Revelation 3:21; 20:4–10).	Matthew 19:27–29; Mark 10:28–30 Luke 18:28–30
	In speaking of the coming kingdom, Jesus told the Parable of the Landowner and the Laborers who worked different hours. Each received the same wage as agreed upon. The Landowner dealt justly with those who thought they were treated unjustly. The Lord always does what is right.	Matthew 19:30; 20:1–16 Mark 10:31
	Jesus spoke for the *fifth or sixth* time about His coming Crucifixion and Resurrection. As they walked, Jesus told them about His going to Jerusalem where He would be delivered to the Gentiles, mocked, scourged, and killed, but would rise again the third day. They did not understand what He meant.	Matthew 20:17–19; Mark 10:32–34; Luke 18: 31–34
	The mother of James and John asked Jesus that her two sons sit on His right and left in His kingdom. The ten other disciples were displeased (and probably envious or ambitious for themselves). Jesus contrasted *"the rulers of the Gentiles"* with *His* way of being a servant and slave to all. Jesus came *"to serve and to give His life a ransom for many."*	Matthew 20:20–28 Mark 10:35–45
March AD 30 Age 33	Near Jericho on the road to Jerusalem, two blind men, one named Bartimaeus, cried to Jesus as *"Son of David,"* a Messianic title. Jesus healed both and they followed Him, giving glory to God, as did many in the crowd.	Matthew20:29–34 Mark 10:46–52 Luke 18:35–43
	At Jericho, Zacchaeus, a chief tax collector, wanted to see Jesus. Jesus went to his house and Zacchaeus declared his faith—he would make restitution to any he had wronged. Jesus spoke of the fruit of faith in his life and stated, *"the Son of Man has come to seek and to save that which was lost."*	Luke 19:1–10
	Jesus told the Parable of the Nobleman and the Ten Minas. He rewarded or judged each servant for his use of the Nobleman's property while the Nobleman was away. They did not know when he would return.	Luke 19:11–28
April AD 30 Age 33	Jesus traveled with His disciples on the Jericho Road to Jerusalem, coming first to Bethphage and arriving in Bethany where Jesus stayed at the home of Mary, Martha, and Lazarus.	Matt 21:1a; Mark 11:1a; Luke 19:28–29a; John 12:1

Events of the Last Week of the Life and Ministry of Jesus			
The Events of the last week of the life and ministry of Jesus are given in varying ways in the Four Gospels. Writers in the First Century AD did not write as some journalists in the Twenty-first Century. Many details are presented more like someone placing several photos of the week on a table in no certain order. The details of each photo or each event occurred at a precise time, but to gather a concise, detailed account one must blend all Four Gospel accounts. Some of the writers did not follow a precise order of events but clustered the events into certain themes or parts of the week. Therefore, this *Chronology* seeks to place these events in the order they occurred, as much as is possible.			
Time	**Place**	**Event**	**Scripture**
April AD 30-Age 33 FRIDAY afternoon and SATURDAY	Jesus and His disciples came to Bethphage, then Bethany on the Mount of Olives.	Traveling on the road from Jericho to Jerusalem, Jesus and His disciples came to Bethany on the Mount of Olives, two miles from Jerusalem. They arrived with several other pilgrims coming for Passover Week.	Matthew 21:1a Mark 11:1a Luke 19:28–29a John 11:55–56; 12:1
SATURDAY night plus the following days	Bethany—Home of Mary, Martha, and Lazarus—2 miles east of Jerusalem	Apparently, Jesus stayed at the home of Lazarus, Mary, and Martha in Bethany during the week.	John 11:55–56; 12:1
SATURDAY night	Bethany Home of Simon the Leper.	Simon the Leper hosted a supper for Jesus and His disciples. Martha and Mary were there helping serve, along with their brother Lazarus. During the supper, in worship, Mary anointed Jesus' body with *"very costly oil of spikenard."* Judas and other disciples complained, but Jesus honored her for anointing Him for *"My burial"* and said her act would be remembered.	Matthew 26:6–13 Mark 14:3–9 John 12:2–8
		Many Jews heard Jesus was at the home of Simon the Leper and came to see Jesus and Lazarus. The chief priests wanted to put Jesus and Lazarus to death, because many were believing in Jesus.	John 12:9–11

NOTE: The Tenth day of the month Nisan was '*Passover lamb selection day*' (Exodus 12:3). After this day, came three days of examining the lamb to make sure there were no external or internal blemishes (Exodus 12:5a) *before* Passover Day, the Fourteenth day of Nisan, when the Passover Lamb would be slain and roasted (Exodus 12:6). When Jesus came into Jerusalem, the people cried out *"Hosanna,"* which means *"save now, O LORD,"* a statement from Psalm 118:25, a Messianic Psalm. Jesus would be the Savior. Jesus went through three days of examination by many different individuals and groups. Jesus then went to the Cross and was crucified as our Sin Offering and spotless Passover Lamb. *"Knowing that you were not redeemed with corruptible things, like silver or gold, from your aimless conduct received by tradition from your fathers, but with the precious blood of Christ, as of a lamb without blemish and without spot"* (1 Peter 1:18–19). No internal or external blemishes. *"For indeed Christ/Messiah, our Passover, was sacrificed for us"* (1 Corinthians 5:7). *"And walk in love, as Christ also has loved us and given Himself for us, an offering and a sacrifice to God for a sweet-smelling aroma"* (Ephesians 5:2). *"For He made Him* [Jesus the Christ] *who knew no sin to be sin* [our Sin Offering] *for us, that we might become the righteousness of God in Him"* (2 Corinthians 5:21). *"Save now, I pray, O LORD; O LORD, I pray, send now prosperity. Blessed is he who comes in the name of the LORD! We have blessed you from the house of the LORD"* (Psalm 118:25–26—NKJV).			
SUNDAY	Descending the Mount of Olives near the towns of Bethany and Bethpage. Then , into Jerusalem.	Triumphal Entry—Jesus sent two disciples to the village on the Mount of Olives to get a colt of a donkey. Jesus rode into Jerusalem on that colt as people spread garments on the path and waved palm branches, shouting *"Hosanna, save now."* This fulfilled various prophecies of the Messiah and His coming (from *Psalms* and *Zechariah*).	Psalm 118:25–26 Zechariah 9:9 Matthew 21:1b–11 Mark 11:1b–11a Luke 19:29b–38 John 12:12–18
SUNDAY	Approaching Jerusalem	The Pharisees called to Jesus to stop the words of praise from the disciples and the people. Jesus said that if all became silent the stones would cry out.	Luke 19:39–40
	Jerusalem	As Jesus came nearer to the city of Jerusalem, He wept over it and lamented their unbelief. He prophesied the future destruction of the city and the Temple.	Luke 19:41–44
SUNDAY late	At the Temple	Jesus walked into the Temple, surveyed the scene, and left since it was *"already late."*	Mark 11:11

SUNDAY night	Bethany	Jesus and the Twelve left Jerusalem and spent the night in Bethany.	Matthew 21:17 Mark 11:11
MONDAY	On the way from Bethany to Jerusalem	As Jesus and the disciples walked from Bethany to Jerusalem, He was hungry and went to a fig tree, but found no fruit. He then cursed the barren fig tree.	Matthew 21:18–19 Mark 11:12–14
MONDAY	Jerusalem Temple area	Jesus came to Jerusalem and went to the Temple. There He cleansed the Temple of moneychangers and merchants, quoting Isaiah 56:7 and Jeremiah 7:11.	Isaiah 56:7 Jeremiah 7:11 Matthew 21:12–13 Mark 11:15–17 Luke 19:45–46
	Jerusalem The Temple area	In the Temple area, many came to Him, and He healed the blind and the lame.	Matthew 21:14
	Jerusalem The Temple area	Many chief priests and scribes complained of children saying, *"Hosanna to the Son of David!"* Jesus quoted from Psalm 8:2 about children praising God, affirming Himself as God.	Psalm 8:2 Matthew 21:15–17
	Jerusalem	Jesus taught the multitudes.	Mark 11:18 Luke 19:47a
		Seeing and hearing Jesus and the people's response, the chief priests (Sadducees) and scribes (Pharisees) sought a way to destroy Him but could not because of the people. They stated, *"Look, the world has gone after Him!"*	Mark 11:18 Luke 19:47b–48 John 12:19
		Greeks who had come for the Passover wanted to see Jesus. Using the picture of planting a grain of wheat, Jesus taught on His coming death, on dying to oneself, serving and following Him, and receiving the Father's honor and eternal life.	John 12:20–26

		Jesus spoke of His soul being *"troubled"* and of *"this hour,"* the hour of His death and resurrection. The Father's Voice thundered from Heaven. Jesus acknowledged that Voice and the judgment coming. He called all to walk in the light (His light) and then He departed.	John 12:27–36
		Quoting Isaiah, the apostle John interpreted all Jesus said and did. John spoke of the unbelief of the people and that Isaiah had seen *"His glory"* (Pre-Incarnate) *"and spoke of Him."*	Isaiah 53:1; 6:1–9–10 and 6:1–8 John 12:37–41
		Some among the rulers of the Jews believed in Jesus but did not acknowledge that publicly because of the Pharisees. They loved the approval of men more than of God.	John 12:42–43
		Jesus called all to believe in Him and the Father. Those who believe will have His light. His words are from the Father. One should believe Him for eternal life.	John 12:44–50
	Mount of Olives and Bethany for the night	Jesus and the Twelve left the city of Jerusalem and spent the night in Bethany.	Mark 11:19 Luke 21:37
TUESDAY	On the way from Mount of Olives (possibly Bethany) to Jerusalem	Jesus' disciples saw the fig tree withered *"from the roots."* Jesus taught on faith and prayer.	Matthew 21:19–22 Mark 11:19–25 Luke 21:37–38
TUESDAY	Jerusalem Temple area	Jesus taught. The chief priests, scribes, and elders challenged His *authority*. He told the Parables of the Two Sons and of the Landowner and Vinedressers. He quoted Psalm 118:22–23 about the rejection of the Chief Cornerstone. He told the Parable of the Invitation to a King's Son's Marriage Feast.	Psalm 118:22–23 Matthew 21:23–46; 22:1–14 Mark 11:27–33; 12:1–11 Luke 20:1–18

TUESDAY	Jerusalem Temple area	Pharisees and Herodians challenged Jesus and tried to set a trap over tribute or taxes to Caesar.	Matthew 22:15–22 Mark 12:12–17 Luke 20:19–26
		The Sadducees challenged Jesus over the reality of the Resurrection.	Matthew 22:23–33 Mark 12:18–27 Luke 20:27–40
		A scribe or lawyer, one of the Pharisees (along with others), asked Jesus about the Great Commandment. Jesus spoke of loving God as first and loving one's neighbor as second.	Matthew 22:34–40 Mark 12:28–34
		Quoting Psalm 110:1, Jesus challenged the Pharisees over Messiah being the Son of David and Lord of David. How? They could not answer, but *"the common people heard Him gladly."*	Matthew 22:41–46 Mark 12:35–37 Luke 20:41–44
		Jesus warned about the scribes' and Pharisees' pride and hypocrisies, and their condemnation. Jesus pronounced Six *"Woes."*	Matthew 23:1–36 Mark 12:38–40 Luke 20:45–47
		Once again, Jesus lamented over Jerusalem and quoted Psalm 118:26.	Matthew 23:37–39; Psalm 118:26
	Temple Treasury in the Court of the Women in the Temple (near the Altar area)	Jesus spoke about contributions of the rich (*"their abundance"*) versus the two mites (*"her poverty"*) of the widow. This was Jesus' last Public Ministry.	Mark 12:41–44 Luke 21:1–4
TUESDAY Afternoon	Leaving the Temple	The disciples spoke about the *beauty* of the Temple. Jesus spoke of the *destruction* of the Temple—*"not one stone shall be left upon another."*	Matthew 24:1–2 Mark 13:1–2 Luke 21:5–6

	Mount of Olives	The disciples asked about *"when"* these things would happen. Jesus spoke to His disciples of the Last Things—their witness and persecution, the destruction of Jerusalem, tribulation to come, His Second Coming, the Parable of the Fig Tree, and their being ready for their redemption.	Matthew 24:3–35 Mark 13:3–37 Luke 21:7–36
TUESDAY Afternoon		On the Mount of Olives, Jesus used several illustrations and parables to speak of Last Things. He used the Illustration of the Days of Noah and the Parables of the Good and Evil Servant, the Ten Virgins, the Talents, and, finally, the Judgment of *"the nations"* as either Sheep (*"righteous"*) or Goats (*"you cursed"*).	Matthew 24:36–51; 25:1–46 Luke 12:41–48
TUESDAY Afternoon		Jesus spoke of the Passover coming in two days (possibly Thursday or Friday) and the Arrest and Crucifixion of the Son of Man.	Matthew 26:1–2 Mark 14:1a
DAILY	Jerusalem and the Mount of Olives (Likely Bethany)	Jesus taught in the Temple every day and spent the night on the Mount of Olives, likely in Bethany. People came to the Temple every morning to hear Him.	Luke 21:37–38
TUESDAY Evening	Jerusalem—At the residence of the High Priest Caiaphas	The chief priests, scribes, and elders of the people discussed how they might put Jesus to death but wanted to avoid the Feast time.	Matthew 26:3–5 Mark 14:1b–2 Luke 22:1–2
	Jerusalem	That night, *"Satan entered Judas"* Iscariot and he went to *"the chief priests and captains"* and settled an agreement to betray Jesus for thirty pieces of silver.	Matthew 26:14–16 Mark 14:10–11 Luke 22:3–6

TWO POSSIBILITIES here.

Some see WEDNESDAY, the next Day as a non-activity day of rest for Jesus.

Some see WEDNESDAY, the next Day as the day Jesus and His disciples prepared for and celebrated the Passover—on Wednesday night. That means Passover occurred on Thursday and Jesus would have been crucified and buried on Thursday, thus being buried for three days and three nights.

WEDNESDAY	POSSIBILITY #1—In Bethany (the likely place Jesus and His disciples would rest.)	POSSIBILITY #1—No Record of any activities by Jesus this day. Thus, some consider this a Day of Rest. This seems unlikely.	
WEDNESDAY or THURSDAY Afternoon	POSSIBILITY #2—Jerusalem and the preparation for the Passover for Jesus and His Twelve disciples	POSSIBILITY #2—Jesus sent Peter and John to make preparations for eating the Passover that night in a large Upper Room, possibly on WEDNESDAY.	Matthew 26:17–19 Mark 14:12–16 Luke 22:7–13
WEDNESDAY or THURSDAY Evening	Jerusalem Upper Room	Jesus and the Twelve began the Passover observance.	Matthew 26:20 Mark 14:17 Luke 22:14–16
		The disciples were arguing over which of them should be considered the greatest. Jesus spoke of the ways of the Gentile leaders, then told them they were to be servants to others. He also promised them a place in His Kingdom.	Luke 22:24–30
		Taking the role of a household servant, Jesus washed the disciples' feet.	John 13:1–20
		Jesus spoke of one of the Twelve who would Betray Him. Judas questioned Jesus. Satan entered Judas. He left Jesus and the disciples in the room, going out, and *"it was night."*	Matthew26:21–25 Mark 14:18–21 Luke 22:21–23 John 13:21–30
		After Judas went out, Jesus spoke of His being glorified (His Crucifixion and Resurrection) and of His disciples loving one another.	John 13:31–35
WEDNESDAY or THURSDAY Evening	Jerusalem Upper Room	Jesus spoke of Satan wanting to *"sift"* the disciples and of His praying for all of them, especially Peter. Jesus gave His *first* warning to the Eleven of their deserting Him and of Peter denying Him. All the disciples denied they would desert Him, and Peter said he would never deny Jesus.	Luke 22:31–34 John 13:36–38
		Jesus spoke of the disciples being ready for the conflict that would come. He quoted Isaiah 53:12 about His being *"numbered with the transgressors"* and that He would fulfill all that was written about Him.	Isaiah 53:12 Luke 22:35–38

WEDNESDAY or THURSDAY Evening	Jerusalem Upper Room	Passover Meal—Lord's Supper—Jesus instituted the Lord's Supper—Jesus blessed and broke the bread and gave the broken bread to His disciples after the traditional supper portion, and said it was *"My body which is given for you."* When Jesus gave the disciples the traditional Passover Supper's Third Cup, the Cup of Redemption (also known as *"the Cup of Blessing"*), He changed the traditional supper and focused them on this common Cup of the *New Covenant in His Blood "which is shed for many for the forgiveness of sins"* [The common cup was a picture of Jewish betrothal between a bridegroom and a bride.]	Matthew 26:26–28 Mark 14:22–24 Luke 22:17–20 1 Corinthians 11:23–26
WEDNESDAY or THURSDAY Evening	Jerusalem Upper Room	Jesus promised not to drink of *"the fruit of the vine"* until the day He would drink it *"new with you in My Father's kingdom."*	Matthew 26:29 Mark 14:25
		Jesus told the disciples to regularly partake of the Lord's Supper—*"do this in remembrance of Me."* Jesus spoke of doing this *"till He comes."*	Luke 22:19c 1 Corinthians 11:24c, 25c, 26
		Jesus promised (spoken in the language and customs of a Bridegroom of that day) to go and *"prepare a place"* for them in the Father's House and return to take them (in language as one talking to a Bride) to that place.	John 14:1–3
		Jesus declared Himself *"the Way"* to the Father, as well as *"the Truth, and the Life."* He promised the coming of the Holy Spirit.	John 14:4–31
	Jerusalem Upper Room	Jesus and the Eleven sang a Hymn (from Psalm 113–118) and went out to the Mount of Olives.	Matthew 26:30 Mark 14:26 John 14:31

	Most likely walking from the Upper Room past the Temple to the Mount of Olives—They could have walked through the Kidron Valley where vineyards grew.	Jesus spoke of Himself as the True Vine, most likely as they passed in view of the Temple with its ornamental Golden Vine on the front of the Temple shining in the light of a full moon. He spoke of abiding in Him as The True Vine and of the work of the Holy Spirit, bearing His fruit. He also spoke of answered prayer in their relationship of abiding in Christ and His words abiding in each one.	John 14:31; 15:1–27, 16:1–33
	Still walking with His disciples.	In *another* veiled statement, Jesus spoke of them not seeing Him and then seeing Him (the *sixth* or *seventh* mention of His death and resurrection). They did not understand.	John 16:16–22
WEDNESDAY or THURSDAY Evening	Before crossing the Kidron Brook. [Likely, the aroma of blood from the Temple altar draining into the Brook Kidron along with the aroma of thousands of roasted lambs filled the air.]	Jesus prayed for His Father to be glorified and offered His Intercessory Prayer for His disciples *then* and for us *now*. Jesus focused on His Father, knowing Him, desiring that all His disciples know the Father. He prayed for each to know His joy, be protected from the evil one, be sanctified in the truth of God's word, be one in Christ as the Father and the Son are one, know His love, and one day see His glory.	John 17:1–26
	Walking from the Upper Room and onto the Mount of Olives toward Gethsemane	Once again Jesus spoke to His disciples of their deserting Him and Peter denying Him—*second* warning. He quoted Zechariah 13:7 about the sheep being scattered after the Shepherd has been struck. Again, Peter and the others declared they would not desert or deny Him.	Zechariah 13:7 Matthew 26:31–35 Mark 14:27–31
WEDNESDAY or THURSDAY Evening, near Midnight	Jesus and the Eleven walked over the Brook Kidron to the Mount of Olives, and to a Garden of "the Oil Press" or *"Gethsemane."*	Jesus *"often"* came to the Garden of Gethsemane with His disciples for a time of prayer. This was a well-known place to each of them, including Judas.	Luke 22:39 John 18:2

WEDNESDAY or THURSDAY Evening, near Midnight	In the Garden of *"Gethsemane"*—"the Oil Press" referring to an Olive Press	Jesus urged His disciples to pray with Him. He began to pray in agony over the *"Cup"*—the Cup of Wrath for the sins of the world—He would have to drink. Jesus prayed three different times. *"Father, ... let this cup pass from Me; nevertheless, not as I will, but as You will."—"Father, if this cup cannot pass away from me unless I drink it, Your will be done."*	Matthew 26:30, 36–46 Mark 14:26, 32–42 Luke 22:39–46 John 18:1–2
WEDNESDAY or THURSDAY Evening, near Midnight	The Garden of Gethsemane	Judas came to the Garden of Gethsemane to betray Jesus accompanied with an armed Roman cohort and Temple officers from the chief priests, elders, and Pharisees. They carried lanterns, torches, and weapons.	Matthew 26:47 Mark 14:43 Luke 22:47–48 John 18:2–3 Acts 1:16
		When they first sought *"Jesus the Nazarene,"* He said, *"I AM He"* and all fell to the ground.	John 18:4–9
		Judas carried out the planned sign of his betrayal, the kiss of a friend. Matthew quoted Jesus calling Judas *"friend,"* using the word *hetaire*, different one, <u>not</u> like Me, not an ally.	Matthew 26:48–50 Mark 14:44–45 Luke 22:47–48
		In defense, Peter pulled out a sword and cut off the ear of Malchus, the High Priest's servant. Jesus healed it instantly. Jesus said He could call 12 legions of angels (72,000 angels, one legion for Himself and each of the Eleven).	Matthew 26:51–54 Mark 14:47 Luke 22:49–51 John 18:10–12
		Jesus was bound and led away. His disciples fled fulfilling the prophecy of Zechariah 13:7 and the two warnings of Jesus.	Zechariah13:7 Matthew 26:55–56 Mark 14:46, 48–52 Luke 22:52–53
THURSDAY or FRIDAY Morning before Dawn	House of Annas, Caiaphas' father-in-law and former High Priest.	*First Jewish Trial—Annas' House* Caiaphas, the current High Priest, asked Jesus about His teachings. An officer of the High Priest struck Jesus.	John 18:12–14, 19–23

	House of Caiaphas, current High Priest	*Second Jewish Trial—Caiaphas' House* False witnesses testified. They asked Jesus, *"Are You the Christ, the Son of God."* He declared, *"I am."* Caiaphas condemned Him. Men mocked, beat, and spit on Him.	Matthew 26:57, 59–68; Mark 14:53, 55–65; Luke 22:54, 63–65 John 18:24
	Courtyard of the House of Caiaphas—At the Gate and at the Charcoal Fire	Peter denied the Lord three times. The cock crowed. Jesus turned and looked at Peter. *"Peter went out and wept bitterly."*	Matthew 26:58, 69–75; Mark 14:54, 66–72; Luke 22:54–62; John 18:15–18, 25–27
THURSDAY or FRIDAY After Dawn, Before 6:00 am	House of Caiaphas	*Third Jewish Trial—Caiaphas' House* The formal council (Sanhedrin) questioned and condemned Jesus to death because He said He was the Son of God. They sought to make a legal decision by making it a 'daylight' verdict. A night verdict was not allowed 'legally.'	Matthew 27:1 Mark 15:1 Luke 22:66–71
THURSDAY or FRIDAY Morning	At the Temple and at a Field outside Jerusalem.	In remorse, Judas returned the thirty pieces of betrayal money and went out and hanged himself (that day or a day soon after).	Matthew 27:3–5 Acts 1:18–20
Sometime after Judas' death	Temple and Field outside the walls of Jerusalem, known in Aramaic as *Akel Dama*, "Field of Blood"	Judas purchased a "field" where he died. The priests used the returned silver to buy this potter's field for burial of strangers.	Matthew 27:6–10 Acts 1:18–20
THURSDAY or FRIDAY Morning Before 6:00 am	Jerusalem—Pilate's Headquarters—*"the Praetorium"*	*First Roman/Gentile Trial—Before Pilate* Accusing Jesus of claiming to be King of the Jews, the Jewish leaders asked Pilate for the death penalty. Jesus and Pilate discussed Jesus' kingship. Jesus declared, *"I am a king,"* and that he was *"born"* to *"bear witness to the truth."* Pilate found *"no fault"* in Jesus.	Matthew 27:2, 11–14; Mark 15:1–5 Luke 23:1–5 John 18:28–38
THURSDAY or FRIDAY Morning Close to 6:00 am	Jerusalem—Quarters of Herod Antipas	*Second Roman/Gentile Trial—Before Herod* Herod questioned Jesus hoping to see a miracle. Jesus remained silent. Soldiers mocked Jesus and put on Him *"a gorgeous robe."* Herod found no fault in Jesus.	Luke 23:6–12, 15

THURSDAY or FRIDAY Morning Close to 6:00 am	Jerusalem—Second Time before Pilate—Pilate's Praetorium and *Gabbatha, "The Pavement,"* place of the Judgment Seat.	*Third Roman/Gentile Trial—Before Pilate* Jesus was brought back to Pilate. Pilate brought up the prisoner release tradition. He suggested releasing Jesus.	Matthew 27:15–18 Mark 15:6–10 John 18:39
THURSDAY or FRIDAY Between 6:00 and 9:00 am	Pilate's Praetorium and *Gabbatha, "the Pavement"*	While deliberating about the prisoner release, Pilate's wife sent word, *"Have nothing to do with that righteous man..."*	Matthew 27:19
		Pilate again declared Jesus innocent, *"I... found no fault in this man."*	Luke 23:13–17
		The chief priests and elders persuaded and stirred up the crowds to *call for* the release of Barabbas (likely scheduled for crucifixion) to fulfill the prisoner release tradition and to *call for* Jesus to be crucified.	Matthew 27:20–21 Mark 15:11 Luke 23:18–19 John 18:40
		Pilate again declared Jesus' innocence, *"Why, what evil has He done?"*	Matthew 27:22–23; Mark 15:12–14; Luke 23:20–22
THURSDAY or FRIDAY Between 6:00 and 9:00 am	Jerusalem—Pilate's Praetorium and *Gabbatha, "The Pavement,"* place of the Judgment Seat.	Pilate used a Jewish ceremony/ symbolism of washing his hands before the crowd, declaring, *"I am innocent of the blood of this just Person."*	Matthew 27:24–25 Deuteronomy 21:6–8
		Pilate had Jesus scourged. A Roman centurion oversaw each scourging, carried out by lictors who used a *flagrum*, a multiple-strand leather whip with pieces of metal and bone, etc. imbedded to tear skin and muscle, inflicting great pain and bloodshed, often bringing a prisoner near death.	Matthew 27:26 Mark 15:15 John 19:1
		Along with the scourging, the soldiers mocked Jesus as king with a crown of thorns, a reed scepter, and a purple/scarlet robe. They beat Him, spit on Him and offered mock praise and worship.	Matthew 27:26–31; Mark 15:15–19; Luke 23:24–25 John 19:1–3
THURSDAY or FRIDAY Between 6:00 and 9:00 am	Jerusalem—Pilate's Praetorium and *Gabbatha, "The Pavement,"* place of the Judgment Seat.	Pilate declared Jesus innocent stating two more times (John 19:4, 6), *"I find no fault in Him."* After the scourging and mocking, Pilate said, *"Behold, the Man!"*	John 19:4, 5, 6

		Pilate questioned Jesus once more. Jesus stated He knew the power to make judgments was given *"from above."* Pilate sought to release Him. Pilate then brought Jesus out and declared *"Behold your King!"* He then gave in to the pressure of the crowds.	John 19:7–16
		The crowds continued yelling *"Crucify Him!"*	Matthew 27:23 Mark 15:14 Luke 23:23 John 19:6, 15
THURSDAY or FRIDAY Before 9:00 am	Jerusalem—Pilate's Praetorium and *Gabbatha, "The Pavement,"* place of the Judgment Seat.	Pilate sentenced Jesus to death and sent Him to be crucified.	Matthew 27:26 Mark 15:15 Luke 23:24–25 John 19:16
Before 9:00 am	On the way to Golgotha, *"The Place of a Skull"*	Soldiers took the purple/scarlet robe off Jesus and put Jesus' own garments on Him.	Matthew 27:31 Mark 15:20 John 19:16–17
		Soldiers compelled Simon of Cyrene (father of Alexander and Rufus—Mark 15:21; Romans 16:13) to carry Jesus' cross to Golgotha.	Matthew 27:32 Mark 15:21 Luke 23:26
		As He was led to Golgotha, Jesus spoke to several women of judgment to come.	Luke 23:27–31
		Jesus refused to drink the wine mixed with myrrh / *"gall"* (as a mild sedative).	Matthew 27:34 Mark 15:23 Psalm 69:21a
	On the Cross at Golgotha	The soldiers *"crucified"* Jesus, nailing His hands and feet to the cross. Four soldiers oversaw each one being crucified.	Matthew 27:35 John 20:25, 27 Psalm 22:16
THURSDAY or FRIDAY 9:00 am to 12:00 Noon	On the Cross at Golgotha	Beginning at 9:00 am, Jesus was crucified with two criminals, *"thieves,"* one on the right and one on the left, with Jesus on the middle cross.	Matthew 27:38 Mark 15:25–28 Luke 23:32, 33 John 19:18

		The "crime" of each criminal was posted over each head. Over Jesus' head the inscription in Hebrew, Latin, and Greek read, "THIS IS JESUS OF NAZARETH, THE KING OF THE JEWS."	Matthew 27:37 Mark 15:26 Luke 23:38 John 19:19–22
		The soldiers gambled for Jesus' garments (see Psalm 22:18). They divided the clothing into four parts (four soldiers) but did not tear the additional seamless *"tunic."*	Matthew 27:35–36; Mark 15:24 Luke 23:34 John 19:23–24
		Many mocked Jesus during these hours. The two thieves began the morning mocking Him.	Matthew 27:39–44 Mark 15:29–32 Luke 23:35–37
THURSDAY or FRIDAY 9:00 am to 12:00 Noon	On the Cross at Golgotha	Jesus made Seven Statements from the Cross. First Statement: *"Father, forgive them, for they do not know what they do."*	Luke 23:34
THURSDAY or FRIDAY 9:00 am to 12:00 Noon	On the Cross at Golgotha	Second Statement. One thief continued to mock Jesus. The other changed, declaring his personal guilt, his just punishment, Jesus' innocence, and then his personal faith request. He asked, *"Lord, remember me when You come into Your Kingdom"* Jesus answered, *"Assuredly, I say to you, today you will be with Me in Paradise."*	Luke 23:39–43
		Third Statement. Jesus, showing His care for His mother Mary, looked at her and His cousin John and said, *"Woman, behold your son!"* ... [and to John] *"Behold, your mother!"*	John 19:26–27
12:00 Noon to 3:00 pm	In the land, *"the sun was darkened,"* or *"failed,"* not an eclipse, since a full moon occurred at Passover, nor was it a cloud cover.	From Noon to 3:00 p.m., supernatural DARKNESS enveloped *"the whole earth"* since *"the sun failed/ceased/was darkened"* (Luke 23:44–45), darkness being a sign of judgment (Joel 2:31). Jesus made NO Statements for three hours [12:00–3:00].	Matthew 27:45 Mark 15:33 Luke 23:44–45

		Near the ninth hour—3:00 pm—Jesus spoke His Fourth Statement: *"Eloi, Eloi, lama sabachthani?"-"My God, My God, Why have You forsaken Me?"*—QUOTE of Psalm 22:1	Matthew 27:46 Mark 15:34 Psalm 22:1
		"Knowing that all things were now accomplished," Jesus uttered His Fifth Statement: *"I thirst!"*	John 19:28
		Some standing there thought He was calling for Elijah and gave Him a sponge soaked with vinegar-like sour wine, the drink of a Roman soldier. This fulfilled the prophecy of Psalm 69:21b.	Matthew 27:47–49; Mark 15:35–36; John 19:28–29 Psalm 69:21b
		After Jesus received the sour wine, He declared in triumph His Sixth Statement: *"It is finished!"* (Greek, *tetelestai*, the Debt is "Paid in Full.")	John 19:30
3:00 pm, the Time of the Slaying of the Passover Lamb	On the Cross at Golgotha	Jesus strongly uttered His Seventh Statement: *"Father, into Your hands I commit My spirit,"* a QUOTE of Psalm 31:5. Jesus yielded up His spirit to His Father and died.	Matthew 27:50 Mark 15:37 Luke 23:46 John 19:30 Psalm 31:5
THURSDAY or FRIDAY at 3:00 pm	In the Temple, Jerusalem, Entryway, Holy of Holies	The Veil of the Temple was torn from top to bottom, revealing the Holy of Holies.	Matthew 27:51a Mark 15:38 Luke 23:45
THURSDAY or FRIDAY Between 3:00 and 6:00 pm	Jerusalem and the area around the Cross	An earthquake occurred which split many rocks and opened up many tombs.	Matthew 27:51b–52a
		When the Roman Centurion and those with him saw the way Jesus died and all that accompanied this moment, he stated that Jesus was *"the Son of God"* and *"a righteous man."* He had seen many men die. This was no ordinary man, no ordinary crucifixion, no ordinary death.	Matthew 27:54 Mark 15:39 Luke 23:47

THURSDAY or FRIDAY 3:00-6:00 pm	Jerusalem and the area around the Cross	Many women, who had followed Jesus, along with others, observed all that occurred.	Matthew 27:55–56; Mark 15:40–41; Luke 23:48–49
THURSDAY or FRIDAY After 3:00 pm	Jerusalem At the Cross at Golgotha	To hasten death, the Roman soldiers used a *crurifragium*, an iron bar, to break the legs of the two thieves, but because Jesus was already dead, they broke no bones of Jesus. This fulfilled the prophecy of Psalm 34:20.	John 19:31–33, 36 Exodus 12:46; Numbers 9:12; Psalm 34:20
THURSDAY or FRIDAY After 3:00 pm	Jerusalem At the Cross at Golgotha	One of the soldiers pierced Jesus' side with a spear. Blood and water came out. John was an eyewitness of this. Zechariah 12:10 speaks of *"Me whom they have pierced."*	John 19:34–35, 37 Zechariah 12:10
After 3:00 p.m.	Pilate's Place	Joseph of Arimathea asked for Jesus' body so he could bury Him. Surprised, Pilate asked the Roman centurion if Jesus was *"already dead"* and he confirmed that Jesus was indeed dead.	Matthew 27:57–58; Mark 15:42–45; Luke 23:50–52; John 19:38
Before sunset on THURSDAY or FRIDAY	The Garden Tomb belonging to Joseph of Arimathea. This was a new tomb, never used before.	After asking Pilate, Joseph of Arimathea and Nicodemus took Jesus' body, wrapped it in linen and spices and buried Him in Joseph's own Garden tomb. The women went to the tomb also, then prepared to bring spices on Sunday after the Sabbath.	Matthew 27:59–61 Mark 15:46–47 Luke 23:53–56 John 19:38–42
FRIDAY or SATURDAY Morning	Jerusalem in a meeting with Pilate	Some of Jesus' enemies, the chief priests and Pharisees, noted that Jesus had said He would rise from the dead *"after three days,"* so they requested a seal and guard.	Matthew 27:62–64
	In Jerusalem with Pilate and at the Tomb	Pilate granted the request for Roman guards and a seal on the tomb; they secured the tomb.	Matthew 27:65–66
After sunset on Saturday	Jerusalem	The women bought spices to bring to Jesus' tomb on Sunday morning.	Mark 16:1
THE *EVENTS* OF RESURRECTION SUNDAY AND THE RESURRECTION APPEARANCES OF JESUS ON RESURRECTION SUNDAY			
SUNDAY Before Dawn	The Garden Tomb	Jesus arose! He resurrected from the dead! He left the Garden Tomb *before* the stone was rolled away.	Matthew 28:6

		"A great earthquake" occurred. An angel of the Lord descended, rolled away the stone, and sat on it. His appearance was like lightning. The Roman soldiers shook with fear and became like dead men.	Matthew 28:1–4
At Dawn	The Garden Tomb JESUS IS ALIVE!!! He is Risen from the Dead just as He said!!!	Mary Magdalene and other women came to the Garden Tomb while it was still dark and as the sun was rising. They found the stone rolled away. They received the message from the angels, *"He is not here, for He has risen, just as He said." … "Go quickly and tell His disciples that He has risen from the dead…."*	Matthew 28:5–8 Mark 16:2–8 Luke 24:1–8 John 20:1 Jesus told them at least six times He would rise from the dead.
After Dawn	Jerusalem	Jesus appeared to *"the women"* as they went to tell the disciples about the risen Jesus.	Matthew 28:9–10
After Dawn	The Disciples' Place and the Garden Tomb	The women ran and told the disciples about Jesus being risen. Peter and John ran to the Garden Tomb and saw the linen wrappings intact without His body in them and the separate *"face-cloth."* He was not there!	Matthew 28:8 Mark 16:8 Luke 24:9–12 John 20:2–10
After Dawn	The Garden Tomb	Mary Magdalene wept at the tomb. She saw the two angels and then the resurrected Jesus spoke to her there. She told the disciples.	John 20:11–18
After Jesus' Resurrection	Throughout Jerusalem, *"the holy city."*	Many saints were raised and seen, part of the First Fruits of the Resurrection.	Matthew 27:52–53
SUNDAY Morning or Afternoon	Jerusalem	Jesus appeared to Simon Peter or Cephas.	Luke 24:33–35 1 Corinthians 15:5
SUNDAY Afternoon	On the Road to Emmaus	Jesus came and began walking on the Emmaus Road with Cleopas and another disciple.	Mark 16:12–13 Luke 24:13–33
SUNDAY Evening	Jerusalem, in a locked room	In Jerusalem, in a locked room, Jesus suddenly appeared to Ten of the Eleven, without Thomas, and with the Two from Emmaus.	Mark 1:14 Luke 24:36–43 John 20:19–25

All the Recorded Resurrection Appearances of Jesus Christ			
Time	Place	Appeared to...	Scripture
1.Sunday Morning	The Garden Tomb	Mary Magdalene	Mark 16:9–11 John 20:11–18
2.Sunday Morning	Jerusalem	Mary Magdalene, the other Mary, and perhaps other *"women"*	Matthew 28:5, 9–10
3.Sunday Morning or Afternoon	Jerusalem	Simon Peter or Cephas	Luke 24:33–35 1 Corinthians 15:5
4.Sunday Afternoon	On the Road to Emmaus	Cleopas and another disciple	Mark 16:12–13 Luke 24:13–33
5.Sunday Evening	Jerusalem, in a locked room	Ten of the Eleven, without Thomas, with the Two from Emmaus	Mark 16:14 Luke 24:36–43 John 20:19–25
6.Sunday Evening, one week later	Jerusalem	The Eleven Disciples, with Thomas	John 20:26–31 1 Corinthians 15:5
7.Daybreak/ Dawn	Shore of the Sea of Galilee/ Tiberias	Simon Peter, Thomas, Nathaniel, James and John (sons of Zebedee), two other disciples	John 21:1–25
8.Unknown Time, During the 40-Day Post-Resurrection period	An appointed mountain in Galilee	The Eleven Disciples plus *"over 500 Brethren at once"*	Matthew 28:16–20; Mark 16:15–18 Possibly those in 1 Corinthians 15:6
9.Unknown Time	Unknown Place	James, the half-brother of Jesus	1 Corinthians 15:7
10. AD 30, Thursday, Day 40, Ascension Day	Mount of Olives, Near Bethany	The Eleven Disciples (perhaps including others)	Mark 16:19–20 Luke 24:44–53 Acts 1:3–12
11. About AD 33–35	Jerusalem	Stephen, during his stoning execution by Jewish leaders. Saul witnessed this.	Acts 7:55–56, 57–60
12.Around AD 35	On the Road to Damascus, Syria	Jesus appeared to Saul / Paul in a blinding light and spoke to him.	Acts 9:3–8; 22:6–11; 26:12–18; 1 Corinthians 9:1
13.Night of June 3, AD 57	Under Arrest in Jerusalem	Paul	Acts 23:11
14.*"The Lord's Day"* (Sunday) ca.AD 95	The Island of Patmos in the Aegean Sea	The Apostle John	Revelation 1:9–20

Time Future	Place	Will Appear to...	Scripture
15. The Rapture	*"Glorious Appearing"* throughout the earth and in the air	All the saints—those who have died physically and those who remain on earth physically alive. Each believer who has *"fallen asleep"* (a picture of the death of the body) will experience the resurrection of his/her body from wherever he/she was buried (or placed). Christians on earth still alive will be caught up [Greek—*harpazo*—to be caught up or raptured] into *"the clouds"* to join the first group that arose from the dead. *"And thus we shall always be with the Lord."*	1 Corinthians 15:22–23, 35–58; 1 Thessalonians 4:13–18; Titus 2:13 (*"the Blessed Hope and glorious appearing of our Great God and Savior Jesus Christ"*)
16. The Judgment Seat of Christ	*In Heaven after the Rapture*	All the Raptured Saints of all the ages	Romans 14:10–12; 1 Corinthians 3:9–15; 2 Corinthians 5:9–10; Rev.22:12
17. The *"Day of the Lord"* judgment era on earth.	Throughout the heavens and the earth	The Lord will reveal His judgments from heaven on all the earth.	Joel 1:15; 2:1, 11; Isaiah 13:6; Ezek 7:19; 13:5; 30:3; Zeph 1:7, 14; 1 Thess 5:2
18. The Second Coming of Christ (for further Judgment on Earth, before His Millennial Reign on Earth)	*Fiery Appearance* Throughout the earth	All that are alive at His Visible Return. The Resurrected, Reigning Christ will return to the earth visibly and victoriously for all then alive to see. This occurs at the end of the Seven-year Tribulation. He will deal with His enemies and then set up His Visible Kingdom and Reign on the earth for *"many days"* (Ezekiel 38:8) or for *"a thousand years"*—The Millennium (Revelation 20:4–6).	Psalm 2:1–9; 22:28; 110:1–7; Daniel 7:13–14; Matthew 24:29–31; 26:64; Mark 13:24–27; Luke 21:25–28; 2 Thessalonians 1:7–10; Jude 14–15
19. The Battle of Armageddon (*"Har-Megiddo"* —Hill of Megiddo overlooking the Valley of Jezreel	*Appearing on a White Horse* In Israel, in the Jezreel Valley / the Valley of Megiddo.	The Lord Jesus Christ—*"Faithful and True,"* "King of kings and Lord of lords," and *"The Word of God,"* comes riding on a White Horse, leading the Armies of Heaven on white horses. His only weapon is the Sword in His Mouth, the Word of God. He speaks and conquers all.	Revelation 16:14–16; 17:14; 19:11–21

20. The *Reign of Christ on Earth* for One Thousand Years—*"the days of the Son of Man"* (Luke 17:22)—also known as *The Millennial Kingdom*	From His Throne in Jerusalem ruling the entire earth (as well as all creation and Heaven)	The Lord Jesus Christ will appear to all on the earth (and heaven) during His Millennial Reign (*"many days"*—Ezekiel 38:8) or *"a thousand years"*—Revelation 20:4) on the earth. Satan will be bound in *"the bottomless pit"* for one thousand years (Revelation 20:1–3).	Psalm 96:10–13; Isaiah 2:1–5; 11:1–16; 12:1–6; Matthew 13:24–30, 36–43; 24:29–51; 25:31–46; Luke 17:22, 2421:27–28. 34–36; John 5:24–29; 2 Thessalonians 1:10; Revelation 19:12–13; 20:4–6
21. At the Close of the Millennial Kingdom Comes the *Final Battle*	Jerusalem, Israel and the area surrounding it—stated as *"the camp of the saints and the beloved city."*	Satan is released from the bottomless pit where he was bound for one thousand years. He deceives the nations, and they gather to battle with God and the Saints. *"And fire came down from heaven and devoured"* all those gathered against God (Revelation 20:9). Satan is cast into *"the lake of fire and brimstone"* forever (Revelation 20:10).	Revelation 20:7–10
22. After the *Final Battle, The Great White Throne Judgment* occurs	God's Appointed Place	Jesus sits as Judge concerning all the unredeemed, *"the dead, the great and the small, standing before the throne."* Each receives the appropriate sentence based on their *"deeds"* as recorded in *"the books"* (Revelation 20:12).	Psalm 9:7–8; 96:13; 98:9; John 5:22–30; Acts 10:42; 17:31; Romans 2:5–6, 8, 16; 2 Timothy 4:1; 1 Peter 4:5; Revelation 20:11–15
23. The Eternal *"Day of God"* (2 Peter 3:12) or *"the Day of Eternity"* (2 Peter 3:18)	The New Earth and Heavens with New Jerusalem	All the redeemed of all the ages. Jesus will Reign in the New Jerusalem on the New Earth *forever.*	Isaiah 65:17; 66:22; 2 Peter 3:12, 13, 18; Revelation 21–22

For maps showing the land in which Jesus traveled and His various ministry sites, see the various maps presented online and in published Bible atlases.

Notes

Leader's Guide

Table of Contents

The best way to become a better discussion leader is to regularly evaluate your group discussion sessions. The most effective leaders are those who consistently look for ways to improve.

But before you start preparing for your first group session, you need to know the problem areas that will most likely weaken the effectiveness of your study group. Commit now to have the best Bible study group that you can possibly have. Ask the Lord to motivate you as a group leader and to steer you away from bad habits.

How to Guarantee a Poor Discussion Group:

1. Prepare inadequately.

2. Show improper attitude toward people in the group (lack of acceptance).

3. Fail to create an atmosphere of freedom and ease.

4. Allow the discussion to wander aimlessly.

5. Dominate the discussion yourself.

6. Let a small minority dominate the discussion.

7. Leave the discussion "in the air," so to speak, without presenting any concluding statements or some type of closure.

8. Ask too many "telling" or "trying" questions. (Don't ask individuals in your group pointed or threatening questions that might bring embarrassment to them or make them feel uncomfortable.)

9. End the discussion without adequate application points.

10. Do the same thing every time.

11. Become resentful and angry when people disagree with you. After all, you did prepare. You are the leader!

12. End the discussion with an argument.

13. Never spend any time with the members of your group other than the designated discussion meeting time.

Helpful Hints

One of the best ways to learn to be an effective Bible discussion leader is to sit under a good model. If you have had the chance to be in a group with an effective facilitator, think about the things that made him or her effective.

Though you can learn much and shape many convictions from those good models, you can also glean some valuable lessons on what not to do from those who didn't do such a good job. Bill Donahue has done a good job of categorizing the leader's role in facilitating dynamic discussion into four key actions. They are easy to remember as he links them to the acrostic ACTS:

*A leader ACTS to facilitate discussions by:

- Acknowledging everyone who speaks during a discussion.
- Clarifying what is being said and felt.
- Taking it to the group as a means of generating discussion.
- Summarizing what has been said.

*Taken from *Leading Life-Changing Small Groups* ©1996 by the Willow Creek Association. Used by permission of ZondervanPublishing House.

Make a point to give each group member ample opportunity to speak. Pay close attention to any nonverbal communication (i.e. facial expressions, body language, etc.) that group members may use, showing their desire to speak. The four actions in Bill Donahue's acrostic will guarantee to increase your effectiveness, which will translate into your group getting more out of the Bible study. After all, isn't that your biggest goal?

Dealing with Talkative Timothy

Throughout your experiences of leading small Bible study groups, you will learn that there will be several stereotypes who will follow you wherever you go. One of them is "Talkative Timothy." He will show up in virtually every small group you will ever lead. (Sometimes this stereotype group member shows up as "Talkative Tammy.") "Talkative Timothy" talks too much, dominates the discussion time, and gives less opportunity for others to share. What do you do with a group member who talks too much? Below you will find some helpfulideas on managing the "Talkative Timothy's" in your group.

The best defense is a good offense. To deal with "Talkative Timothy" before he becomes a problem, one thing you can do is establish as a ground rule that no one can talk twice until everyone who wants to talk has spoken at least once. Another important ground rule is "no interrupting." Still another solution is to go systematically around the group, directing questions to people by name. When all else fails, you can resort to a very practical approach of sitting beside "Talkative Timothy." When you make it harder for him (or her) to make eye contact with you, you will create less chances for him to talk.

After taking one or more of these combative measures, you may find that "Timothy" is still a problem. You may need to meet with him (or her) privately. Assure him that you value his input, but remind him that you want to hear the comments of others as well. One way to diplomatically approach "Timothy" is to privately ask him to help you draw the less talkative members into the discussion. Approaching "Timothy" in this fashion may turn your dilemma into an asset. Most importantly, remember to love "Talkative Timothy."

Silent Sally

Another person who inevitably shows up is "Silent Sally." She doesn't readily speak up. Sometimes her silence is because she doesn't yet feel comfortable enough with the group to share her thoughts. Sometimes it is simply because she fears being rejected. Often her silence is because she is too polite to interrupt and thus is headed off at the pass each time she wants to speak by more aggressive (and less sensitive) members of the group.

It is not uncommon in a mixed group to find that "Silent Sally" is married to "Talkative Timothy." (Seriously!) Don't mistakenly interpret her silence as meaning that she has nothing to contribute. Often those who are slowest to speak will offer the most meaningful contributions to the group. You can help "Silent Sally" make those significant contributions. Below are some ideas.

Make sure, first of all, that you are creating an environment that makes people comfortable. In a tactful way, direct specific questions to the less talkative in the group. Be careful though, not to put them on the spot with the more difficult or controversial questions. Become their biggest fan—make sure you cheer them on when they do share. Give them a healthy dose of affirmation. Compliment them afterward for any insightful contributions they make. You may want to sit across from them in the group so that it is easier to notice any nonverbal cues they give you when they want to speak. You should also come to their defense if another group member responds to them in a negative, stifling way. As you pray for each group member, ask that the Lord would help the quiet ones in your group to feel more at ease during the discussion time. Most of all, love "Silent Sally," and accept her as she is—even when she is silent!

Tangent Tom

We have already looked at "Talkative Timothy" and "Silent Sally." Now let's look at another of those stereotypes who always show up. Let's call this person, "Tangent Tom." He is the kind of guy who loves to talk even when he has nothing to say. "Tangent Tom" loves to chase rabbits regardless of where they go. When he gets the floor, you never know where the discussion will lead. You need to understand that not all tangents are bad, for sometimes much can be gained from discussion that is a little "off the beaten path." But diversions must be balanced against the purpose of the group. What is fruitful for one member may be fruitless for everyone else. Below are some ideas to help you deal with "Tangent Tom."

Evaluating Tangents

Ask yourself, "How will this tangent affect my group's chances of finishing the lesson?" Another way to measure the value of a tangent is by asking, "Is this something that will benefit all or most of the group?" You also need to determine whether there is a practical, spiritual benefit to this tangent. Paul advised Timothy to refuse foolish and ignorant speculations, knowing that they produce quarrels. (See 2 Timothy 2:23.)

Addressing Tangents:

1) Keep pace of your time, and use the time factor as your ally when addressing "Tangent Tom." Tactfully respond, "That is an interesting subject, but since our lesson is on _______________, we'd better get back to our lesson if we are going to finish."

2) If the tangent is beneficial to one but fruitless to the rest of the group, offer to address that subject after class.

3) If the tangent is something that will benefit the group, you may want to say, "I'd like to talk about that more. Let's come back to that topic at the end of today's discussion, if we have time."

4) Be sure you understand what "Tangent Tom" is trying to say. It may be that he has a good and valid point, but has trouble expressing it or needs help in being more direct. Be careful not to quench someone whose heart is right, even if his methods aren't perfect. (See Proverbs 18:23.)

5) One suggestion for diffusing a strife-producing tangent is to point an imaginary shotgun at a spot outside the group and act like you are firing a shot. Then say, "That rabbit is dead. Now, where were we?"

6) If it is a continual problem, you may need to address it with this person privately.

7) Most of all, be patient with "Tangent Tom." God will use him in the group in ways that will surprise you!

Know–It-All Ned

The Scriptures are full of characters who struggled with the problem of pride. Unfortunately, pride isn't a problem reserved for the history books. It shows up today just as it did in the days the Scriptures were written.

Pride is sometimes the root-problem of a know-it-all group member. "Know-It-All Ned" may have shown up in your group by this point. He may be an intellectual giant, or only a legend in his own mind. He can be very prideful and argumentative. "Ned" often wants his point chosen as the choice point, and he may be intolerant of any opposing views—sometimes to the point of making his displeasure known in very inappropriate ways. A discussion point tainted with the stench of pride is uninviting—no matter how well spoken!

No one else in the group will want anything to do with this kind of attitude. How do you manage the "Know-It-All Neds" who show up from time to time?

Evaluation

To deal with "Know-It-All Ned," you need to understand him. Sometimes the same type of action can be rooted in very different causes. You must ask yourself, "Why does 'Ned' come across as a know-it-all?" It may be that "Ned" has a vast reservoir of knowledge but hasn't matured in how he communicates it. Or perhaps "Ned" really doesn't know it all, but he tries to come across that way to hide his insecurities and feelings of inadequacy.

Quite possibly, "Ned" is prideful and arrogant, and knows little of the Lord's ways in spite of the information and facts he has accumulated. Still another possibility is that Ned is a good man with a good heart who has a blind spot in the area of pride.

APPLICATION
"Know-It-All Ned" may be the most difficult person to deal with in your group, but God will use him in ways that will surprise you. Often it is the "Neds" of the church that teach each of us what it means to love the unlovely in God's strength, not our own. In 1 Thessalonians 5:14, the apostle Paul states, *"And we urge you, brethren, admonish the unruly, encourage the fainthearted, help the weak, be patient with all men."* In dealing with the "Neds" you come across, start by assuming they are weak and need help until they give you reason to believe otherwise. Don't embarrass them by confronting them in public. Go to them in private if need be.

Speak the truth in love. You may need to remind them of 1 Corinthians 13, that if we have all knowledge, but have not love, we are just making noise. First Corinthians is also where we are told, *"knowledge makes arrogant, but love edifies"* (8:1). Obviously, there were some "Neds" in the church at Corinth. If you sense that "Ned" is not weak or faint-hearted, but in fact is unruly, you will need to admonish him. Make sure you do so in private, but make sure you do it all the same. Proverbs 27:56 tells us, *"Better is open rebuke than love that is concealed. Faithful are the wounds of a friend, but deceitful are the kisses of an enemy."* Remember the last statement in 1 Thessalonians 5:14, *"be patient with all men."*

Agenda Alice
The last person we would like to introduce to you who will probably show up sooner or later is one we like to call "Agenda Alice." All of us from time to time can be sidetracked by our own agenda. Often the very thing we are most passionate about can be the thing that distracts us from our highest passion: Christ. Agendas often are not unbiblical, but imbalanced. At their root is usually tunnel-vision mixed with a desire for control. The small group, since it allows everyone to contribute to the discussion, affords "Agenda Alice" a platform to promote what she thinks is most important. This doesn't mean that she is wrong to avoid driving at night because opossums are being killed, but she is wrong to expect everyone to have the exact same conviction and calling that she does in the gray areas of Scripture. If not managed properly, she will either sidetrack the group from its main study objective or create a hostile environment in the group if she fails to bring people to her way of thinking. "Agenda Alice" can often be recognized by introductory catch phrases such as "Yes, but . . ." and "Well, I think. . . ." She is often critical of the group process and may become vocally critical of you. Here are some ideas on dealing with this type of person:

1) Reaffirm the group covenant.
   At the formation of your group you should have taken time to define some ground rules for the group. Once is not enough to discuss these matters of group etiquette. Periodically remind everyone of their mutual commitment to one another.

2) Remember that the best defense is a good offense.

Don't wait until it is a problem to address a mutual vision for how the group will function.

3) Refocus on the task at hand.
   The clearer you explain the objective of each session, the easier it is to stick to that objective and the harder you make it for people to redirect attention toward their own agenda. Enlist the whole group in bringing the discussion back to the topic at hand. Ask questions like, "What do the rest of you think about this passage?"

4) Remind the group, "Remember, this week's lesson is about ____________."

5) Reprove those who are disruptive.
   Confront the person in private to see if you can reach an understanding. Suggest another arena for the issue to be addressed such as an optional meeting for those in the group who would like to discuss the issue.

Remember the words of St. Augustine: "In essentials unity, in non-essentials liberty, in all things charity."

Adding Spice and Creativity
One of the issues you will eventually have to combat in any group Bible study is the enemy of boredom. This enemy raises its ugly head from time to time, but it shouldn't. It is wrong to bore people with the Word of God! Often boredom results when leaders allow their processes to become too predictable. As small group leaders, we tend to do the same thing in the same way every single time. Yet God the Creator, who spoke everything into existence is infinitely creative! Think about it. He is the one who not only created animals in different shapes and sizes, but different colors as well. When He created food, He didn't make it all taste or feel the same. This God of creativity lives in us. We can trust Him to give us creative ideas that will keep our group times from becoming tired and mundane. Here are some ideas:

When you think of what you can change in your Bible study, think of the five senses: (sight, sound, smell, taste, and feel).

SIGHT:
One idea would be to have a theme night with decorations. Perhaps you know someone with dramatic instincts who could dress up in costume and deliver a message from the person you are studying that week.

Draw some cartoons on a marker board or handout.

SOUND:
Play some background music before your group begins. Sing a hymn together that relates to the lesson. If you know of a song that really hits the main point of the lesson, play it at the beginning or end.

SMELL:
This may be the hardest sense to involve in your Bible study, but if you think of a creative way to incorporate this sense into the lesson, you can rest assured it will be memorable for your group.

TASTE:

Some lessons will have issues that can be related to taste (e.g. unleavened bread for the Passover, etc.). What about making things less formal by having snacks while you study? Have refreshments around a theme such as "Chili Night" or "Favorite Fruits."

FEEL:
Any way you can incorporate the sense of feel into a lesson will certainly make the content more invigorating. If weather permits, add variety by moving your group outside. Whatever you do, be sure that you don't allow your Bible study to become boring!

Handling an Obviously Wrong Comment
From time to time, each of us can say stupid things. Some of us, however, are better at it than others. The apostle Peter had his share of embarrassing moments. One minute, he was on the pinnacle of success, saying, *"Thou art the Christ, the Son of the Living God"* (Matthew 16:16), and the next minute, he was putting his foot in his mouth, trying to talk Jesus out of going to the cross. Proverbs 10:19 states, "When there are many words, transgression is unavoidable. . . ." What do you do when someone in the group says something that is obviously wrong? First of all, remember that how you deal with a situation like this not only affects the present, but the future. Here are some ideas:

1) Let the whole group tackle it and play referee/peacemaker. Say something like, "That is an interesting thought, what do the rest of you think?"

2) Empathize. ("I've thought that before too, but the Bible says. . . .")

3) Clarify to see if what they said is what they meant. ("What I think you are saying is. . . .")

4) Ask the question again, focusing on what the Bible passage actually says.

5) Give credit for the part of the answer that is right and affirm that before dealing with what is wrong.

6) If it is a non-essential, disagree agreeably. ("I respect your opinion, but I see it differently.")

7) Let it go —some things aren't important enough to make a big deal about them.

8) Love and affirm the person, even if you reject the answer.

Transitioning to the Next Study

For those of you who have completed leading a Following God Group Bible Study, congratulations! You have successfully navigated the waters of small group discussion. You have utilized one of the most effective tools of ministry—one that was so much a priority with Jesus, He spent most of His time there with His small group of twelve. Hopefully yours has been a very positive and rewarding experience. At this stage you may be looking forward to a break. It is not too early however, to be thinking and planning for what you will do next. Hopefully you have seen God use this study and this process for growth in the lives of those who have participated with you. As God has worked in the group, members should be motivated to ask the question, "What next?" As they do, you need to be prepared to give an answer. Realize that you have built a certain amount of momentum with your present study that will make it easier to do another. You want to take advantage of that momentum. The following suggestions may be helpful as you transition your people toward further study of God's Word.

- Challenge your group members to share with others what they have learned, and to encourage them to participate next time.
- If what to study is a group choice rather than a church-wide or ministry-wide decision made by others, you will want to allow some time for input from the group members in deciding what to do next. The more they have ownership of the study, the more they will commit to it.
- It is important to have some kind of a break so that everyone doesn't become study weary. At our church, we always look for natural times to start and end a study. We take the summer off as well as Christmas, and we have found that having a break brings people back with renewed vigor. Even if you don't take a break from meeting, you might take a breather from homework—or even get together just for fellowship.
- If you are able to end this study knowing what you will study next, some of your group members may want to get a head start on the next study. Be prepared to put books in their hands early.
- Make sure you end your study with a vision for more. Take some time to remind your group of the importance of the Word of God. As D. L. Moody used to say, "The only way to keep a broken vessel full is to keep the faucet running."

Evaluation

Becoming a Better Discussion Leader

The questions listed below are tools to assist you in assessing your discussion group. From time to time in the Leader's Guide, you will be advised to read through this list of evaluation questions in order to help you decide what areas need improvement in your role as group leader. Each time you read through this list, something different may catch your attention, giving you tips on how to become the best group leader that you can possibly be.

Read through these questions with an open mind, asking the Lord to prick your heart with anything specific He would want you to apply.

1. Are the group discussion sessions beginning and ending on time?

2. Am I allowing the freedom of the Holy Spirit as I lead the group in the discussion?

3. Do I hold the group accountable for doing their homework?

4. Do we always begin our sessions with prayer?

5. Is the room arranged properly (seating in a circle or semicircle, proper ventilation, adequate teaching aids)?

6. Is each individual allowed equal opportunity in the discussion?

7. Do I successfully bridle the talkative ones?

8. Am I successfully encouraging the hesitant ones to participate in the discussion?

9. Do I redirect comments and questions to involve more people in the interaction, or do I always dominate the discussion?

10. Are the discussions flowing naturally, or do they take too many "side roads" (diversions)?

11. Do I show acceptance to those who convey ideas with which I do not agree?

12. Are my questions specific, brief and clear?

13. Do my questions provoke thought, or do they only require pat answers?

14. Does each group member feel free to contribute or question, or is there a threatening or unnecessarily tense atmosphere?

15. Am I allowing time for silence and thought without making everyone feel uneasy?

16. Am I allowing the group to correct any obviously wrong conclusions that are made by others, or by myself (either intentionally to capture the group's attention or unintentionally)?

17. Do I stifle thought and discussion by assigning a question to someone before the subject of that question has even been discussed? (It will often be productive to assign a question to a specific person, but if you call on one person before you throw out a question, everyone else takes a mental vacation!)

18. Do I summarize when brevity is of the essence?

19. Can I refrain from expressing an opinion or comment that someone else in the group could just as adequately express?

20. Do I occasionally vary in my methods of conducting the discussion?

21. Am I keeping the group properly motivated?

22. Am I occasionally rotating the leadership to help others develop leadership?

23. Am I leading the group to specifically apply the truths that are learned?

24. Do I follow through by asking the group how they have applied the truths that they have learned from previous lessons?

25. Am I praying for each group member?

26. Is there a growing openness and honesty among my group members?

27. Are the group study sessions enriching the lives of my group members?

28. Have I been adequately prepared?

29. How may I be better prepared for the next lesson's group discussion?

30. Do I reach the objective set for each discussion? If not, why not? What can I do to improve?

31. Am I allowing the discussion to bog down on one point at the expense of the rest of the lesson?

32. Are the members of the group individually reaching the conclusions that I want them to reach without my having to give them the conclusions?

33. Do I encourage the group members to share what they have learned?

34. Do I encourage them to share the applications they have discovered?

35. Do I whet their appetites for next week's lesson discussion?

Getting Started

The First Meeting of Your Bible Study Group

Main Objectives of the First Meeting: The first meeting is devoted to establishing your group and setting the course that you will follow through the study. Your primary goals for this session should be to . . .

- Establish a sense of group identity by starting to get to know one another.
- Define some ground rules to help make the group time as effective as possible.
- Get the study materials into the hands of your group members.
- Create a sense of excitement and motivation for the study.
- Give assignments for next week.

BEFORE THE SESSION

You will be most comfortable in leading this introductory session if you are prepared as much as possible for what to expect. This means becoming familiar with the place you will meet, and the content you will cover, as well as understanding any time constraints you will have.

Location—Be sure that you not only know how to find the place where you will be meeting, but also have time to examine the setup and make any adjustments to the physical arrangements. You never get a second chance to make a first impression.

Curriculum—You will want to get a copy of the study in advance of the introductory session, and it will be helpful if you do the homework for Lesson One ahead of time. This will make it easier for you to be able to explain the layout of the homework. It will also give you a contagious enthusiasm for what your group will be studying in the coming week.

You will want to have enough books on hand for the number of people you expect so that they can get started right away with the study. You may be able to make arrangements with your church or local Christian Bookstore to bring copies on consignment. We would encourage you not to buy books for your members. Years of small group experience have taught that people take a study far more seriously when they make an investment in it.

Time—The type of group you are leading will determine the time format for your study. If you are doing this study for a Sunday school class or church study course, the time constraints may already be prescribed for you. In any case, ideally you will want to allow forty-five minutes to an hour for discussion.

WHAT TO EXPECT

When you embark on the journey of leading a small group Bible study, you are stepping into the stream of the work of God. You are joining in the process of helping others move toward spiritual maturity. As a small group leader, you are positioned to be a real catalyst in the lives of your group members, helping them to grow in their relationships with God. But you must remember, first and foremost, that whenever you step up to leadership in the kingdom of God, you are stepping down to serve. Jesus made it clear that leadership in the kingdom is not like leadership in the world. In Matthew 20:25, Jesus said, *"You know that the rulers of the Gentiles lord it over them, and their great men exercise authority over them."* That is the world's way to lead. But in Matthew 20:26–27, He continues, "It is not so among you, but whoever wishes to become great among you shall be your servant, and whoever wishes to be first among you shall be your slave." Your job as a small group leader is not to teach the group everything you have learned, but rather, to help them learn.

If you truly are to minister to the members of your group, you must start with understanding where they are, and join that with a vision of where you want to take them. In this introductory session, your group members will be experiencing several different emotions. They will be wondering, "Who is in my group?" and deciding "Do I like my group?" They will have a sense of excitement and anticipation, but also a sense of awkwardness as they try to find their place in this group. You will want to make sure that from the very beginning your group is founded with a sense of caring and acceptance. This is crucial if your group members are to open up and share what they are learning.

DURING THE SESSION

GETTING TO KNOW ONE ANOTHER

Opening Prayer—Remember that if it took the inspiration of God for people to write Scripture, it will also take His illumination for us to understand it. Have one of your group members open your time together in prayer.

Introductions—Take time to allow the group members to introduce themselves. Along with having the group members share their names, one way to add some interest is to have them add some descriptive information such as where they live or work. Just for fun, you could have them name their favorite breakfast cereal, most (or least) favorite vegetable, favorite cartoon character, their favorite city or country other than their own, etc.

Icebreaker—Take five or ten minutes to get the people comfortable in talking with each other. Since in many cases your small group will just now be getting to know one another, it will be helpful if you take some time to break the ice with some fun, nonthreatening discussion. Below you will find a list of ideas for good icebreaker questions to get people talking.

____ What is the biggest risk you have ever taken?

____ If money were no object, where would you most like to take a vacation and why?

____ What is your favorite way to waste time?

____ If you weren't in the career you now have, what would have been your second choice for a career?

____ If you could have lived in any other time, in what era or century would you have chosen to live (besides the expected spiritual answer of the time of Jesus)?

____ If you became blind right now, what would you miss seeing the most?

____ Who is the most famous person you've known or met?

____ What do you miss most about being a kid?

____ What teacher had the biggest impact on you in school (good or bad)?

____ Of the things money can buy, what would you most like to have?

____ What is your biggest fear?

____ If you could give one miracle to someone else, what would it be (and to whom)?

____ Tell about your first job.

____ Who is the best or worst boss you ever had?

____ Who was your hero growing up and why?

DEFINING THE GROUP: 5–10 MINUTES
SETTING SOME GROUND RULES

There are several ways you can lay the tracks on which your group can run. One is simply to hand out a list of suggested commitments the members should make to the group. Another would be to hand out 3x5 cards and have the members themselves write down two or three commitments they would like to see everyone live out. You could then compile these into the five top ones to share at the following meeting. A third option is to list three (or more) commitments you are making to the group and then ask that they make three commitments back to you in return. Here are some ideas for the types of ground rules that make for a good small group:

Leader:

____ To always arrive prepared

____ To keep the group on track so you make the most of the group's time

____ To not dominate the discussion by simply teaching the lesson

____ To pray for the group members

____ To not belittle or embarrass anyone's answers

____ To bring each session to closure and end on time

Member:

____ To do my homework

____ To arrive on time

____ To participate in the discussion

____ To not cut others off as they share

____ To respect the different views of other members

____ To not dominate the discussion

It is possible that your group may not need to formalize a group covenant, but you should not be afraid to expect a commitment from your group members. They will all benefit from defining the group up front.

INTRODUCTION TO THE STUDY:
15–20 MINUTES

As you introduce the study to the group members, your goal is to begin to create a sense of excitement about the Bible characters and applications that will be discussed. The most important question for you to answer in this session is "Why should I study _________?" You need to be prepared to guide them to finding that answer. Take time to give a brief overview of each lesson.

CLOSING: 5–10 MINUTES

Give homework for next week. In addition to simply reminding the group members to do their homework, if time allows, you might give them 5–10 minutes to get started on their homework for the first lesson.

Key components for closing out your time are a) to review anything of which you feel they should be reminded, and b) to close in prayer. If time allows, you may want to encourage several to pray.

PREPARATION OF THE DISCUSSION LEADER

I. Preparation of the Leader's Heart

A. Pray. It took the inspiration of the Holy Spirit to write Scripture, and it will require His illumination to correctly understand it.

B. Complete the Bible Study Yourself

1. Prayerfully seek a fresh word from God for yourself. Your teaching should be an overflow of what God taught you.

2. Even if you have completed this study in the past, consider using a new book. You need to be seeking God for what He would teach you this time before looking at what He taught you last time.

3. Guard against focusing on how to present truths to class. Keep the focus on God teaching you.

II. Keeping the Big Picture in Sight

One value of discussion: It allows students to share what God's Word says.

A. Looking back over the homework, find the one main unifying truth. There will be a key emphasis of each day, but all will support one main truth. Keep praying and looking until you find it (even if the author didn't make it clear).

B. Begin to write questions for each day's homework. Do this as you go through the study.

1. Consider key passage(s) for the day and ask questions of the text. For example, use the 5 Ws and an H (Who, What, When, Where, Why, and How): What was Jesus' main point? What is the context here? Do you see any cultural significance to this statement? How did this person relate to... (God? His neighbor? An unbeliever? The church? etc.)

2. Don't ask, "What do you think" questions unless it's "What do you think GOD is saying...?" It's easy to slip into sharing opinions if we don't carefully guide students to consider what God says. What I think doesn't matter if it differs from what God thinks.

3. Ask application questions as well. For example, "What steals our joy?" "How are we like these Bible characters?" "How can we learn from __________'s lessons so that we don't have to learn it the hard way?" "How can I restore/protect my __________ (joy, faith, peace...)?" Consider making a list where you write answers to "So what?" questions: So, what does this mean to me? How do I put this truth into practice?

4. Include definitions, grammar notes, historical/cultural notes, cross references, and so forth, from your own study. Go back over your notes/questions and add/delete/re-write after further prayer and thought. Go through your notes again, highlighting

(underlining, color coding, whatever works for you) what you believe is MOST important. This will help when time gets cut short. It will also jog your memory before moving to next day's homework,

III. Leading the Discussion

A. Begin with prayer

1. Consider varying the method - this will help to remind the group that we pray not as habit but as needy children seeking our loving Father Who teaches us by His Spirit.

2. If having a time of prayer requests, consider ways to make it time effective and to avoid gossip disguised as a prayer request. Time management is a way you can serve the group.

B. Start the Study with Review—Briefly review context of the study (or have a student come prepared to do it). This keeps the group together for those joining the study late or who've missed a week. This also serves as a reminder since it's been a week or so since your previous study session.

C. Go through the study questions day by day.

1. You may offer a "unifying theme" of study or ask if students can identify a theme.

2. Follow the Holy Spirit. Remember that you can't cover everything from every day. As you prepare, highlight any notes He leads you to consider as being most important.

3. Watch your time! When you are leading a group Bible study, you enter into a different dimension of the physical realm. Time moves at a completely different pace. What is 20 minutes in normal time flies by like 5 minutes when you are in the speaking zone.

4. Manage the questions raised by students and consider their value to the whole group within time constraints. Turn any questions raised back to the group.

5. Whether you make application day by day (probably best) or make application at end, be sure to allow time for students to name ways to put knowledge into practice.

IV. Evaluation

1. After 1-2 days, evaluate how the lesson went.

2. Thank God—thank Him for using His Word in all participants' lives and ask Him to guard the good seed planted!

V. Begin Preparation for the Next Lesson

Lesson 1

The Early Days of David

From Shepherd Boy to His Anointing as King

Memory Verses: Psalm 78:71–72

"From the care of the ewes with suckling lambs He brought him, to shepherd Jacob His people, and Israel His inheritance. So he shepherded them according to the integrity of his heart, and guided them with his skillful hands."

BEFORE THE SESSION

- Pray for your group as they study through this week's lesson.
- Spread your study time over the week. Allow the Scripture passages to soak in your head and heart. This is like a large meal. You need time to chew each truth and digest it fully.
- As you walk through this lesson, keep in mind that times and cultures change, but the human heart does not unless God works His work.
- As you study, remember to jot down those ideas and questions you want to discuss or ask as you go through this lesson with your small group.

What to Expect
Many have heard of King David, perhaps about his being a shepherd boy or about the David and Goliath incident. Few have studied the details of David's life and how he grew in knowing and following the Lord. In spending time considering David's decades, it is essential to apply the spiritual truths he learned in those many years. He was not a perfect son or man or soldier, not a perfect king or leader, but he had a "heart for God." That one factor affects everything. Each of us needs to know and follow the Lord from the heart; it's not a matter of merely knowing historical figures or facts, life principles or life lessons. It is important to genuinely know and follow the Lord and His Word in a personal way. It mattered in the life of David and those around him; it matters in each of our lives. Help your group see the essentials without getting lost in the details. Help focus the group on the personal applications of that time in history as well those that apply today. As you walk through David's life and times, encourage them to share their insights, ideas, and applications.

Main Point: The main point to be seen in "The Early Days of David" is how God worked to bring him from shepherd boy to Shepherd King. God works in unique ways in each of our lives to bring each to know and walk with Him.

During the Session

Opening: 5–10 Minutes

Opening Prayer—Have one of the group members open the time with prayer.

Opening Illustration—Assets or Treasures?—So many hope that some skill, some item, something in their lives will prove to be more than a normal asset, perhaps it would be a great treasure. In the days of David, children were considered assets to help around the house, to contribute to the family well-being through hard work and team effort, and a help for the parents in later years. Sometimes that is *all* parents and society thought of a child, hopefully another asset. However, that asset could be a treasure. David proved to be that. Though seen as only *"the youngest,"* not necessarily a favorable term, he was a treasure, a 'king in waiting' that no one saw. We can make the same error; what we consider a possible asset, or sometimes a liability, can in fact be a treasure from God. Help your group grasp that truth as you walk through the life of David.

DISCUSSION: 30 MINUTES

Study diligently in your preparation time. This will help you guide the discussion as well as answer many of the questions that arise in your group. Seeing the 'hidden' ways of God in David's life can help your group in many areas of their Christian walk. And seeing David's heart can help any heart redirect from a wrong focus to a right focus. As you trek through the lesson, seek to keep the main point the main point and be sure to leave time for the application points in Day Five. There is nothing more important than emphasizing personal application.

Main Objective in Day One: In Day One, the main objective is to see a clear overview of David, "Another Child—The Eighth Son," and how God viewed him. In addition to any discussion questions you may have in mind, the list of questions below may also contain useful discussion-starter ideas.

___ What is so important about taking care of daily details whether in the home, at school, or at the job?

___ How can mundane things be meaningful things? Is that possible? How so?

___ How essential is "integrity" in the home, in school, on the job, in the neighborhood or community?

___ David was a young man with a great "heart," but that is not enough. First Samuel 16:13 also notes the work of *"the Spirt of the LORD"* in his life. How crucial is the Holy Spirit and His work in each life?

Main Objective in Day Two: In Day Two, the main objective is to see how important obedience to the Lord is in any life. Check which discussion questions you will use from Day Two.

___ How does obedience to the Lord and His Word reveal our trust in the Lord?

___ What essential characteristic do we consistently see in Samuel? What does that say to each of us?

___ God's surprises sometimes baffle us and sometimes amaze us. What should we do with these?

___ Most of the time, God's timing is different from our ideas. How can we handle this fact?

<u>Main Objective in Day Three</u>: In Day Three, our main objective is to see the Lord *and* David's heart in Psalm 23. Below, are some suggested discussion starters for you to consider.

___ How important is a *personal* relationship with the Lord? How important does this seem in David's life?

___ David used everyday terms familiar to him. What everyday terms could we use to talk about knowing God?

___ Someone said no one is ready to live until he or she is ready to die. How does David show this?

___ What comfort or strength can we find in thinking of matters of time *and* eternity?

<u>Main Objective in Day Four</u>: Day Four's main objective is to see some of the main details about David and the incident with Goliath. Check any questions that are applicable for your Day Four-discussion time.

___ Normal life means "do the next thing" or "take the next step," nothing unusual. How did David show this in his life?

___ Pressures squeeze us and reveal some of what's on the inside. How did Goliath's challenge affect David?

___ What did *"five smooth stones"* and *"his sling"* mean in David's life? In this incident with Goliath?

___ David revealed his skill, but there was more. What responses do you see from Saul and from Jonathan?

<u>Day Five—Key Points in Application</u>: The most important application point in "The Early Days of David" is *personally* following the Lord. Check which discussion questions you will use to help focus the applications from Day Five.

___ What is the most significant factor in *your* life about personally knowing Jesus as Lord and Savior?

___ How is the Lord like a *"Shepherd"* in your life? What does He know about each "sheep"?

___ How are David's early days an encouragement to you?

___ What one or two psalms have become particularly meaningful to you?

CLOSING: 5–10 MINUTES

- Summarize—Restate the key points the group shared.
- Focus—Using the memory verses (Psalm 78:71–72), focus the group again on what a personal walk of integrity means today. Remind the members of your group that each life is unique; none of us is "David," but each of us is responsible for the choices he/she makes and how he/she lives.
- Ask them to share their thoughts about the key applications from Day Five.
- Preview—Take a few moments to preview next week's lesson, "On the Run: David's Days Running from Saul and Seeking the Lord." Encourage your group members to do their homework in proper fashion by spacing it out over the week.
- Pray—Close in prayer.

Tools for Good Discussion

Some who are reading this have led small group Bible studies many times. Here is an important word of warning: experience alone does not make you a more effective discussion leader. In fact, experience can make you less effective. You see, the more experience you have the more comfortable you will be at the task. Unfortunately, for some that means becoming increasingly comfortable in doing a bad job. Taking satisfaction with mediocrity translates into taking the task less seriously. It is easy to wrongly assert that just because one is experienced, he or she can successfully "shoot from the hip" so to speak. If you really want your members to get the most out of this study, you need to be dissatisfied with simply doing an adequate job and make it your aim to do an excellent job. A key to excellence is regularly evaluating yourself to see that you are still doing all that you need to be doing. We have prepared a list of over thirty evaluation questions for you to review from time to time. This list of questions can be found on pages 224–225 in the Leader's Guide. The examination questions will help jog your memory and, hopefully, will become an effective aid in improving the quality of your group discussion. Review the evaluation questions list, and jot down below two or three action points for you to begin implementing next week.

ACTION POINTS:

1.

2.

3.

Lesson 2

On the Run

David's Days Running from Saul and Seeking the Lord

Memory Verses: Psalm 56:3–4

"When I am afraid, I will put my trust in You, in God, whose word I praise, in God I have put my trust; I shall not be afraid. What can mere man do to me?"

BEFORE THE SESSION

- Pray for your group as they study through this week's lesson.
- Remember, your goal is not to teach the lesson, but to facilitate discussion and help lead to application.
- As you walk through this lesson, keep in mind that the LORD does not change, that He listens to the needy heart and works in answer to the fervent, honest cry of a needy person.
- As you study, remember to highlight key statements and jot down those ideas and questions you want to discuss or ask as you go through this lesson with your small group.

What to Expect

Several people know about David running from Saul, but do not know many of the details. Further, many do not apply what David was learning to their own lives. We are all "on the run" in some ways, running from one problem to another, trying to get away from those we do not like, and in some cases, dealing with those who are treating us wrongly, facing some of what David faced. The circumstances, events, and people David encountered give many illustrations for today's believer. None of us is facing the same challenges David faced, but we face similar situations. Jesus faced those as well and He continually looked to His Father and to His Word. David often did that, though not perfectly. We can do the same, seeking the Lord for what we are facing, calling out to Him in prayer, reading His Word, and looking to Him for the next step. Because we face similar circumstances, it is essential to help focus the group on personal application of what David faced and how he handled these days in his life.

Help your group grasp the significance of what David was going through and how he sought the Lord. These truths apply to every age of history and to every life currently. Encourage your group members with clear applications and help them to share insights that God has shown them.

Main Point of "On the Run: David's Days Running from Saul and Seeking the Lord":
The main point in the overview of these years in David's life is to see how he sought and followed the Lord and led others to do the same. David did not follow perfectly, but he learned much over these years and helped many.

During the Session

Opening: 5–10 Minutes

Opening Prayer—Have one of the group members open the time with prayer.

Opening Illustration—Tired or Dehydrated?—For a Marathon, 5K, or 10K, organizers provide 'water tables' for the runners along the way. Each can grab a small cup, guzzle it down, and stay hydrated for the journey. What if someone ignores those tables? Dehydration (and extreme harm) could come quickly. In his weariness, even Samson cried out for water (Judges 16:18–19). Many believers claim to be "weary" or overly "tired" when in fact they are spiritually dehydrated, or simply spiritually "thirsty," not drinking in Scripture or not surrendering moment by moment to the *"living water"* work of the Holy Spirit. "On-the-run" David stayed 'hydrated.' One time, when certain men spoke unjustly of stoning him, he *"strengthened himself in the LORD his God"* and the Lord worked on his behalf (1 Samuel 30:6). Help your group grasp these truths and their application points.

Discussion: 30–40 minutes
Make your preparation time a priority this week. Diligent preparation can help you as you guide the discussion. It can also aid you in answering many of the questions that arise in your group. We all face times like that of David's "on the run" season; we too can rely on the Lord in prayer and in His Word like David did. As you walk through this Scripture Adventure, seek to keep the main point the main point and be sure to leave time for the application points in Day Five. Knowing how these truths apply to any and every heart can encourage and help each believer grow.

Main Objective in Day One: In Day One, the main objective is to see the first years of David "on the run" and how he sought to do the right thing. Think through your discussion questions as well as the list of questions given below as you look for useful discussion-starter ideas.

___ David went from favored by Saul to hated by Saul, partly because of God's presence with David and the Lord's leaving Saul. How did David handle these days?

___ How did Jonathan help David in these early days? How important is the counsel of a loving friend?

___ How does Psalm 59 reveal David's trust in the Lord during the events surrounding the attempt on his life at David's and Michal's house?

___ When David faced Goliath, he acted *"in the name of the LORD of hosts"* and said, *"the battle is the LORD'S"* (1 Samuel 17:45, 47). How did he show that faith in dealing with Saul in the early days?

Main Objective in Day Two: In Day Two, the main objective is to see how David sought wise counsel (Samuel then Jonathan) and a hiding place. Check which discussion questions you will use from Day Two.

___ How important is it to seek wise counsel when we are facing a perplexing or even dangerous situation?

___ David, while not a perfect man, knew he must run from those seeking to kill him. How valid is time and distance from those trying to take one's life?

___ David feigned madness before Achish in Gath, Philistia. Does this show David's fear or faith or both?

___ How does David reveal his faith in Psalm 34 (likely written after his escape from Achish and his men)?

Main Objective in Day Three: In Day Three, our main objective is to see how David's and Saul's characters were further revealed and how David sought the Lord and his ways. Below, are some suggested discussion starters for you to consider.

___ What leadership abilities do you see in David in these days? What makes a good leader?

___ What do you learn about Saul's anger? How did it affect him and others?

___ How did David show prayer as a priority in his life?

___ How was David's character more clearly revealed in these days?

Main Objective in Day Four: Day Four's main objective is to see David's leadership and growth in character in a variety of situations. Check any questions that are applicable for your Day Four-discussion time.

___ How did David reveal a 'learner's' heart in the incidents with Nabal and Abigail?

___ What do David's many escapes have to say about David, his circumstances, and the will of God?

___ What are some ways David experienced protection and provision in this season of his life?

___ What do you see about the timing of God in David's life in the dealings with the Philistines, then the Amalekites?

Day Five—Key Points in Application: The most important application points in "On the Run" are the ways David dealt with people and how important relationships are in daily life. Check which discussion questions you will use to help focus the applications from Day Five.

___ What can we learn from David about how to relate to others?

___ How does God's work in David's life encourage you about His work in your life?

___ How should we relate to God; what kind of relationship should we have with Him?

___ In what ways can we encourage and lead others day by day? What does God's gifting and equipping mean to you?

CLOSING: 5–10 MINUTES

- Summarize—Restate the key points the group shared.
- Focus—Using the memory verses (Psalm 56:3–4), focus the group again on what it means to focus on the Lord and His Word. Remind the members of your group that focusing on the Lord is always the right direction to take.
- Ask them to share their thoughts about the key applications from Day Five.
- Preview—Take a few moments to preview next week's lesson on "King David: The First Half of David's Reign as King." Encourage your group members to dig into Scripture each day, spacing the Scripture Adventure out over the week.
- Pray—Close in prayer.

Tools for Good Discussion

While wayward discussions can be a waste of time and actually hurtful to spiritual growth, healthy discussion can help each member of your group grow. There are four actions that can help you in your small group discussion times—just remember the acrostic *"A.C.T.S."* and review the four actions given on page 217. This is part of the broader "Helpful Hints" section of How to Lead a Small Group Bible Study which begins on page 216.

Lesson 3

King David

The First Half of David's Reign as King

Memory Verse: Daniel 2:21

"And it is He ["the God of Heaven"] who changes the times and epochs; He removes kings and establishes kings; He gives wisdom to wise men, and knowledge to men of understanding.'"

BEFORE THE SESSION

- Praying for each member of your group can make a difference as each studies this week's lesson and as you discuss this lesson. God can make an eternal difference in each life; He uses prayer.
- Remember, your goal is to facilitate discussion, help lead people to clear applications, and encourage each person in the group.
- As you walk through this lesson, recall that the LORD works to fulfill His will, even as He did in David's life. Always, the key is who *God* is, not who any person is (or thinks he or she is).
- Highlight key statements. Jot down ideas and questions you want to discuss or ask as you go through this lesson with your small group.

What to Expect

As with each season of David's life, his first twenty years as king of Israel were filled with the activity of God, with opposition from some, with a mostly consistent testimony of David's trust in God, as well as some of the failures of David and others. The events and lessons surrounding David help us see better what it means to look to the Lord day by day. Help the group grasp something of these days of David's reign and the challenges he faced. Not everyone wanted David as king, just as today not everyone wants the will of God in their lives, relationships, or circumstances. Following God is always the right way, for He knows which way to go and is willing to guide in that way. Help focus the group on personal application, how God worked in and through David's life, and how He is willing to work in each of His children's lives. Encourage them to share the insights and applications God has given.

Main Point of "King David": The main point in this look at the first half of David's reign is to see how God worked, how David and others responded, and how this applies to each of us today.

During the Session

Opening: 5–10 Minutes

Opening Prayer—It is good to pray. Have one of the group members open the time with prayer.

Opening Illustration—"We're in this Together"—When we look at David as king, we must never think that he reigned without several working with him. As the saying goes, "no one is an island;" there are no true "solo" ventures. Each of us needs others. This is obvious in infancy; no baby could survive without others. It is also true throughout life; we need each other. That being true, we can learn from David through his friends and foes, through his seeking the Lord, seeking the wise counsel of others, even through his attempts at trying to go it alone. We need each other as followers of Christ, and we can help one another in a small group Bible study. Help your group see and apply these truths.

Discussion: 30–40 minutes
Prioritize your preparation, study, and prayer times this week. These times can certainly aid your thought processes, your leadership in the discussion, and your ability to answer many questions that could arise. Remembering that God is the God who leads in the *Best* way in spite of our weaknesses can encourage those going through difficult seasons as well as those seemingly living in the calm areas of life. As you walk through this Scripture adventure, focus on what it means to seek the Lord and follow Him and His Word. Seek to keep the main point the main point. Always be thinking of ways to make the application points clear, especially in Day Five.

<u>Main Objective in Day One</u>: In Day One, the main objective is to see that God continues to guide His people even in the light of the failures and wrongs of others. Think through the list of questions given below as you look for useful discussion-starter ideas.

___ In light of David's examples of prayer, what should each of us do *first* when facing daily decisions? How?

___ What does it mean to honor others? What are some ways we can show care and honor?

___ What does it mean to seek to do what is right? How can we know what is right?

___ How did David show the right way to receive the help of others? What are some ways we can do that today?

<u>Main Objective in Day Two</u>: In Day Two, the main objective is to see how David began to reign and desired to seek and follow the Lord in his reign. Review these questions and check which ones you will use.

___ What is significant about David's response to the aggression of the Philistines?

___ What can we learn from David's leadership in conquering Jerusalem?

___ What do you see in the relationship between David's *"mighty men"* and David? What do you see in David's heart toward the Lord and toward them?

___ David dedicated to the Lord the many treasures he won in battle. Why is this significant? What does it show about David?

Main Objective in Day Three: In Day Three, our main objective is to see how to face enemies and battles God's way and how to lead others. Consider these questions as you ponder the ways and works of David.

___ What is significant about the Lord helping David in his battles? What does that say to each of us?

___ How important is it to show care for others? What are some God-honoring ways each of us can do that?

___ How important is it to follow the Lord and His Word in our relationships with others?

___ Offenses come. How should we deal with any offenses we may have committed against someone? How should we handle offenses from others?

Main Objective in Day Four: Day Four's main objective is to see how easily wrongs can arise and how to deal with them God's way. Look over these questions and check any that are applicable for your discussion time.

___ David's men convinced him to stay in Jerusalem and not go out to battle. It is good to have wise counsel, but how much more important is it to follow the Lord and His Word in the decision-making process?

___ What do we learn from David about how to handle or not handle temptation, wrong, and guilt?

___ How crucial is it to see how God sees sin and evil? What do we learn from the events of David's life?

___ What do we learn about God in the events surrounding David, Bathsheba, Uriah, and Nathan?

Day Five—Key Points in Application: Application points matter very much for Christian growth. In "King David," we find several practical applications from David's life during his first twenty years as king. Check which discussion questions you could use to help focus applications.

___ In what different ways did David experience the grace and mercy of God in his reign as king?

___ How vital is the grace and mercy of God in our lives?

___ How did David see the holiness and love of God in the various experiences of his first twenty years as king?

___ How important is God's forgiveness? What did this mean for David? What does this mean to you?

CLOSING: 5–10 MINUTES

- Summarize—Restate the key points the group shared.
- Focus—Using the memory verse (Daniel 2:21), focus the group on the place of the Lord in dealing with the leaders of the world, of each nation, even of each area or community.
- Ask for some key application points from Day Five.
- Preview—Take a few moments to preview next week's lesson on "The Shepherd King in New Pastures." Encourage your group members to focus intently on the Scriptures like one searching for buried treasure. Work each day, giving time over the week for this Scripture adventure.
- Pray—Close in prayer.

Tools for Good Discussion

Often a "Talkative Timothy" will show up in a Study Group. He (or she) tends to talk too much and dominate the discussion, which gives less time for others to give their input or share their insights. What should you do with a group member who talks too much? In the "Helpful Hints" section of How to Lead a Small Group Bible Study (page 217), you'll find some practical ideas on managing the "Talkative Timothy" situation.

Lesson 4

The Shepherd King in New Pastures

The Challenges of Reigning in the Present and Preparing for the Future

Memory Verses: Psalm 23:1–3

"The LORD is my shepherd, I shall not want. He makes lie down in green pastures; He leads me beside quiet waters. He restores my soul; He guides me in the paths of righteousness for His name's sake."

BEFORE THE SESSION

- Pray for your group—each member—as they study through this week's lesson.
- Don't feel that you have to use all of the discussion questions listed below. You may have come up with others on your own, or you may find that time will not allow you to use them all. These questions are to serve you, not for you to serve them.
- You are the gatekeeper of the discussion. Do not be afraid to "reel the group back in" if they get too far away from the subject of the lesson.
- Remember to keep a highlight pen ready as you study to mark any points you want to be sure to discuss.

What to Expect

We enter the stream of David's life at a new point. Now in his fifties and early sixties, he has new challenges. No one can please everyone, and David came to understand this in many new ways. He faced family and national challenges, as well as the encouragement of God's work and God's Word in his life. It is vital to understand that all these relationships are important—family, friends, those we lead (but may not know very well), those who oppose, and the Lord (the most important relationship). As you walk through this lesson, it is essential to help focus the group on personal application, ever aware that Scripture was not written simply for information, but *"for our instruction"* and for obedience, as well as for our well-being (Romans 15:4).

Help your group understand the many challenges each faces today—not the same as David, but often similar and dealing with all kinds of people. Encourage your group members to share insights God has shown them.

Main Point of "The Shepherd King in New Pastures": The main point in viewing David's life during this season is to see how God worked and how David responded year by year. We can learn from David's life.

During the Session

Opening: 5–10 Minutes

Opening Prayer—Have one of the group members open the time with prayer.

Opening Illustration—"Pardon Our Dust"—Sometimes we enter a building or room and find a sign with the words "Pardon Our Dust" or "Please Excuse the Mess" or "Progress at Work" or something like that. We can identify with this whether in a business situation, a church renovation, something at school or even at home. It is also true of our personal lives; we always have some area that needs some "work" and that means some "dust" and some "messes." That was true of David, of his family, even of the nation of Israel. Your group members need to grasp this truth about David and about life today. In this week's lesson, carefully look at this in this season of David's life. Look for clear applications.

Discussion: 30–40 minutes

Good preparation time is vital to help you in guiding the discussion as well as in answering various questions from the members of your group. Seeing what David faced and how he faced those matters can help each of us better see how the Lord works in our lives and situations. Knowing God is the Great King can help us see His hand in our lives. We can learn from Him (as well as from David) how to make wise choices in line with the character of God and His Word. As you walk through this Scripture adventure, make sure you keep the main point the main point. Leave time for the application points in Day Five.

Main Objective in Day One: In Day One, the main objective is to see how David sought to instruct and train his son Solomon in his early years and how vital it is for families to follow God. Look over the questions listed here along with others you may have as you consider what might be the most useful discussion-starters.

___ How crucial is obedience to God and His Word? What is the difference between 'knowing about' and 'knowing' through doing?

___ The *"heart"* is crucial to God and to each family member. What are some ways to help one another in *"heart"* matters?

___ What is valuable in a father or mother helping a child better see who God is and how rich His Word is?

___ What are some ways to help a child *"hold fast"* the words of a parent and the Word of God?

Main Objective in Day Two: In Day Two, the main objective is to see some of the issues and wrong choices that come about in a family situation or in close relationships. Check which discussion questions you will use from Day Two.

___ What do Scriptures tell us to do when facing a temptation?

___ Amnon and others had many Scriptures available. How could the Ten Commandments alone have helped him and those in league with him?

___ Does personal vengeance ever accomplish good? How did Absalom's actions affect others?

___ What is needed to make wrongs right? How can relationships be restored?

Main Objective in Day Three: In Day Three, our main objective is to see the continued work of God in David's life and how he responded. Listed below are some suggested discussion starters for you to consider.

___ David had a new palace, but there was nothing more significant in Israel's life than their covenant relationship with God. How important was the Ark of the Covenant? What do you learn from David's words and actions?

___ What did David learn and what can we learn from the events surrounding Uzzah's death?

___ Worship matters, as David revealed. What are some ways we can show or tell others of the value of the Lord? What are some ways each of us can better worship the Lord?

___ What can we learn from David's plans to build a *"house"* for God? How important is it to 'pray first' before doing anything in 'daily life' or in matters of 'ministry'?

Main Objective in Day Four: Day Four's main objective is to see David's response to God in prayer. Look over the questions here and choose those that are applicable for your Day Four-discussion time.

___ How did God point to His relationship with David and his descendants in His revelation to David in 2 Samuel 7? Why is the matter of a personal relationship with God so important? What matters to God forever?

___ How important is humility in our relationship with the Lord? How can we show a humble heart or attitude?

___ David prayed based on God's *"word"* to him. How can we pray God's Word day by day? What difference could this make?

___ What does it mean to pray for God's *"blessing"*? What difference could this make in a life or situation?

Day Five—Key Points in Application: The most important application point in "The Shepherd King in New Pastures" is the *direction* of the heart, along with the *condition* of the heart. Check which discussion questions you will use to help focus the applications from Day Five.

___ What does it mean to be a person *"after"* God's *"heart"*?

___ How does one maintain a right heart? What does it take to follow God consistently?

___ How important is the Word of God in one's relationship and walk with God?

___ Many opinions and ideas bombard us each day. Some are clear distractions to following God and others are more subtle. How can we best know the difference and how can we best deal with distractions so that we follow the Lord in the right way?

CLOSING: 5–10 MINUTES

- Summarize—Restate the key points the group shared.
- Focus—Using the memory verses (Psalm 23:1–3), focus the group on the Lord as *The* Shepherd. What are some practical ways we can know and follow Him?
- Ask them to share their thoughts about the key applications from Day Five.
- Preview—Take a few moments to preview next week's lesson on "The Final Season: The Leadership and Legacy of King David." Encourage your group members to be diligent in searching the Scripture each day, and to anticipate God speaking to each of them throughout the week.
- Pray—Close in prayer.

Tools for Good Discussion

As mentioned earlier, there are certain people who show up in every discussion group. Last week we looked at "Talkative Timothy." Another person who is likely to show up is "Silent Sally." She doesn't readily speak up. Sometimes, her silence is because she doesn't yet feel comfortable enough with the group to share her thoughts. At other times, perhaps she simply fears being rejected. Often, her silence is because she is too polite to interrupt and thus is headed off at the pass each time she wants to speak by more aggressive (and less sensitive) members of the group. In the "Helpful Hints" section of How to Lead a Small Group Bible Study (p. 218), you'll find some practical ideas on managing the "Silent Sally's" in your group.

Lesson 5

The Final Season

The Leadership and Legacy of King David

Memory Verses: 2 Samuel 23:3–5

"The God of Israel said, the Rock of Israel spoke to me, 'He who rules over men righteously, who rules in the fear of God, is as the light of the morning when the sun rises, a morning without clouds, when the tender grass springs out of the earth, through sunshine after rain.' Truly is not my house so with God? For He has made an everlasting covenant with me, ordered in all things, and secured; for all my salvation and all my desire, will He not indeed make it grow?"

BEFORE THE SESSION

- Resist the temptation to do all your homework in one sitting or to put it off until the last minute. You will not be as prepared if you study this way.

- Make sure to mark down any discussion questions that come to mind as you study. Don't feel that you have to use all of the suggested discussion questions included in this leader's guide. Feel free to pick and choose based on your group and the time frame with which you are working.

- Make some personal applications of "The Final Season" in your time this week. Your testimony and example can be a powerful encouragement to your group members.

- In preparation for your discussion time, review the two Charts at the end of this lesson, "The Angel of the LORD" and "How to Deal with Sin." Consider what discussion or application points could come out of the truths presented in those charts along with the events of David's life.

What to Expect

David is known far and wide; his life yields much discussion. The Scriptures reveal much about his legacy as a boy, as a man, and as a king. We know David had a *"heart"* turned towards the Lord, but we also know he did not have a perfect heart. In this 'final season' of his life and reign, David reveals successes and failures. It is vital to see these from God's perspective and to apply them to our daily lives. Success or failure in God's eyes is always tied to *His* definition of success or failure. For the most part, David succeeded in following God and His Word; where he failed, we see some of the tell-tale signs of unbelief and disobedience. Help your group members see and apply the vital relationship between trust and obedience, as well as the importance of paying careful attention to Him and His Word.

Main Point of "The Final Season: The Leadership and Legacy of King David": The main message from "The Final Season" is that God continued to work in David's life even with his weaknesses and failures. God never gives up on His purposes and plans, nor on His people.

During the Session

Opening: 5–10 minutes

Opening Prayer—Remember to have one of your group members open your time together in prayer.

Opening Illustration—More than a Game—Many games such as "Simon Says" or "Red Rover-Red Rover..." use the idea of following a leader or his words. In sports, how vital it is to listen to and obey the coach, the quarterback, the point guard, or some other leader! It can be the difference between moving forward or losing ground, scoring or not, even winning or losing. Following God and His Word is so much more than a game; as a matter of fact, it can matter forever. David illustrates this as do so many with whom he crossed paths; some succeeded, many failed.

Discussion: 30–40 minutes

Remember that your job is not to teach this lesson, but to facilitate discussion. Do your best to guide the group to the right answers, but don't be guilty of making a point someone else in the group could just as easily make.

Main Objective in Day One: The main point in Day One is to see the ways and works of Absalom, how this affected David and Israel, and how these matters ended. Choose a discussion question or two from the list below.

___ How did Absalom *"steal"* the hearts of several in Israel? What does this say about our words to others?

___ What does Absalom's use of deceit say about him? What lessons can we learn from viewing his words and actions?

___ What do you learn from David's responses, his words to others, and his attitude during Absalom's attempted coup?

___ What insights do you glean from reviewing Absalom's death and defeat, David's grief, and the many different responses of people in those days?

Main Objective in Day Two: In Day Two, we look at the issue of pride, discovering the ongoing challenges David faced guiding people, dealing with his own heart, and seeking to follow the Lord. Below, check any discussion questions you might use from Day Two.

___ What lessons can we learn from the ways and words of Sheba?

___ How did David's census reveal his pride?

___ How does God view pride? How did God view David's motives and actions?

___ What did David's worship offering say about his heart? About God's heart?

Main Objective in Day Three: Day Three guides us through David's preparations for Solomon's future reign and the future Temple his son would build. Review the questions below and see if any are suitable to your group discussion on Day Three.

___ How important is courage and fearlessness in leading others? How does the fear of God fit in with this?

___ What does the multitude of details about the Temple service say about worship among the people of God? What are some heart essentials for any worship leader?

___ What are some of the key elements in one's relationship with the Lord and with others?

___ Principles of "Giving" abound in the Scriptures. What are several principles about giving found in David's words and his preparations for the Temple?

Main Objective in Day Four: In Day Four, we see the final days of David and how he continued to respond, ever faithful to the Lord, His Word, and His covenant promises. Check which discussion questions you will use from Day Four.

___ David's final words reveal a lifetime of understanding and walking with God. What one or two statements he made mean most to you?

___ What kind of heart did Adonijah reveal in David's last days? What can we learn from Adonijah, his upbringing, his words, and his actions?

___ What do you learn from Nathan, Bathsheba, and those who sided with them?

___ What matters (really matters) in David's life and reign or in Solomon's life and reign?

Day Five—Key Points in Application: Day Five, "Following My Shepherd," focuses on pride and humility as well as on what matters most in life. Decide on some discussion-starter topics for the application section of Day Five. These questions are suggested questions you may want to use for your discussion:

___ David spoke of the essential of *"the fear of God."* How does pride match or not match with that?

___ How does God's view of pride inform each of us? What should be our view, our attitude toward pride?

___ What are some evidences of pride? What are evidences of humility? What's the difference?

___ How we spend our time reveals our priorities? What do we need to *make sure* is in our schedule?

Closing: 5–10 minutes

- Summarize—Go over the key points of your study of "The Final Season."
- Focus—Using the memory verses (2 Samuel 23:3–5), focus the group on David's attention to the details of one's heart and the results that could come, especially in leading others.
- Ask the group members what they thought were the key applications from Day Five.
- Preview—Take a few moments to preview next week's lesson "Jesus Christ, the "*Son of David*": Jesus, the God-Man, Born into the Line of David, Revealing Himself as King, Lord, Messiah, and Savior." Encourage them to be sure to complete their homework.
- Pray—Close in prayer.

Tools for Good Discussion

Hopefully your group is functioning smoothly at this point, but perhaps you recognize the need for improvement. In either case, you will benefit from taking the time to *evaluate* yourself and your group. Without evaluation, you will judge your group on subjective emotions. You may think everything is fine and miss some opportunities to improve your effectiveness. You may be discouraged by problems you are confronting when you ought to be encouraged that you are doing the right things and making progress. A healthy Bible-study group is not one without problems but one that recognizes its problems and deals with them the right way. At this point in the course, it is important to examine yourself and see if there are any corrections needed. Again, review the evaluation questions list found on pages 224–225 of the Leader's Guide, and jot down two or three action points for you to begin implementing next week. Perhaps you have made steady improvements since the first time you answered the evaluation questions at the beginning of the course. If so, your improvements should challenge you to be an even better group leader for the final lesson in the study.

ACTION POINTS:

1.

2.

3.

Lesson 6

Jesus Christ, "Son of David"

Jesus, the God-Man, Born into the Line of David, Revealing Himself as King, Lord, Messiah, and Savior

<u>Memory Verses</u>: John 1:1, 14

"In the beginning was the Word, and the Word was with God, and the Word was God.... And the Word became flesh, and dwelt among us, and we beheld His glory, glory as of the only begotten from the Father, full of grace and truth."

BEFORE THE SESSION

- George MacDonald said, "The best preparation for the future is the present well seen to, and the last duty done" [www.brainyquote.com, accessed April 28, 2020]. One of the main reasons a Bible study flounders is because the leader comes in unprepared and tries to "shoot from the hip."
- Make sure to jot down any discussion questions that come to mind as you study.
- Keep in mind the importance of personal daily application of these lessons for *your* life. As your group members ponder those who have gone astray, they will be warned, challenged, and encouraged to follow the Lord and His Word.
- Don't forget to pray for the members of your group and for your time studying together. You don't want to be satisfied with what you can do—you want to see God do what only He can do!

What to Expect

In viewing Jesus Christ, *"Son of David,"* one ventures into a vast arena. As *"Son of David,"* there are numerous connections between Jesus and King David, more than most realize. The Messiah (or Christ) coming as the *"Son of David"* was an oft-repeated topic of conversation and an oft-prayed-for reality. People wanted the conquering Messiah to come and deal with Rome (and any other enemies of the Jews). However, most did not understand all that His coming would mean. This overview of the Scriptures will help many gain a fuller understanding and hopefully see several life applications. Be sensitive to any discussion questions that may surface in this lesson and guard your group from applying it only to others rather than to themselves.

<u>Main Point of "Jesus Christ, "Son of David": Jesus, the God-Man, Born into the Line of David, Revealing Himself as King, Lord, Messiah, and Savior</u>": The main point to be seen in this lesson is the faithfulness of God to His plans and promises for Israel and for the nations, as well as His gracious ways with each person.

During the Session

Opening: 5–10 Minutes

Opening Prayer—Remember to have one of your group members open your time together in prayer.

Opening Illustration—"*A Promise is a Promise*"—Many "promises" are made every day. Some are very accurate and trustworthy; others are extremely suspect and should be treated like a pet rattlesnake—not to be trusted. When God made a promise to anyone, His character and power were on the line, and He has fulfilled promise after promise. There are more yet to be fulfilled. While we may not trust some promises whether about a product or service or 'guarantee,' we can trust God. He is *"faithful and true,"* as is His Word (Revelation 3:14; 19:11; 21:5; 22:6). Jesus came as the *"Son of David,"* fulfilling numerous promises; He has more yet to fulfill. *"A Promise is a Promise"* and He and His promises are trustworthy; each will be fulfilled in greater ways than we can now see. Help your group members better understand what it means to know and follow the *"Son of David"* daily and into eternity and to trust His promises. Pray for yourself and each member to grow and experience what it means to follow faithfully.

Discussion: 30–40 minutes

Remember to pace your discussion so that you will be able to bring closure to the lesson at the designated time. You are the one who must balance lively discussion with timely redirection to ensure that you don't end up finishing only part of the lesson.

Main Objective in Day One: In Day One, the main objective is to see many of the older promises made by God and how He has kept those promises. Check which discussion questions you will use from Day One.

___ What are some things God revealed about Himself and His plans from the Beginning (Genesis 1–3)?

___ How did God work in the life of Abram/Abraham over the years?

___ What 'king' factors do you discover about the *"seed"* in God's words to David?

___ What are some ways the Messiah Jesus matches the various promises given through the years?

Main Objective in Day Two: In Day Two, we see a few of the details about Jesus' birth and how others thought how the Messiah might come. Choose a discussion question or two from the list below.

___ How could Jesus be the *"Son of David"*? What streams came together to fulfill this prophecy?

___ What were some of the people's expectations about the prophesied *"Son of David"*?

___ In John 8, what stands out in Jesus' conversation with the leaders in Jerusalem? What did they think of Him? What did He think of Himself?

___ How could Jesus be the *"Son of David"* and David's *"Lord"*?

Main Objective in Day Three: Day Three focuses on the *"mercy"* of the *"Son of David,"* that which was expected and that which was shown. Decide on some discussion-starter questions for your session in "The Merciful Son of David." Below are some possible discussion questions to consider.

___ What were some of the thoughts of Mary, Elizabeth, and Zacharias about the *"mercy"* of God? What do their words, prayers, and mention of *"mercy"* reveal about each of them?

___ Jesus questioned the two blind men near Capernaum, and He acted on their behalf? What do His question *and* His actions reveal about the mercy of God?

___ What does one's cry for *"mercy"* reveal about the person doing the asking?

___ What kind of response should one have who has received the mercy of God?

Main Objective in Day Four: In Day Four, we see the strength and compassion of the triumphant *"Son of David."* Check which discussion questions you will use from Day Four.

___ What truly mattered to Jesus? On what did He focus during those final few days in Jerusalem?

___ What were Jesus' thoughts about being *"king"*? What did He reveal, especially to Pilate, during these days in Jerusalem?

___ What does it mean that Jesus is the *"Eternal King"*? What does that mean to *you*?

___ What does it mean that Jesus is *"the root and offspring of David"*? How does this apply to daily life?

Day Five—Key Points in Application: The most important application point in Day Five is what it means to know and follow Jesus as our Eternal Shepherd. Below, check any discussion questions that are best suited to your group for application.

___ What meaning and personal applications does Jesus' designation as *"the Good Shepherd"* have for you or for others?

___ What are some ways Jesus has shown or continues to show Himself as *"the Great Shepherd"*?

___ How do you see Jesus as *"the Chief Shepherd"*? What does that mean to *you*?

___ Thinking back over the life and ministry of Jesus, what are some of the prominent characteristics of Jesus as the *"Son of David"*? What are some ways we can relate to Him as the *"Son of David"*?

Closing: 5–10 minutes

- Summarize—Restate the key points. Ask the group to express their thoughts about the most significant applications.
- Focus—Using the memory verses (John 1:1, 14), direct the group's focus to *Who* Jesus is—in Eternity Past, in His earthly life and ministry, today, and for Eternity Future. Note the practical applications to everyday life this can have for each person. To better grasp some of what this means, it may help for each to walk through the Chart at the end of Lesson Six, *A Chronology of the Life and Ministry of the Lord Jesus Christ.*
- Think back over the life and reign of David and the life and ministry of Jesus. Recall some of the practical applications from the lives of both. What does it mean to have a *"heart after"* God? It may be helpful to review the thoughts in "Having a Heart for God" at the end of this book.
- Pray—Close in prayer, thanking the Lord for the journey He has led you on over the past six weeks.

Tools for Good Discussion

Congratulations! You have successfully navigated the waters of small group discussion. You have finished all six lessons in *Following God: David, the Shepherd King*, but there is so much more to learn, so many more paths to take on our journey with the Lord, so much more to discover about what it means to follow the Lord. Now What? It would be wise for you and your group to not stop with this study. In the front portion of this leader's guide (in the "Helpful Hints" section of How to Lead a Small Group Bible Study, pp. 223), there is information on how you can transition to the next study. Share those insights with your group. Encourage them to continue in some sort of consistent Bible study. Time in the Word is much like time at the dinner table. If we are to stay healthy, we will never get far from physical food, and if we are to stay nourished on "sound" or "healthy" doctrine, then we must stay close to the Lord's "dinner table" found in His Word. Job said it well, *"I have not departed from the command of His lips; I have treasured the words of His mouth more than my necessary food"* (Job 23:12).

Having a Heart for God

God noted David as *"a man after My heart"* (Acts 13:22; see 1 Samuel 13:14). Jesus, the *"Son of David,"* also had a heart for God, for all His Father wanted Him to do or say (see John 8:28–29). What does it mean to have a *"heart"* for God? Paul described God's heart about David, noting him as one *"who will do all My will."* That is certainly true of Jesus, even as His words in Gethsemane revealed, *"My Father, ... not as I will, but as You will"* (Matthew 26:39), and yet again, *"My Father, ... Your will be done"* (Matthew 26:42).

The many psalms David penned reveal this desire to follow God, to do His will. In Psalm 40:8a, David stated, *"I delight to do Your will, O my God."* Psalm 40:6–8 is quoted in Hebrews 10:5–7 referring to the readiness and willingness of Jesus *"to do Your will, O God,"* even going to the Cross to fulfill God's will, accomplishing full salvation for any who would come to Him repentant of sin, placing faith in Him, receiving His life, and beginning to follow Him (Luke 24:46–47; John 1:12; Acts 20:21). That person is changed forever, desiring to do His will, even in the midst of struggles about His will.

One of the clearest expressions of bowing to His will are the actions and words of worship written by the Apostle John as he viewed those before the Lamb in Revelation 4:8, 11 and 5:9–10, 12–14 [NASB, 1995 Edition].

"HOLY, HOLY, HOLY IS THE LORD GOD, THE ALMIGHTY, WHO WAS AND WHO IS AND WHO IS TO COME... *Worthy are You, our Lord and our God, to receive glory and honor and power; for You created all things, and because of Your will they existed, and were created."*

"And they sang a new song, saying, 'Worthy are You to take the book, and to break its seals; for You were slain, and purchased for God with Your blood men from every tribe and tongue and people and nation. You have made them to be a kingdom and priests to our God; and they will reign upon the earth.'"

"'Worthy is the Lamb that was slain to receive power and riches and wisdom and might and honor and glory and blessing.' And every created thing which is in heaven and on the earth and under the earth and on the sea, and all things in them, I heard saying, 'To Him who sits on the throne, and to the Lamb, be blessing and honor and glory and dominion forever and ever.' And the four living creatures kept saying, "Amen." And the elders fell down and worshiped."

David was noted as *"the sweet psalmist of Israel"* (2 Samuel 23:1e); that is clearly seen in his psalms of worship, praise, thanks, even agony. In the twenty-first century, several have helped us worship with greater focus and more heart; one of the most vivid expressions of worship and adoration based on Revelation 4 and 5 is *"Revelation Song"* penned by Jennie Lee Riddle (copyright, 2004). That and other hymns and spiritual songs help us and call us to worship and surrender our wills to "THE LORD GOD, THE ALMIGHTY," and they aid us in developing, growing, and maturing in a personal *"heart for God,"* as well as directing each in loving God with all one's heart, soul, mind, and strength.

Take some time to spend before the Lord. Worship Him. Sing to Him. Surrender afresh to Him and His will. Be like David and like Jesus, the *"Son of David"*; cultivate a *"heart for God,"* love Him and live in His will in everyday life, and help others do the same.

Made in the USA
Columbia, SC
14 June 2022